Human Resource Management for Sports and Recreation Programs

Human Resource Management for Sports and Recreation Programs

Richard Leonard

Flager College

PUBLISHING

A Division of the International Center for Performance Excellence
West Virginia University
375 Birch Street, WVU-CPASS
PO Box 6116
Morgantown, WV 26506-6116

Library of Congress Card Catalog Number: 2019949943

ISBN: 9781940067438

Cover Design: Wendy Lazzell
Cover Photos: Shutterstock.com | EtiAmmos | ID: 732086635
Back cover image: istock.com | Yuri_Arcurs | ID: 531113851
Production Editor: Eileen Harvey

10 9 8 7 6 5 4 3 2 1

PUBLISHING

A Division of the International Center for Performance Excellence
West Virginia University
375 Birch Street, WVU-CPASS
PO Box 6116
Morgantown, WV 26506-6116
800.477.4348 (toll free)
304.293.6888 (phone)
304.293.6658 (fax)
Email: fitcustomerservice@mail.wvu.edu
Website: www.fitpublishing.com

Table of Contents

Table of Contents

List of Exhibits

Appendices

Acknowledgments

More than a few talented professionals supplied their knowhow and passion to this textbook. I would first like to communicate my profound thanks to Ms. Barbara Ridenour Dalton for her leadership at FiT Publishing at West Virginia University. Her assistance during the creation of this textbook, as well as my previous books with FiT/WVU, has been extraordinary.

Because the creation of a textbook is a multidimensional and intricate process, a special note of appreciation goes to this book's editor Eileen Harvey. Eileen was incredibly attentive to the book's features and displayed a remarkable dedication to the project. Simply stated, her hard work is evident in quality of the final product.

I am also indebted to Mr. Jeff Kelly, Esquire, for his legal expertise and exceptional contributions to this textbook. Not only did Jeff write Chapter 2: Human Resource Management and the Law, he also functioned as legal expert and technical proofreader for the project. It was a true pleasure to be connected with someone who is dedicated to his profession, as well as the formation of this all-inclusive (and legally sound) textbook.

Finally, I would like to communicate my deepest thanks to my wife, Shuli. As a human resource professional, she has been a fantastic sounding board. Her specialized insights and suggestions added greatly to the book, and I am indebted to her for all of her assistance.

Preface

The fundamental inspiration for the creation of this textbook is to underscore the importance of human resource management principles for both sport and recreation management students/scholars for their future careers, and real-world sports and recreation administrators presently in the field. My sincere desire is to integrate the most up-to-date human resource concepts and functions into a single text that could be used for college level instruction as well as a functional reference guide. The ultimate aspiration for the final product is to provide a wide-ranging and sequentially coherent manual for use as a core foundation for anyone to devise, systematize, and execute human resource strategies. Whether one is studying to enter the field or is currently working as a professional sports or recreation program executive, administrator, coach, or staff member, having a competent knowledge of human resource management is essential for achieving personal and program success.

As stated throughout this text, a sports or recreation program's most indispensable resource is its people. By understanding the efficient development and utilization of this most precious asset, a sports or recreation program can experience sustainable advantages over its competitors. Well thought out and executed human resource management strategies ensure a sports or recreation program's consistent performance and entails everything from tactical planning, structuring operations, hiring and onboarding personnel, training and developing program members, and monitoring and adapting human relations systems. The skillful deployment of human resource fundamentals can and will provide practical systems for "big picture" decision-making and achievement of long-term objectives. Sport and recreation organizations, no matter the level or status, are impacted by an ever-increasing quantity and intensity of competition. Sports and recreation administrators can no longer think of human resource management as an addendum or an expensive extravagance. In order to succeed, the application of human resource principles and strategies examined in this textbook could be the difference between the progress and achievement, or decline and collapse of one's operation.

Introduction

Human Resource Management for Sports and Recreation Programs is divided into 11 chapters with 6 appendix sections. Each chapter contains learning objectives for the reader, key terms, review and discussion questions, application exercises and term projects for students. The following is a synopsis of the textbook:

Chapter 1 embraces topics such as the significance of human resource management in sports and recreation programs, the primary operational elements and universal practices in human resource management, strategic human resource management, and human resource information systems.

Chapter 2 is an abridgment of human resource laws and regulations that impact all U.S. businesses—sports and recreation programs included—from both historical and contemporary perspectives.

Chapter 3 is divided into two parts that covers planning from a high-level sports or recreational program perspective and subsequent human resource perspective, and include the delineation of factors, strategic approaches and techniques to create executie, and monitor a human resource plan.

Chapter 4 discusses the function of occupational modeling, including (1) conducting a job analysis, (2) researching job structuring and design, (3) composing job descriptions, and (4) constructing organizational structures and hierarchical charts.

Chapter 5 is also in two parts that discuss the recruitment and selection of new sports or recreation program personnel, with a comprehensive step-by-step selection process, and a discussion of onboarding principles and strategies for new program personnel that even details a sports or recreation program employee's first day.

Chapter 6 is focused on sports and recreational program training that includes conducting needs assessments, delineating established training methodologies, both individual and group oriented, implementing strategies for training programs, and evaluating and improving training programs.

Chapter 7 discusses performance management and performance evaluations in sports and recreation programs. The chapter provides the steps in the performance management process and different approaches to final performance reviews, including performance evaluations and tips on conducting performance assessment reviews. The chapter also includes a discussion of performance improvement action planning.

Chapter 8 examines the basic concepts and motivation behind rewards systems for sports and recreation programs and their value in human resource management. Elements such as intrinsic versus extrinsic rewards, different types of financial compensation, designing reward systems, adjustments and compensation augmentation, incentive and bonus practices, benefits, and pay equity are discussed.

Chapter 9 examines human relation systems that deal with issues and grievances and methods for handling them. Included in the discussion are methods for systematizing formal employee interactions, disciplinary systems, grievance procedures, corrective action planning, and employee separations management.

Chapter 10 is divided into two parts that examine safety management and employee wellness programs. Safety management strategies discussed here focus on developing a safety culture with relevant safety policy and procedures, establishing safety protocols, and methods of training and measuring workplace safety, and accident reporting procedures. This chapter also explores methods and strategies to create and manage wellness programs for the ongoing health and wellness of employees in the sports and recreation program.

Introduction

Chapter 11 examines the need for and value of ethics in sports and recreation programs, such as what drives people to behave unethically, a discussion of standards for ethical workplace behavior, and constructing an ethical code of conduct for the sports and recreation program are all discussed.

The supplementary appendices supply the reader with a complete template and topics for the composition of a oral presentation; resume review strategies and pointers for sports and recreation program administrators; an undergraduate internship program template for use by industry professionals in a sport and recreation program; IRS rules/regulations concerning employment classifications for structuring an organizational chart and job descriptions and requirements; and, a practicum project that can be utilized in any sports management curriculum.

chapter one

A Framework of Human Resource Principles for Sports and Recreation Programs

Chapter Objectives

- Understand human resource management and its influence on program administration
- Understand the role and value of program stakeholders
- Understand the concept of relationship building through communication systems
- Understand the legal and regulatory concepts that guide HR management and their impact
- Understand human resource planning and occupational modeling
- Understand the concepts and value of recruiting, selection, and onboarding functions
- Understand performance evaluation concepts and functions
- Understand strategic development concepts and their application within HR policies and practices.
- Understand the value and function of information systems in HR management
- Understand the criteria and functions needed for a robust information system

Key Terms

Human Resource Management
Demographic Shifts
Societal Perception
Laws/Regulations Technology
Career Planning
Mentorships
Overstaffing
Understaffing
Human Resource Management
   Systems (HRIS)
Compensation
Strategic Objectives and Goals
Cultural Diversity
Stakeholders
Workplace Safety

Relationship Building
Communication Policies and
   Procedures
Human Capital
Psychological Contract
Core Values
Federal Human Resource Laws
State Human Resource Laws
Sport Governing Body
Occupational Modeling
Forecasting and Trend Analysis
Internal Competencies
Job Analysis
Hierarchical Charts
Recruitment

Onboarding
Orientation
Performance Evaluation
Reward Systems
Human Relations
Action Planning
Wellness Programs
Strategic Human Resource
   Management
Stretch Objectives
Security Protocols
Paperless/Virtual System
Data Backup Systems

What is Human Resource Management?

When defining human resource management in sports and recreation programs, one must clarify the basic similarities and differences between the concepts of general business management and human resource management. Rue, Ibrahim, and Byars (2013) describes the theory of general business management as "a form of work that involves deciding the best way to use an organization's resources to produce goods or services" (p. 3). In comparison, Price (2011) characterizes the more specific principle of human resource management as

> a philosophy of people management based on the belief that human resources are uniquely important to sustain business success. An organization gains competitive advantage by using its people effectively, drawing on their expertise and ingenuity to meet clearly defined objectives. (p. 29)

Both concepts analyze and employ the efficient use of an organization's assets and resources, with efficiency designated as the less and most proficient utilization of an operation's resources and assets to make a quality product or service. The primary divergence between general business management and human resource management is in their focus. General management examines the use of resources in a sports and recreation program, while human resource management mainly focuses on the organization's most indispensable possession: its workforce.

> **HR Tip**
>
> In any organization, human resource management is a support activity. It does not directly produce any specific product or service, but it does provide the most capable and skilled personnel who work directly towards producing a program's product or service.

The Significance of Human Resource Management

The overriding premise of this textbook is to accentuate the often-overlooked reality that a program's most valuable asset is its people. These individuals are the "life force" of the operation and directly impact the achievements and, unfortunately, the failures of the program. Forward thinking businesses (and sports and recreation programs are business enterprises) value human resource management enough that it has a direct input into crafting organizational objectives, as well as subsequent short- and long-term strategic decision-making. There are numerous, significant reasons why capable internal stakeholders (program employees and the professional management of those individuals) are necessary for a program's fruition.

Impact Elements and Benefits

The significance and impact of strong human resource management has on sports and recreation programs are many. Human resource management is widely acknowledged to have a direct connection with productivity and organizational success. By applying human resource management concepts, a sports or recreation program will experience (1) enhanced morale and positive attitudes, (2) marked increases in internal proficiencies, (3) minimized litigation and regulatory compliance issues, and (4) beneficial foundations for competitive advantage and growth.

Utilizing sound human resource management strategies is essential in dealing with volatile current and future external environmental forces (nature, economy, law/regulations, societal perception, technology, demographic shifts, and competition). Snell, Morris, and Bohlander (2013) assert that external environmental forces (also known as remote environments) are "forces that generally affect some, if not all, firms—forces over which they have virtually no control... By and large, a firm can only adapt to these changes rather than influence them." (p. 45). For example, one of the largest demographic groups in the United States' history is "baby boomers," who are progressing into modified or full retirement within the next 10 to 15 years. Human resource management can proactively adapt to this imminent demographic shift by career planning, mentorship, adjusting job responsibilities, and exercising innovative retention tactics.

In practical terms, human resource management systems help circumvent over- or under-staffing predicaments. While understaffing program operations is an instantly noticeable concern, overstaffing contributes to squandered resources and unproductive personnel, who could be employed in other program areas.

Similarly, human resource management systems help prevent over- or under-compensation of sports and recreation program personnel. Under- compensation leads to elevated levels of employee dissatisfaction and diminished productivity. Conversely, overcompensating sports or recreation program employees is an acute mismanagement of internal and frequently limited financial resources.

The use of relevant human resource management systems in a sports or recreation program are concentrated directly on strategic objectives. To attain strategic objectives, a sports or recreation program's human resource management strategies should converge on procuring the most skilled, competent staff with the necessary skills to complete identifiable program functions. Human resource management can help sports and recreation program administrators, coaches, and staff appreciate societal forces and cultural diversity. Acknowledging the evolving transformation in the local, regional, and national labor force is significant and can be a definitive strength of a sports or recreation program.

By exercising human resource management approaches, a sports or recreation program can augment the value of its human resource asset by creating or acquiring targeted training packages that are strategy-centered.

HR Tip

Having effective human resource management systems conveys a sense of professionalism to in-house personnel, outside program stakeholders, and prospective recruits. This leads to enhanced retention as well as "drawing in" the best possible program members.

Human resource management in a sports or recreation program should be directly involved in all facets of workplace safety. From generating safety protocols, monitoring safety, reporting safety issues, and providing broad-spectrum guidance, human resource management is an integral component in the welfare and well-being of all program members.

All of the strategies employee by human resource management speaks to its role as a conduit in stakeholder relationship building, and contributes considerably to open lines of communication throughout an operation. Additionally, human resource management can facilitate:

- how people in a program communicate with each other;
- when (and whether) people in a program can communicate with each other;
- who communicates directly with whom; and
- what program related materials can be transferred through internal communication channels.

Sound human resource management communication policies and procedures in relation to the program's internal operation can (1) alleviate numerous misunderstandings, (2) amplify strategic efficiencies, (3) positively influence the program's culture, and (4) strengthen stakeholder work satisfaction. Unquestionably, an entrenched and well-organized human resource communication system is a fundamental component in an all-inclusive operating system. It fosters a high performance environment and culture and how individuals interact with it.

Human resource management is an advocate for the investment in human capital. This investment is the underpinning of a psychological contract (formal and informal) between the executives, ownership, director levels and the program's operational and functional personnel. If a sports or recreation program commits time and resources to advance its members, the members will, by and large, dedicate themselves to the organization. An important part of this psychological contract depends on human resource management policies and procedures that establish the ethical core values of the operation. These "big picture" core values guide sports and recreation program members in day-to-day "small picture" actions.

By establishing comprehensive human resource management systems in a sports or recreation program, the finite element of time (a precious resource) can be maximized. Instead of a reactionary atmosphere that squanders time, a program can experience a proactive environment that has an even and time-effective feeling.

> **HR Tip**
> While the human resource asset of a sports or recreation program is characteristically one of the most (if not the most) expensive component of operation, it is essential. The program's health and performance precisely correlate with its human resource asset. Thus, human resource management stands separate from other departments in an organization's hierarchical structure and directly reports to ownership, CEO, COO, and executive level administration.

Primary Operating Practices

This textbook identifies and discusses five pivotal human resource management elements and practices that are indispensable in sports and recreation program administrators.

1. The legal environment of human resource management (chapter 2)
2. Planning and modeling strategies in human resource management (chapters 3 and 4)
3. Obtaining and developing the sports human resource asset (chapters 5 and 6)
4. Evaluating and rewarding a human resource personnel (chapters 7 and 8)
5. Human resource relations (chapters 9, 10, and 11)

Legal Environment of Human Resource Management

"One of the most important external factors that affect HRM is the legal environment. The management cannot manage the human resources unilaterally. It is now compelled to manage its employees according to the legislation enacted" (Aquinas, 2009, p. 9). For sports and recreation programs, the legal/legislative aspect of human resource management can be explained and examined in multiple tiers. The first tier is federal human resource laws (historical and contemporary). The second tier relates to geographic or state human resource laws and regulations not encompassed in federal statutes and regulations. The third tier embodies (1) an organization's established internal human resource policies and procedures, (2) the organization's governing body (intercollegiate sports include NCAA, NJCAA, NAIA, and for recreation organizations the YMCA, YWCA, JCC, city and local municipalities), or (3) the specific sport's governing body (USA Wrestling, USA Gymnastics, and others). Each tier can have an extreme impact on a sports or recreation program's day-to-day processes as well as long-term goals and objectives. For this reason, it is imperative that program administrators, coaches, counselors, and staff members are familiar with and have access to all noteworthy legal mandates and regulations from all three regulatory tiers.

Planning and Modeling Strategies in Human Resource Management

Every area of sports and recreation program administration—from general operations, marketing, human resource management, and accounting and finance, planning—contributes critical strategies. The human resource plan is a critical part of the organization's operational plan. Human resource-driven strategic planning incorporates long-term goal development and meticulous short-term actions to accomplish those goals. Human resource planning necessitates forecasting and trend analysis, assessment of internal competencies and requisite qualifications, creation and implementation systems for complying an inventory of sports or recreation program skills and capabilities, and delineating straightforward approaches to achieving organizational goals through the engagement of the human resource asset.

The information conveyed in a human resource plan is derived from examining and extrapolating program-wide objectives from the organization's operational plan. This concept, known as unity of strategy, is central for both plans to reach fruition. In other words, both plans must be interdependent and have a symbiotic connection. From a practical standpoint, a coherent human resource plan should "mirror" in many (if not all) ways the operational plan.

Occupational Modeling. In this context, occupational modeling is creating and structuring work positions in the sports or recreation program. Once a program has a coherent, comprehensive human resource plan, the main emphasis shifts to instilling in the program personnel the steps responsibilities and guiding principles necessary to realize objectives. Job analysis, job designing, and job descriptions are developed with meticulous attention to detail and within the program hierarchy as specified in the human resource plan.

Obtaining and Developing Human Resource Assets. No matter how well a sports or recreation program plans and structures its human resource component, without procuring and cultivating the right people, the enterprise will never achieve any of its existing objectives or future aspirations. The talent one secures and enhances is everything, in every facet of the program. It is not an oversimplification to declare that the more sophisticated and skilled the personnel are within a program—through external acquisition, internal training or promotion—the higher the probability of reaching, and even exceeding, program goals.

Recruitment and Selection. Obtaining the best suited candidate for a sports or recreation program is a balance between having a valid, reliable, and equitable recruitment and selection process and one's own intangible skill in observation and opinion of the individual (or "gut feeling"). Is the systemized methodology for recruiting and selecting new program employees a guarantee for success? Categorically, no. However, instituting a controlled recruitment and selection process can minimize hiring ill-suited or inappropriate individuals, while also ensuring legal compliance.

Onboarding. After devoting significant time to constructing recruitment sources, identifying the best possible candidates, completing the selection process for each, and hiring the best possible candidate, it is vital that the sports or recreation program have a smooth, stress-free onboarding process. Anything less could jeopardize the hard work expended finding the right match for the position. A well defined orientation program, with a review of policy and procedures, operating systems, and organizational and job training is required for the efficacious onboarding of new program employees.

HR Evaluation and Rewards

Greene (2011) asserts that performance management must fit logically within the organization. This idea creates a very distinct definition of the program's evaluation and reward system in a context in line with the organization's stated vision, goals, and objectives. Further,

> [T]he definition of performance must also enable an organization to measure results and to compare the actual results to what is required. Performance must be defined and managed in a way that is viewed as fair and appropriate by employees, as well as by other parties of interest. (p. 29)

Evaluating Performance. To verify whether a program employee is meeting, exceeding, or deficient in job requirements, performance evaluations are an exceptional analytical tool in this regard. Through a sincere and candid human resource performance assessment, program employees will know which of their specific job areas are (1) fulfilling, (2) surpassing, or (3) underperforming in established job requirements.

From a human resource management viewpoint, performance evaluations are non-emotional, non-disciplinary valuations of an employee's contribution to the sports or recreation program. Employees who exceed expectations should be commended and, if possible and appropriate, compensated. Program employees should meet expectations, and if the situation warrants, to go beyond an average performance level. Program employees who are deficient in particular aspects of their position should work cooperatively with administrators to develop and implement an action plans for improving performance in deficient areas.

Rewarding Program Employees. No other aspect of human resource management is more scrutinized than the equitable creation and monitoring of a reward system. Whether it is salary, benefits, incentive packages, or recognition, stakeholder rewards are considered a "hot-button topic" in program operations. Rewards systems in any program necessitates a definitive and justifiable structure, while maintaining complete transparency. An operational misstep in this area could yield unfortunate legal and public relations consequences for the overall program.

Rewarding program employees has evolved from basic wage and salary increases to a fully developed reward system.

Total reward describes a reward strategy that incorporates components including learning and development, aspects of the working environment, into a total benefits package. It brings together all types of reward—direct and indirect, intrinsic as well as extrinsic. Each aspect of reward (base pay, contingency pay, employee benefit and non-financial rewards, including intrinsic rewards from the work itself) are linked together and treated as a coherent whole. (Martin, 2010, p. 267)

Human Resource Relations. Traditionally, human resource management has examined human relations from a single perspective: employee discipline. The primary goal of human relations has shifted increasingly from employee discipline to employee retention. While employee discipline is still a factor of human relations, it has evolved to encompass:

- corrective action planning (based on performance criteria and assessments);
- efficient and compassionate separation processes;
- stakeholder wellness programs;
- teambuilding and extracurricular social functions; and
- ethical standards and training.

Compensation and benefits aside—compensation is not to be minimized, but is in a class by itself—managers can take a number of steps to raise levels of motivation and keep employees from wanting to leave. For example, managers can:

- Provide opportunities to learn and to grow within the job.
- Frequently praise and reward those who perform well.

- Conduct personal development discussions that focus on what's important to the employee, in addition to annual performance evaluations.

- Keep employees informed of any challenges the company faces.

- Provide ongoing training opportunities. A well-taught, cross-trained, and multiskilled workforce is especially valuable when you have fewer workers trying to cover all the bases.

(Arthur, 2015, pp. 203-204)

> **HR Tip**
>
> Enlightened sports and recreation programs recognize that to amplify employee satisfaction and performance, a holistic human relations approach must be incorporated into the philosophy of the organization.

Strong internal communication should be at the core of sound employee relations and retention policies in a sports or recreation program.

Strategic Human Resource Management. In the business world over the past 40 years, the evolution of human resource management has been nothing short of astonishing. The discipline has progressed from a clerical-based occupation to one of indispensable consequence in strategic planning for the organization.

> The involvement that an organization's HR function has in the development and implementation of strategy —how much and what kind—is a critical determinant of its influence and the value it adds. There is a growing consensus among executives and researchers that human capital needs to be given more and better-informed consideration because it should be an important determinant of what strategies an organization can and should pursue. (Lawler & Boudreau, 2015, p. 28)

Today's proactive human resource systems and functions, which will be the principal substance of this text, are the future driving forces in sports and recreation program administration. To have a thriving program now and, more importantly, in the future, one needs to appreciate the people who comprise the main component required for strategic development and execution. To accomplish program objectives, goals, and strategies, the quantity and quality of a program's employees are the salient asset. If a program has habitually regarded human resource functions as a superfluous time and financial expense, a philosophical transformation, while problematic, is possible. The solution is to consider all of the program's human resource systems as value creators rather than contributors to program resource depletion.

Human resource management, as a strategic factor of the operation, (1) acquires the most competent program members, (2) configures their jobs to strengthen productivity, (3) furnishes targeted training programs which enhance skills and competencies to complete strategies, (4) analyzes group and individual efficiency and output, and (5) retains and inspires employees to commit to the strategic objectives of the overall sports or recreation program.

HR Tip

In every aspect of the operational plan (marketing, operational management, accounting/finance, fundraising, etc.), human resource managers must focus on the organization's overall vision and mission as well as long- and short-term goals. Human resource functions emanate directly from the program's projected strategic future. Failing to do so would place the program in jeopardy of wasting critical resources, putting itself at a competitive disadvantage, and, ultimately, failure.

Human resource management is often the bridge between projected strategic objectives and what can, in reality, be accomplished by the program. In many instances, a program's strategic goals and objectives can either be impracticable or impossible to obtain or, conversely, too easily accomplished. With sound human resource systems in place, stretch objectives, which are described as setting "performance targets high enough to stretch an organization to perform at its full potential and deliver the best possible results" (Thompson, Peteraf, Gamble, & Strickland, 2018, p. 28), are not only conceivable, but plausible. Additionally, because sports and recreation programs are considered high performance enterprises, stretch objectives are even more significant to institute and undertake.

Characteristics of a Successful Human Resource Manager

When assembling a human resource department for a sports or recreation program, unquestionably the most significant position is the Human Resource Manager. The selection of this candidate must precisely correspond with the sports or recreation program's future vision, operational mission, and principal values, as well as dedication to the organization's personnel. The multitude of traits that make-up a talented human resource professional is incalculable. However, consider below, a list of some of the obligatory prerequisites for an exemplary human resource manager. These ideal characteristics include, but are not limited to:

- well developed cognitive abilities;
- high-level of personal organization;
- fosters strong social and interpersonal relationships;
- exhibits decisive decision-making skills;
- appreciates and leading organizational change;
- develops sound communication skills and the ability to disseminate information over a wide variety of mediums;
- balances an employee-centered attitude within the sports or recreation program's policies and procedures;
- skilled in conflict resolution, leading individual and group negotiations;
- emotionally stable and professional persona;
- blends day-to-day job responsibilities with creating long-term strategic goals and objectives;
- understands balancing employee empowerment with definitive accountability standards;
- remains objective in critique and constructive feedback of personnel (when applicable);

- employs hands-on management approach; and
- possesses intuitive ability to judge and assess talent.

From these essential characteristics, the selection of a talented and dynamic Human Resource Manager is more assured for a sports and/or recreation program's achievement. An ill-suited individual could likely produce operational anarchy, depreciated moral standards, and, in due course, program failure.

Human Resource Information Systems

Human Resource Information Systems (HRIS) are built to enhance operational efficiency by organizing human resource management data and curtailing time expended on these program recordkeeping requirements. Through technology and software innovations, HRIS are cost effective and exceedingly user-friendly. Grensing-Pophal (2010) have developed a number of criteria administrators can consider when in the process of procuring a HRIS for one's sports or recreation program.

System compatibility. Will the system you are considering be compatible with your existing hardware and software needs?

Value. You can purchase a system at any range of the price spectrum, from very low cost to exorbitantly expensive. The challenge is to find the price and value that most closely meets your company's needs and budget.

Ease of access. A set of questions to ask, will help determine the most easily accessible system for the program: Who will be entering and accessing information? How readily accessible will the HRIS be? What level of training will be required, and how long will it take to become proficient in the system? Can the HRIS run parallel with other commonly accessed systems?

Support. Will the vendor provide ongoing support, regular updates, and training? Will there be additional charges for these services?

Reporting. The types of reports available to administrators are a key driver in selecting a system. What types of reports can be generated automatically? What ability will users have to modify reports, or to create new reports?

Personal Compatibility. An HRIS is a long-term commitment, and it requires a long-term relationship with a vendor. While administrators will select a system based, to a large degree, on the capabilities of the system, an open working relationship with the vendor will also be important.

Future needs. Consider any potential organizational changes that may affect operations over the next three to five years. (p. 170)

The inventory of tasks that corporate human resource information systems can accomplish is vast. For a sports or recreation program, base-level systems can characteristically meet operational demands, both now and in the future. However, it is of great consequence to understand that each program must determine which human resource data functions to incorporate into its tailored HRIS, which allows for overlap and a need to tailor functions. Some of the possible areas a program could integrate within an HRIS are detailed in Table 1.1.

There are some final considerations when setting up an HRIS for a sports or recreation program. First and foremost, an all-inclusive HRIS is a virtual system that is entirely paperless. The central advantages to a paperless system are:

TABLE 1.1 Functional HRIS Areas

General Program Information	*Personnel Information*
Online policy and procedure manual	Applications and resume database
Job descriptions for all program positions	Audio/visual messaging
Program hierarchical chart	Transcripts
Governing body's resources (compliance manuals, report forms, general information)	IRS/tax information
	Payroll, benefit data, e-paychecks
Program strategic plan	Employee evaluations
Electronic media guides and bio information	Employee discipline records and action plans
E-training programs and certifications	Employee assistance programs
Program event calendar/schedule	
Program directory (public contact information)	
Orientation program and information	

Note: HRIS, security protocols based on clearance levels should be established. For instance, recreation program events and schedules should be accessible by all recreation program members at any security level. Conversely, personnel data should only be available to top recreational organization administrators, based on need and job title/level. Prior to launching an HRIS, these protocols must created with the sports or recreation program's legal counsel.

- *Cost savings.* Printed materials are expensive. The never-ending expenditure of printing, reprinting, copying, and distributing human resource materials can be exorbitant for a sports or recreation program.

- *Information accessibility.* Data compiled in an HRIS are consolidated so that all program data can be obtained immediately within the physical operation or remotely.

- *Modification efficiency.* Modifying any of the human resource function and data in an HRIS can be instantaneous. Conversely, amending printed materials can be a painstakingly arduous process and costly.

The fact that computer systems, no matter how sophisticated and sound, are not infallible and can crash or be hacked. This conspicuous disadvantage is why a sports or recreation program must support and maintain a data backup storage system. Data backup systems can be (1) an uncomplicated, but secured, in-house external hard drive, (2) a cloud-based secured storage mechanism, or (3) both. Data backups updates and revision should be periodically scheduled or automatically built into the HRIS to occur regularly.

Setup and data entry consideration in HRIS should answer before selecting an HRIS are: (1) Who is going to set up the required functions? (2) Who is going to input new data? (3) Who will be responsible for data maintenance? (4) When should data reports be generated? Not only do these questions help define job responsibilities among program employees, they help determine many of the layers of functionality required by the system for daily efficacious use and maintenance.

> ## HR Tip
>
> When considering purchasing an HRIS (which is highly recommended due to the affordability, remarkable functionality, and tailoring capabilities of most HRIS packages), a chief topic of conversation with the software vendor should be customer support. From assisting in set-up, going live, and helping with any possible system glitches, 24-hour competent tech support is a critical consideration.

Challenges in Today's Volatile Environment

Never before has human resource management confronted more precarious and ever-evolving operational issues. These difficulties are pertinent to all business enterprises, sports and recreation programs included. Ongoing and potential areas of focus for human resource management should be identified and actively considered for current and future incorporation into program management policies.

Social Media. Owing to the popularity of social media use, human resource management necessitates the development of coherent, fair policies and procedures for staff, administrators, and executives in the use of social media in and outside of the workplace. These policies must balance personal freedoms with organizational interests.

Public Relations. Due to expanding media technology and program access, the handling of public relation incidents and crises (internally and externally) should be an ongoing principal concern for human resource managers.

Revolving Workplace. The conundrum associated with the escalating volatility of employment is twofold. Internally, mounting outside competitive pressures and new internal operating strategies amplify outsourcing, layoffs, and downsizing. Externally, workforce mobility continues to intensify, allowing talented individuals to change positions at will.

Training. Every distinct industry must embrace innovative, exponentially increasing technology and modernization. Personnel training, lead by human resource management, must proactively welcome these changes with strategic technology and transformation training.

Equality. Rectifying inequities and the lack of organizational diversity is a vital function of human resource management now, and in the future. Items such as addressing fair pay policies, equitable hiring, impartial promotions, systemic discrimination, and eliminating human prejudice in business operations are all important, ongoing concerns for human resource management.

Team Synergy. Because of fluctuating structural dynamics in organizations, more project based, cross-function teams will be created and applied in the future. This team structure will be founded on an empowered, self-managed employment philosophy.

Health and Quality of Personal Lives. Balancing workforce productivity with individual quality of life is a critical component of human resource management's employee retention policy.

Internal Politics. While not a new dilemma, dealing with politicized organizational environments falls directly on human resource management.

Aging Personnel. As previously mentioned, the demographic group known as "baby boomers" is leaving the workforce in what can best be described as a mass exodus. The loss of intellectual capital from these departures could cause a significant impact to many operations. Human resource management must develop unique creative strategies to preserve and transfer as much of this experiential knowledge as possible.

Labor Laws. Staying abreast and in compliance with current and future federal, state, and local labor laws is an ongoing, fundamental consideration for all human resource professionals.

Ethical Operating Standards. Human resource management must develop, cultivate, and monitor internal ethics principles and actions for all sports and recreation program stakeholders.

Professional Development. Through career mapping and job improvements, human resource managers must foster professional development activities for all in-house employees. These activities, such as continuing education units, tuition reimbursement, seminars, will be fundamental tools in boosting an organization's human resource retention.

Economic Unpredictability. The assessment of local, state, and national economic volatility and its impact on a sports and recreation programs human resource is an growing priority for human resource managers.

Personnel Recruiting. Winning the recruitment battle for the most qualified and prized individuals will escalate in the future and fall clearly on human resource managers.

From these challenges and more, the question then becomes, How can a sports or recreation program's human resource manager deal with all of these daunting and sometimes overwhelming issues? The salient key is to establish human resource systems, policies and procedures, and operational strategies that can be used as guideposts for precise actions to be taken.

Summary

For program success, it is necessary to distinguish and appreciate the most valuable asset in the program: the operation's people. Contemporary human resource management strategies and functions have become essential elements in this respect. A program administrator, coach, counselor, or staff member who utilizes human resource management tools can experience better productivity, less personnel turnover, increased cultural awareness, increased safety and health of the program's stakeholders, better internal communication and relationships, and, ultimately, a strategic advantage over direct and indirect competitors.

As a factor in sports or recreation program planning and strategic development, human resource management can and should be a prominent factor in the fulfillment of the operation's vision, mission, and values, along with long- and short-term goals. By underscoring the human element in strategic planning, a program can experience a marked proliferation in the quality, development, monitoring, and retention of its people. This will compound, often dramatically, the success of the program's goals and objectives.

To minimize opportunity costs, human resource clerical functions should be incorporated into a tailored human resource information system (HRIS). This HRIS can contribute to superior internal efficiencies and, consequently, increase the precious commodity of time to pursue and execute program aspirations.

References

Aquinas, P. (2009). *Human resource management: Principles and practices.* New Delhi, India: Vikas Publishing House.

Arthur, D. (2015). *Fundamentals of human resources management: A practical guide for today's HR professional.* New York, NY: American Management Association International.

Greene, R. J. (2011). *Rewarding performance: Guiding principles; Custom strategies.* New York, NY: Routledge.

Grensing-Pophal, L. (2010). *Human resource essentials: Your guide to starting and running the HR function.* Alexandria, VA: Society for Human Resource Management.

Lawler, E. E., & Boudreau, J. W. (2015). *Global trends in human resource management: A twenty-year analysis.* Stanford, California: Stanford Business Books.

Martin, J. (2010). *Key concepts in human resource management.* Thousand Oaks, CA: Sage Publishing.

Price, A. (2011). *Human resource management* (4th ed.). Andover/Hampshire, United Kingdom: Southwestern Cengage Learning.

Rue, L. W., Ibrahim, N. A., & Byars, L. L. (2013). *Management: Skills and application* (14th ed.). New York, NY: McGraw-Hill/Irwin.

Snell, S., Morris, S., & Bohlander, G. (2013). *Managing human resources* (17th ed.). Boston, MA: Cengage Learning.

Thompson, A. A., Peteraf, M. A., Gamble, J. E., & Strickland, A. J. (2018). *Crafting and executing strategy: The quest for competitive advantage* (21st ed.). New York, NY: McGraw-Hill/Irwin.

Review and Discussion Questions

1. What is a sports or recreation program's most valuable asset?

2. What are the benefits of human resource management's professionalism?

3. How can human resource management help with workplace safety?

4. What are the advantages of having strong human resource communication policies and procedures?

5. Define the term psychological contract.

6. List the five major human resource management elements and universal practices.

7. What are the three tiers of human resource laws and regulations for a sports or recreation program?

8. What is human resource management modeling?

9. How have human relations evolved?

10. Describe human resource onboarding.

11. When purchasing an HRIS for a sports or recreation program, what are the criteria to consider?

12. What are HRIS security protocols?

13. What are the advantages of a paperless system? What is the major disadvantage of a paperless system?

Application Exercises

1. You are the new coach for an NAIA baseball program. List 10 core values that emphasize a philosophy of employee-centered operations for that program. Elaborate on each human resource value.

2. Through online research, find three policy and procedure templates that could be adapted to a city-wide recreation program. Highlight areas for program consideration. Use APA to cite sources.

Term Project
Oral Presentation

You are the Owner/Athletic Director of a mid-sized United States Volleyball Association Junior Olympic club program. The program has:

12 Teams (3 at each age level – 12's, 14's, 16's, and 18 Elite)

36 Coaches

12 Parent Chaperons (volunteers)

2 Program Administrators

2 Administrative Office Staff

The organization is sorely lacking a human resource information system in its operation. Most functions are still done by hand. Using Figure 1.1, design, from the ground up, an HRIS that will increase internal operational efficiency in your organization.

Elements:

- Research human resource software that can be used by the operation. Use HR sources (online and journals) to conduct your research.
- Select and compare the top 3 most appropriate programs. Justify what each software package provides and why it would be appropriate for the operation.
- Determine the cost factors and the long-term savings potential for each.
- Discuss hardware requirements, costs, and benefits for each.
- Define the conversion time, training requirements, and estimated learning curve for each..

Criteria:

- Develop a 30-minute presentation on the top HRIS program and detail the functions to be utilized by the club program
- Prepare for a 15-minute Q & A session after main presentation
- Create PowerPoint slides and visual aids to supplement the presentation (hard copy to be submitted prior to presentation).
- Conduct extensive external research to justify your selections.

chapter two

Human Resource Management and the Law

Jeffrey Kelly, Esquire

Chapter Objectives

- Categorize the sources of human resource laws that can apply to sport and recreation programs as employers
- Provide resources for researching and complying with federal state human resource laws
- Illustrate how human resource laws apply to employers.
- Emphasize the difference(s) between independent contractors and employees
- Discuss the concept of at-will employment
- Summarize the major federal human resource laws that can apply employers
- Recognize difference(s) between federal law and state and local human resource laws
- Identify human resource requirements of other governing bodies

Key Terms

Independent Contractor	Discrimination	Reinstatement
Minimum Wage	Retaliation	Unpaid Leave
FICA Tax	Disparate Treatment	Shared-Responsibility Payment
Unfair Labor Practice	Disparate Impact	Small Business Health Options
Collective Bargaining	Business Necessity	Program (SHOP)
Right-to-Work State	Sexual Harassment	Genetic Information
I-9 Verification	Disability	
Protected Class	Reasonable Accommodation	

This chapter will cover the major areas of human resource law, with a focus on certain provisions of federal laws and regulations, as well as corresponding state and some local laws. The chapter begins with historical federal laws (pre-1990) and corresponding state laws and local laws, and then focuses on contemporary (post-1990) federal laws and corresponding state and local laws.

While this chapter will cover major provisions of certain human resource laws, most of the laws also contain requirements pertaining to recordkeeping and providing notice to employees who, either through postings in the workplace or written notice to employees at specific times, are not covered by this chapter. Human resource law can be very complex, ever-changing, and can vary widely between the federal, state, and local levels. Therefore, it is also strongly advised to consult with your legal counsel in all aspects of employment to ensure compliance with all applicable federal, state, and local laws.

Although consulting with legal counsel is ultimately recommended to ensure compliance with all applicable laws, there are many resources to aid employers, including, but not limited to, the U.S. Department of Labor, Equal Employment Opportunity Commission, and other agencies that are charged with enforcing certain laws. Resources to aid employers in complying with state and local laws are also available through state and local agencies. The U.S. Department of Labor provides a list of state labor offices and their contact information on its website.

Applicability of Human Resource Laws

Whether the various employment and labor laws covered in this chapter apply to a program and its workers depends on several factors. First, is the worker considered an employee of the program or an independent contractor? Second, how many of the program workers are considered employees?

Employees v. Independent Contractors

Whether workers in any business are classified as employees or independent contractors is important in determining whether various employment and labor laws apply (most of which are covered in this chapter). According to the Internal Revenue Service, employer obligations, such as withholding wages, and in some cases contributing their own money, and paying certain employment taxes such as Social Security, Medicare, worker's compensation, and unemployment tax only apply for workers who are considered employees. Businesses normally do not have to withhold or pay any taxes on *payments* to *independent contractors*. Additionally, the rights of workers and what procedures are followed when it comes to hiring, employing, separating, and providing benefits generally only apply when the workers are employees, not independent contractors.

What determines whether a worker is an employee or independent contractor? Even though a worker may be designated as an independent contractor, this determination requires a more in-depth analysis using several factors. For additional information, please see Appendix D IRS Rules and Regulations Concerning Employment Classifications.

Minimum Number of Employees and How "Employee" is Defined. For those workers who are determined to be employees, whether certain federal and state laws and regulations apply also depends on how many employees an employer has, and how the term *employee* is defined by that law. For example, many federal laws, such as the Family Medical Leave Act (FMLA), only apply to employers with at least 50 employees, while state laws pertaining to family medical leave often have a lower minimum threshold. However, employment and labor laws also vary on how they define employees. For example, according to the EEOC, most federal anti-discrimination laws consider the definition of employee to include those who work full-time, part-time, or on a temporary or seasonal basis.

Conversely, the Patient Protection and Affordable Care Act only counts full-time employees as those who work an average of 30 or more hours during a calendar month or a combination of part-time employees that, together, equal a full-time employee.

Interns and Volunteers. According to the U.S. Department of Labor, whether an intern is considered an employee can depend on several factors, one of which is whether the intern is promised any compensation. (According to the EEOC, even volunteers can be considered employees and covered under the federal anti-discrimination laws under certain circumstances, such as the volunteer opportunity often leading to employment opportunities.

States may also have their own laws that determine whether interns and volunteers are considered employees. Therefore, it is important for any business to be clear with how they use interns and volunteers and what rights and protections volunteers may have under federal and applicable state laws.

Employment-at-Will. Although a worker may be classified as an employee, the terms and conditions of that individual's employment depend on whether that employee is an at-will employee or an employee who is covered under an employment contract. Such employment contracts may be expressly laid out upon the employee being hired, or may be established through certain documents given to the employee, such as employee handbooks or standards of conduct. However, in instances where there is no established employment contract, employment relationships have historically been governed by the common law* concept of employment-at-will . When the relationship between an employer and an employee is considered to be at-will, either party can terminate the employment relationship at any time and for any reason (or no reason at all) without notice, as long as no laws are being violated.

In many cases, employees choose to terminate the relationship with their employer for a number of reasons (see Appendix F Employee Generated Separations: A New Attitude). However, when the termination of the relationship of an at-will employee is initiated by the employer, particularly without cause or notice, the employer must be aware of any exceptions to the at-will concept that may apply. Such exceptions arise out of both federal and state laws and can significantly reduce how and when the concept of employment-at-will applies. For example, under federal law and all state laws, employees may not be fired for any illegal reasons such as the employee being a whistleblower (in violation of federal and state whistleblower laws), or for some discriminatory reason, such as the employee's race or gender that would violate federal and state anti-discrimination laws.

As of the publication of this textbook, all states except Montana still recognize the concept of employment-at-will, but vary on the exceptions that can apply, including exceptions that fall under public policy, implied contract, or covenant of good faith in fair dealing. Additional information on a state's laws can be obtained at that state's labor office.

---

* Common law is a body of English law as adopted and modified separately by the different states in the U.S. and by the federal government.

> ### HR Tip
> Due to the exceptions to at-will employment, a sport and recreation program's legal counsel should be involved in the drafting of employee handbooks, standards of conduct, or any other materials that may contain terms or conditions of employment. To ensure that the at-will status of employees remain clear, legal counsel should also be involved in establishing systems pertaining to discipline, corrective action, grievances, and separation, as detailed in Chapter 9.

Historical Employment/Labor Laws (Pre-1990)

Fair Labor Standards Act of 1938

The Fair Labor Standards Act (FLSA) is a federal law that was first enacted in 1938. The FLSA establishes minimum wage, overtime, child labor, and record keeping requirements, and is enforced by the Wage and Hour Division of the U.S. Department of Labor. The FLSA applies to all employers whose annual sales total $500,000 or more OR who are engaged in interstate commerce, regardless of the number of employees the employer has. However, certain types of employees are exempt from the minimum wage and overtime pay provisions of the FLSA. According to the U.S. Department of Labor exemption regulations, employees who are considered executive, administrative, professional, and outside-sale employees, as well as employees in certain computer-related occupations (as defined in DOL regulations), are exempt from both the minimum wage and overtime pay provisions of the FLSA.

> ### HR Tip
> Whether an athletic program employee is exempt from the provisions of the FLSA depends on the duties that the employee performs, and not the employee's title. Consequently, it is crucial that job descriptions for each position are clear and accurately reflect the actual duties of the position.

Minimum Wage

Federal Minimum Wage Laws. The FLSA requires employers of covered employees who are not otherwise exempt to pay these employees a minimum wage, which, as of the publication of this textbook, currently is $7.25 an hour. There are certain exceptions. For example, youth under 20 years of age may be paid a minimum wage of currently not less than $4.25 per hour during the first 90 consecutive calendar days of employment with an employer. Employers may not displace any employee to hire someone at the youth minimum wage.

State and Local Minimum Wage Laws. In addition to the federal minimum wage, employers may be subject to state or local minimum wage laws. Nearly all U.S. states have their own minimum wage laws, many of which establish a minimum wage that exceeds the federal minimum wage. If an employer is subject to both federal and state minimum wage laws, the employer generally must pay eligible employees the higher of the two. Please see Table 2.1 for state minimum wage laws and how they compare to the FLSA, which is based on information provided by the U.S. Department of Labor.

TABLE 2.1   State Minimum Wage Laws

States with minimum wage laws higher than federal: 29	Alaska, Arkansas, Arizona, California, Colorado, Connecticut, D.C., Delaware, Florida, Hawaii, Illinois, Massachusetts, Maryland, Maine, Michigan, Missouri, Montana, Minnesota, Nebraska, New Jersey, New Mexico, Nevada, New York, Ohio, Oregon, Rhode Island, South Dakota, Vermont, Washington, West Virginia
States with minimum wage laws equal to federal: 14	Iowa, Idaho, Indiana, Kansas, Kentucky, New Hampshire, North Carolina, North Dakota, Oklahoma, Pennsylvania, Texas, Utah, Virginia, Wisconsin
States with no minimum wage laws (federal applies): 5	Alabama, Louisiana, Mississippi, South Carolina, Tennessee
States with lower minimum wage (federal applies): 2	Georgia, Wyoming

In addition to state laws, localities may have even higher minimum wage. For example, the minimum wage in Chicago, Illinois, is $12.00 an hour, while the minimum wage in New York City ranges from $13.50 to $15.00 an hour depending on the size of the employer.

When employers are subject to varying federal, state, and local minimum wage laws, they must pay the highest of the minimum wages that are required.

Overtime

Federal Overtime Law. In addition to establishing a minimum wage, the FLSA also requires employers to pay eligible employees overtime pay for hours worked over 40 in a workweek at a rate no less than time and one-half their regular rates of pay. According to the U.S. Department of Labor, the FLSA overtime provisions apply on a workweek basis, although it should be noted that there is more than one type of workweek, and different workweeks may be established for different employees or groups of employees. Regardless of the type of workweek, averaging of hours over a payroll period (such as two or more weeks) is not permitted. Normally, overtime pay earned in a particular workweek must be paid on the regular pay day for the pay period in which the wages were earned.

As stated previously, some employees are exempt from the overtime provisions and are therefore not eligible to earn overtime. For those who are eligible, the FLSA does not require employers to authorize such employees to earn overtime. However, according to the Department of Labor,

> Employees must be paid for work "suffered or permitted" by the employer even if the employer does not specifically authorize the work. If the employer knows or has reason to believe that the employee is continuing to work, the time is considered hours worked. (See Regulation 29 CFR 785.11.)

Furthermore, the FLSA does not require overtime pay for work on Saturdays, Sundays, holidays, or regular days of rest unless overtime is worked on such days.

State Overtime Laws. Many states have their own overtime laws that may still apply to employers who are exempt from the FLSA. In those cases where an employee is subject to both federal and state overtime laws, the employee is entitled to overtime according to the higher standard that will provide higher overtime pay.

Employees who may be exempt from overtime under the FLSA may still be eligible for overtime under a state's laws. While state overtime laws can vary from the FLSA on which employees are eligible, some states allow covered employees to earn overtime on a daily basis by working over 8 hours per day, regardless of whether they exceed 40 hours for the week. For example, Nevada requires employers to pay overtime to employees who work more than 8 hours in a 24-hour period, regardless of whether they exceed 40 hours for the week. However, this Nevada provision only applies to employees who make less than one and half times the current state minimum wage in Nevada, while employees whose pay exceeds this threshold are only eligible for overtime if they exceed 40 hours for the week.

Child Labor

Federal Child Labor Laws. The FLSA prohibits oppressive child labor and establishes restrictions on child labor that vary by age group as follows:

- **Under 14.** Children can only perform very limited types of work, such as delivering newspapers, performing certain types of work for their parents, or being employed in the child entertainment industry.
- **Ages 14–15.** Children are allowed to work in non-hazardous occupations, subject to the following conditions:
  - Hours per week: No more than 18 hours per week when school is in session, and 40 hours per week when school is not in session.
  - Work hours: Cannot work during school hours, and must be between 7:00 am and 7:00 pm (9:00 pm during the summer).
  - **Note:** The FLSA regulations allows children who provide specific sports-attending services at professional sporting events (e.g., batboys or batgirls) to work any hours so long as they occur outside of school hours. (29 C.F.R. § 570.35(c)(2)).
- **Ages 16–17.** Children can work in non-hazardous occupations, but there are no restrictions on the working times or number of hours.

According to the U.S. Department of Labor, employers who violate the FLSA child labor provisions may be assessed a civil penalty of up to $11,000 for each employee who was the subject of a child labor violation, and up to $50,000 for each violation that causes the death or serious injury of a minor employee; penalties may be doubled for repeat or willful violations - 29 U.S.C. § 216(e).

State Child Labor Laws. In addition to the FLSA provisions on child labor, employers must be aware of state child labor laws; all 50 states have them. While many states' child labor provisions mirror the FLSA, other states have stricter standards. For example, Florida prohibits 16- and 17-year old from working more than 30 hours per week during the school year, and they cannot work between 11:00 pm and 6:00 am prior to a school day (Section 450.081(2), Florida Statutes).

While information about state child labor laws can be obtained from a state's labor office, the U.S. Department of Labor also provides a comprehensive chart of child labor laws by state on its website.

HR Tip

Employers should be aware of any state requirements and procedures for verifying an employee's age. While the FLSA does not require minors to obtain working permits or working papers, many states do have such requirements and can vary on how such documentation is obtained. In addition to a state's labor office, the U.S. Department of Labor provides a chart on its website containing information on state requirements and procedures for obtaining a minor's proof of age.

Updates and Amendments to the FLSA. The FLSA has been updated several times since its inception. According to the Equal Employment Opportunity Commission (EEOC), the Equal Pay Act of 1963 was passed as an amendment to the FLSA and began requiring that men and women in the same workplace be given equal pay for equal work. To be considered equal work, jobs must be substantially similar, and equal pay includes equal salary, overtime pay, bonuses, stock options, profit sharing, bonus plans, life insurance, vacation and holiday pay, and benefits.

In 2010, the Patient Protection and Affordable Healthcare Act (PPACA) amended the FLSA to include protection for employees who are nursing mothers. Additional information on this provision can be found in the section on the PPACA.

Federal Insurance Contributions Act of 1935

The Federal Insurance Contributions Act (FICA) requires employers to withhold certain amounts of an employee's compensation to pay FICA taxes, which include Social Security and Medicare taxes. The law requires employers to not only withhold a portion of an employee's wages to pay these taxes, but employers generally must also match the amount of FICA taxes withheld from its employees. FICA also requires employers to report employee wages annually so that the proper amount of Social Security and Medicare benefits for workers and their dependents can be calculated.

Federal Unemployment Tax Act of 1939 (FUTA)

The Federal Unemployment Tax Act of 1939 was created to provide payments of unemployment compensation to eligible workers who lost their jobs. The law requires employers to pay both a federal unemployment tax and a state unemployment tax at regular intervals so the proceeds can be used to fund the unemployment compensation programs. Although it is a federal law, it is administered through state programs, each of which have certain eligibility requirements. Such requirements usually include the individual working for a certain period of time prior to being separated and the individual must be actively seeking employment to continue receiving benefits. However, individuals who were terminated for some level of misconduct or left their jobs voluntarily are generally disqualified from receiving benefits.

National Labor Relations Act of 1935

The National Labor Relations Act (also called the Wagner Act) of 1935 (NLRA) is one of the most prominent federal laws that was passed to protects employee's rights pertaining to joining labor unions and bargaining collectively with employers over the terms and conditions of employment. It was preceded by the Clayton Act of 1914 and the Norris-LaGuardia Act of 1932, both of which protected employees rights to organize and engage in peaceful strikes, but not to the extent that the NLRA did.

Unfair Labor Practices. Under the NLRA, employers are prohibited from engaging in unfair labor practices, such as interfering with employees' rights to form and/or join labor unions. Employer actions that can be considered unfair labor practices include threatening employees with loss of jobs or benefits if they engage in certain "concerted activities," such as joining or voting for a union, or promising benefits to employees to discourage them from doing so. Other employees protections include an employee's right to strike. However, the NLRA also provides employees who are not represented by a union with the right to engage their employer about the terms and conditions of employment such as pay, workplace, conditions, or addressing safety concerns.

Collective Bargaining in Good Faith. When unions are chosen to represent a group of employees (bargaining unit) after an election among the employees takes place, the NLRA requires both the employer and the union to bargain collectively and in good faith with one another over the terms and conditions of employment. Whether a good faith attempt was made can be determined on a case-by-case basis, but it generally requires "an open mind and a sincere desire to reach an agreement, as well as a sincere effort to reach common ground." However, even though the employer and union are required to bargain in good faith, they are not compelled to reach an agreement.

National Labor Relations Board. Another main provision of the NLRA was that it created the National Labor Relations Board (NLRB) to act as an independent agency to administer and enforce the NLRA. The NLRB has the authority to conduct and oversee union elections as well as investigate employee charges of unfair labor practices, decide cases, and enforce orders which can eventually lead to monetary remedies.

Applicability of the NLRA. The NLRA covers most private-sector workers in industries whose operations affect interstate commerce. However, the NLRA specifically does not apply to supervisors (in most circumstances), or non-private sector workers such as federal, state, and local government workers.

State Labor Laws. Although the NLRA doesn't apply to federal, state, and local government workers, such workers can still be covered under state laws. For example, in the State of Florida, public employees have the right to form, join, or participate in any labor organization or union of their own choosing, and also have the right to be represented by any labor organization or union of their own choosing. (Section

447.301, F.S.) However, Florida does not provide public employees with the right to strike. (Section 447.505, F.S.)

Right-to-Work States. It should be noted that, in certain states, known as right-to-work states, employees can never be compelled to join a union as a condition of maintaining employment. This does not mean that unions do not exist in those states, but only that employees can never be compelled to join a union as a condition of maintaining employment. However, according to the National Labor Relations Board, such employees may still be protected by the collective bargaining agreement negotiated by the union.

Janus v. AFSCME Council 31. Although employees could decide not to be members of a labor union, those non-union members who are public employees could be compelled to pay "fair share agency fees" under the rationale that they still benefitted from the collective bargaining of the employer even though they were not union members. In June, 2018, the Supreme Court of the United States in Janus v. AFSCME Council, 128 S. Ct. 2448 (2018), reversed this long-standing precedent by issuing a decision stating that public employers could not deduct such fees from non-members wages, nor may a labor union otherwise collect agency fees from a non-member without the non-member's consent.

Occupational Safety and Health Act of 1970

Federal OSHA Law. The primary federal law that covers workplace health and safety is the Occupational Safety and Health Act (OSHA). This law was passed in 1970 with the purpose of ensuring the "safe and healthful working conditions for working men and women by setting and enforcing standards and by providing training, outreach, education, and assistance." The law covers most private sector employees nationwide, as well as those employed by federal agencies.

The law is administered and enforced by OSHA under the U.S. Department of Labor. OSHA creates and enforces safety standards in the workplace. Employer's responsibilities include providing workplaces that are free from serious recognized hazards and compliance with standards, rules, and regulations set by OSHA; examining workplace conditions to ensure compliance with OSHA standards; establishing, updating, and communicating operating procedures so that employees follow safety and health requirements; and posting OSHA posters in prominent locations within the workplace to inform employees of their rights and responsibilities.

Failure to comply with OSHA standards can result in substantial fines to employers. According to OSHA, the current penalties are $12,934 per violation, and $129,336 for willful or repeated violations, and are regularly adjusted for inflation.

State OSHA Plans. Although OSHA is a federal law that applies to all private sector and federal government employees in all states and territories, it does not apply to state and local government employees. However, according to OSHA, the law does allow states and territories to adopt their own OSHA plans (which can be submitted to, and approved by, OSHA) as long as the state plans are considered to be "at least as effective in preventing work-related injuries, illnesses, and deaths."

It is important to note state and local employees may still be covered by OSHA if there is a state plan in place that extends OSHA protection to those employees. According to OSHA, 26 states plus Puerto

Rico and the Virgin Islands have OSHA-approved plans, all of which expand OSHA coverage to state and local government employees, as well as private employees.

Fair Credit Reporting Act of 1970

Federal FCRA Law. The Fair Credit Reporting Act of 1970 (FCRA) is a federal law that imposes certain requirements on employers who use third-party companies (known as consumer reporting agencies) to compile background information on applicants and employees. Such background information often includes information relating to consumer credit, criminal background, driving records, and dates of employment. The FCRA is enforced by the Federal Trade Commission (FTC) and, as provided by FTC's website.

The FCRA requires employers to take the following steps prior to obtaining a background check:

- Obtain the applicant or employee's written permission to conduct the background check;
- Provide clear written notice to applicants or employees that such background information may be used to make employment decisions. Such notice must be in a stand-alone document that is separate from the employment application; and
- Inform such individuals of their right to a description of the nature and scope of any investigations that are requested by the employer.

Employers must also certify compliance to the company from which they are obtaining the applicant or employee's information. Compliance includes certifying that the employer:

- notified the applicant or employee and obtained their permission to request a consumer report;
- complied with all of the FCRA requirements;
- will not discriminate against the applicant or employee or otherwise misuse the information, as provided by any applicable federal or state equal opportunity laws or regulations.

Once the background check is completed, the employer must take the following steps if it is considering taking any type of negative employment action (not hiring, not promoting, or not retaining) against an applicant or employee, based on information obtained in the background check:

- Notify the applicant or the employee of the potential adverse decision and provide a copy of the report and summary of rights to the individual.
- Allow the individual an opportunity to contact the consumer reporting agency and dispute the report.
- Inform the individual of the final decision and certain information about the consumer reporting agency.

When conducting background checks, some employers use "investigative reports," which are reports based on personal interviews concerning a person's character, general reputation, personal characteristics, and lifestyle. The FCRA imposes additional obligations on employers when using investigative reports, such as giving written notice that you may request or have requested an investigative consumer report, and giving a statement that the person has a right to request additional disclosures and a summary of the scope and substance of the report.

State FCRA Laws. Many states have provisions that are similar to the FCRA. However, other states such as Illinois and Oregon go further in that they prevent certain types of employers from making employment decisions based on an individual's credit reports, subject to certain exceptions. Therefore, employers should be aware of both federal and state law requirements when conducting employee background checks.

Employment Retirement Income Security Act of 1974

The Employee Retirement Income Security Act of 1974 (ERISA) was passed to protect the interests of employees who participate in their employer's retirement and/or welfare benefit plans. According to the U.S. Department of Labor, it protects employee's retirement savings from mismanagement and abuse, and promotes transparency and accountability by requiring plan sponsors to provide plan information to participants. ERISA also establishes standards of conduct for plan managers and other fiduciaries. However, ERISA does not require any employer to establish a retirement plan; it only requires those who establish such plans to meet federal standards.

ERISA is administered and enforced by the Employee Benefits Security Administration of the United States Department of Labor (EBSA). According to the EBSA, many states have similar laws concerning retirement plans, but these state laws are mostly pre-empted (with certain exceptions) by the federal law.

Consolidated Omnibus Budget Reconciliation Act of 1985

Federal Law. The Consolidated Omnibus Budget Reconciliation Act of 1985 (COBRA) was passed as an amendment to ERISA, and requires employers with group health plans to offer continuation of coverage to any covered employees or former employees and their spouses and dependents when coverage would otherwise be lost due to termination of their employment (voluntarily or involuntarily) or due to a reduction in work hours that would affect the employee's coverage. COBRA also allows spouses and dependents to continue coverage due to events such as death of the covered employees, divorce, or a child's loss of dependent status.

Depending on the type of event, the period of continued coverage required to be offered can range from 18 to 36 months after the qualifying event. However, the law does not require employers to pay for any portion of the premium. According to the EBSA, COBRA general applies to all private sector group health plans maintained by employers who have at least 20 or more employees (full or part-time), as well as state and local governments.

State Laws. Although COBRA only applies to private sector employers of 20 or more employers, most states have their own similar laws, most of which apply to businesses with fewer than 20 employees. State laws also vary on the time period for which continuation of coverage must be offered. For example,

Florida's COBRA law applies to any employer with fewer than 20 employees, and it extends coverage to employees for 11 additional months if the separation from employment is due to a disability. (Florida Health Insurance Coverage Continuation Act, Section 627.6692, Florida Statutes)

Immigration Reform and Control Act of 1986

The main provision of the Immigration Reform and Control Act of 1986 (IRCA) is that it prohibited the hiring or recruiting of individuals who are not authorized to work in the United States. IRCA was passed as an amendment to the Immigration and Nationality Act of 1952 by adding in sanctions against employers, and the sanctions were later updated with the passage of the Immigration Act of 1990 and the Illegal Immigration Reform and Immigrant Responsibility Act of 1996.

To comply with IRCA, employers must verify the identity of each individual hired, as well as confirm that individual's authorization to work. This requirement includes completing and retaining records of I-9 verifications for each employee. I-9 verification includes having the individual provide certain types of documentation to establish their identify and authorization to work, and the employer certifying that the applicant produced such documents.

Although IRCA requires employers to confirm their identity and authorization to work, IRCA prohibits employers from discriminating against individuals on the basis of national origin, citizenship, or immigration status. Also, employers must not hire, recruit for a fee, or refer for a fee, any individuals whom the employer knows to be unauthorized to work in the U.S.

IRCA is enforced by the U.S. Immigration and Customs Enforcement (ICE) within the Department of Homeland Security. According to ICE, penalties for employers who violate IRCA can include civil fines and even criminal penalties if the employer is shown to have engaged in a pattern or practice of violations.

Civil Rights Act of 1964

Federal Law. Title VII of the Civil Rights Act of 1964 (Title VII) is one of the first laws to prohibit discrimination by employers in all aspects of employment *including hiring, firing, pay, job assignments, promotions, layoffs, training, benefits, and any other term or condition of employment (U.S. EEOC).* This 1964 law was preceded by the Civil Rights Act of 1866 (Section 1981), but this earlier law only prohibited discrimination based on race or color, while Title VII expanded to include the factors of national origin, gender, and religion.

The Pregnancy Act of 1970 amended Title VII to prohibit discrimination against a woman because of pregnancy, childbirth, or a medical condition related to pregnancy or childbirth. The Civil Rights Act of 1991 further amended Title VII to allow for trial by jury and expand the types of remedies that could be awarded in discrimination cases.

Sexual Orientation and Gender Identity. Although sexual orientation and gender identity are not explicitly mentioned in Title VII, employers should be aware that the EEOC interprets Title VII as also prohibiting discrimination based on both of these factors, and a growing number of court decisions have endorsed the EEOC's interpretation of Title VII.

Retaliation. In addition to the factors mentioned above, Title VII also makes it illegal for employers to retaliate against employees who either complain about discrimination, file a charge of discrimination, or participate in an employment discrimination investigation or lawsuit. With respect to religion, not only does Title VII prohibit discrimination based on an employee's religion, but it also requires that employers reasonably accommodate applicants' and employees' sincerely held religious practices, unless doing so would impose an undue hardship on the operation of the employer's business.

Disparate Treatment v. Disparate Impact. While Title VII prohibits intentional discrimination (i.e., disparate treatment) based on the factors mentioned above, it also prohibits unintentional discrimination (disparate impact). Unintentional discrimination can include the use of neutral employment policies and practices that have a disproportionately negative effect on applicants or employees of a particular race, color, religion, sex (including gender identity, sexual orientation, and pregnancy), or national origin, if the polices or practices at issue are not job-related and necessary to the operation of the business. For example, a help-wanted advertisement that seeks "females" may discourage men from applying and therefore may violate the law unless there is a business necessity for the business not to seek males.

Sexual Harassment. Title VII's prohibition of discrimination includes sexual harassment as a form of gender discrimination. The following information is taken straight from the EEOC's web page:

> Unwelcome sexual advances, requests for sexual favors, and other verbal or physical conduct can constitute sexual harassment when this conduct explicitly affects an individual's employment, unreasonably interferes with an individual's work performance, or creates an intimidating, hostile, or offense work environment.

> Sexual harassment can occur in a variety of circumstances, including but not limited to the following:
> - The victim as well as the harasser may be a woman or a man. The victim does not have to be of the opposite sex.
> - The harasser can be the victim's supervisor, an agent of the employer, a supervisor in another area, a co-worker, or a non-employee.
> - The victim does not have to be the person harassed but could be anyone affected by the offensive conduct.
> - Unlawful sexual harassment may occur without economic injury to or discharge of the victim.
> - The harasser's conduct must be unwelcome.

As recommended by the EEOC, employers should make efforts to prevent sexual harassment from occurring, which could be done by clearly communicating to employees that sexual harassment will not be tolerated, providing sexual harassment training to all employees, and establishing an effective complaint or grievance process that allows the employer to take immediate and appropriate action upon receiving an internal complaint.

Title VII generally applies to employers with 15 or more employees, including federal, state, and local government employers. Title VII allows for the remedies of back pay, front pay, reinstatement, attorney's fees, compensatory and punitive damages.

State Anti-Discrimination Laws. While Title VII prohibits discrimination in the workplace based on race, gender, skin color, national origin, and religion, nearly all states have enacted employment discrimination laws that prohibit workplace discrimination based on additional factors as well, such as marital status, sexual orientation, gender identity, and gender expression. States may also vary on the scope of a certain protected class, and even differ from federal law on which employers are covered by these laws. Therefore, it is important to be aware of the laws of your state.

Age Discrimination in Employment Act of 1967

Federal Age Discrimination Law. The Age Discrimination in Employment Act of 1967 (ADEA) added age as a protected class in all aspects of employment, but only prohibits age discrimination against individuals that are age 40 and over. According to the EEOC, the ADEA was amended a number of times since its passage, including once in 1986 to eliminate the maximum age in which individuals could claim discrimination, and again in 1990 with the passage of the Older Workers Benefit Protection Act, which clarified that protections given to older workers under the ADEA also pertained to employee benefit plans.

Currently, the ADEA applies to employers with 20 or more employees, as well as federal, state, and local government employers. However, it only provides remedies of back pay, front pay, reinstatement, and attorney's fees, but not compensatory or punitive damages.

State Age Discrimination Laws. While the ADEA only applies to individuals who are age 40 and over, many states have a lower age threshold and minimum employee threshold. For example, Oregon prohibits age discrimination against individuals who are age 18 or over, and applies to any employer with at least one employee. (ORS § 659A.030 and ORS § 659A.001).

Contemporary Human Resource Laws (1990 – Present)

Americans with Disabilities Act of 1990

Federal ADA Law. The Americans with Disabilities Act (ADA) was passed in 1990 and has been amended several times (most recently in 2008). The ADA prohibits disability-based discrimination in all workplaces (public and private) with 15 or more workers, and its primary provision is that it prohibits disability-based discrimination in any aspect of employment, including hiring, firing, pay, job assignments, promotions, layoffs, training, fringe benefits, and any other term or condition of employment, from being based on an individual's disability.

What is a Disability? In order to be covered by the ADA, a person must be qualified for the job to which they are applying and have a disability as defined by the law. A person can show that he or she has a disability in one of three ways.

1. A person may be disabled if he or she has a physical or mental condition that substantially limits a major life activity (such as walking, talking, seeing, hearing, or learning).
2. A person may be disabled if he or she has a history of a disability (such as cancer that is in remission).

3. A person may be disabled if he is believed to have a physical or mental impairment that is not transitory (lasting or expected to last six months or less) and minor (even if the person does not have such an impairment).

According to the EEOC, the ADA prohibits discrimination not only against individuals who have a record or history of a disability, but also against individuals who are perceived as having a disability. It can also apply to individuals who associate with an individual with a disability (such as refusing to hire the parent of a child with a disability due to the assumption that the parent will be taking time off of work).

Reasonable Accommodation. The ADA also requires that employers "reasonably accommodate" the needs of person with disabilities during any aspect of employment unless to do so would be too difficult or expensive to provide, thereby constituting an undue hardship on the employer. What constitutes an undue hardship depends on several factors and must be determined on a case-by-case basis. Example of reasonable accommodations for applicant can include adjusting or modifying examinations and providing sign language interpreters during job interviews. Examples of reasonable accommodations for employees can include regularly scheduled work breaks, modified work schedules, or re-assignment of the employee to a vacant position that is equal in pay and status.

While the ADA does require employers to provide reasonable accommodations, the ADA does not:

1. require that the employer accommodate the needs of job applicants or employees with disabilities who do not otherwise qualify for the work. For example, if having a specific certification for a degree is an essential qualification for a job, then any individual with a disability who does not possess the required certification or degree is not required to be considered by the potential employer.

2. require employees to create *new* positions for disabled employees as a reasonable accommodation or promote disabled employee as a reasonable accommodation.

3. require the employer to provide the exact reasonable accommodation requested by disabled individual if other reasonable accommodations would also allow the disabled employee to perform their jobs. When more than one accommodation would work, the employer may choose the one that is less costly or easier to provide as long as it is effective.

4. require the employer to alter the essential functions of the job. While job restructuring can be required as a reasonable accommodation, the restructuring only pertains to those job functions that are marginal or minor in nature. Essential functions, on the other hand, are the basic job duties that an employee must be able to perform, with or without reasonable accommodation.

HR Tip

When drafting position descriptions (Chapter 4), it is recommended to be clear on what job duties/functions are considered essential to the position, as well as duties that are considered marginal/secondary in nature. According to the EEOC regulations, factors to consider in determining if a function is essential includes: a) whether the reason the position exists is to perform that function, b) the number of other employees available to perform the function or among whom the performance of the function can be distributed, and c) the degree of expertise or skill required to perform the function. [29 C.F.R. § 1630.2(n)]

ADA Facts and Misconceptions. According to the Office of Disability Employment Policy (ODEP) with the U.S. Department of Labor, there are common misconceptions about the ADA. The following myths and facts are taken straight from the ODEP's website at:

TABLE 2.2   ADA Facts and Misconceptions

Myth: The ADA forces employers to hire unqualified individuals with disabilities.	**Fact:** Applicants who are unqualified for a job cannot claim discrimination under the ADA. Under the ADA, to be protected from discrimination in hiring, an individual with a disability must be qualified, which means he or she must meet all requirements for a job and be able to perform its essential functions with or without reasonable accommodations.
Myth: When there are several qualified applicants for a job and one has a disability, the ADA requires the employer to hire that person.	**Fact:** An employer is always free to hire the applicant of its choosing as long as the decision is not based on disability. If two people apply for a data entry position for which both speed and accuracy are required, the employer may hire the person with the higher speed and level of accuracy, because he or she is the most qualified.
Myth: The ADA gives job applicants with disabilities advantages over job applicants without disabilities.	**Fact:** The ADA does not give hiring preference to persons with disabilities.
Myth: Under the ADA, an employer cannot fire an employee who has a disability.	**Fact:** Employers can fire workers with disabilities under three conditions: • The termination is unrelated to the disability or • The employee does not meet legitimate requirements for the job, such as performance or production standards, with or without a reasonable accommodation or • Because of the employee's disability, he or she poses a direct threat to health or safety in the workplace.

Employers should also be aware of the following concerning the ADA:

1. An applicant or employee's request for an ADA accommodation is considered medical information. Therefore, an employer must keep this information confidential. Employers must not disclose the medical information of employees with disabilities, and this includes the fact that the employee was diagnosed with a disability.

2. When hiring, employers cannot ask about disability or medical examination prior to offering a position.

3. Once a request for an accommodation is received from an applicant or employer, it is critical that the employer must engage in an interactive process with the individual to clarify what the individual needs and identify any appropriate reasonable accommodations.

Further information and guidance on ADA issues can be found by visiting online resources, such as the Job Accommodation Network (Office of Disability Employment Policy) and the EEOC website.

State ADA Laws. While the ADA applies to employers with 15 or more employees, some states have their own similar laws that have lower minimum employee thresholds. For example, the State of Massachusetts's ADA law applies to employers with 6 or more employees.

Uniformed Services Employment and Reemployment Rights Act of 1994

Federal Law. The Uniformed Services Employment and Reemployment Rights Act (USERRA) was passed in 1994 and provides certain protections and benefits to individuals who are past and present members of the military (Army, Navy, Marines, Air Force, Coast Guard, and National Guard, including reserves). USERRA applies to all employers in the United States, public or private, regardless of size. USERRA is administered and enforced by the U.S. Department of Labor.

Right to Reinstatement. One of USERRA's primary provisions is that it requires employers to reemploy individuals who left their jobs (voluntarily or involuntarily) to perform military service. Subject to certain restrictions and requirements that must be met—such as providing adequate notice to the employer when possible and obtaining an honorable discharge—eligible individuals must be restored to the job (or comparable job) with benefits that they would have attained had they not been absent due to the military service. Additionally, employees leaving their jobs to perform military service have the right to elect to continue their employer-based health plan coverage for themselves and their dependents for up to 24 months while in the military.

Discrimination and Retaliation. USERRA also prohibits employers from discriminating or retaliating against past or present members of the military. Specifically, employers may not deny initial employment, reemployment, retention in employment, promotions, or any other employment benefits, based on an individual's past, present, or future military service. Employers are also prohibited from discriminating or retaliating against anyone, regardless of whether they have performed military service, who is assisting in the enforcement of USERRA rights, such as testifying or making a statement in connection with a USERRA proceeding.

State Laws. Most states have their own laws that provide similar protections and benefits as those provided by USERRA, and cover state national guard members and other entities as well. For example,

California extends USERRA protections for employees who are members of the California National Guard. Also, employers with 16 or more employees must provide up to ten days of unpaid Civil Air Patrol leave to an employee who responds to an emergency operational mission of the California Wing of the Civil Air Patrol. (Cal. Mil. & Vet. Code §§ 394, 394.5, 395.06; Cal. Lab. Code §§ 1503, 1504)

Family Medical Leave Act of 1993

Federal Law. The Family Medical Leave Act (FMLA) was passed in 1993 to allow employees to balance their work and family life by taking reasonable unpaid leave for certain qualifying family and medical reasons. This law requires covered employers to grant eligible employees up to a total of 12 workweeks of unpaid leave (which can be taken consecutively or intermittently) in a 12-month period for one or more of the following reasons:

- for the birth of a son or daughter, and to care for the newborn child;
- for the adoption or foster care placement of a child with the employee, and to care for the newly placed child;
- to care for an immediate family member (spouse, child, or parent, but not a parent in-law) with a serious health condition; and
- when the employee is unable to work because of a serious health condition.

According to the Department of Labor, the FMLA applies to all public agencies employers, including state, local, and federal employers, as well as private sector employers who employ 50 or more employees. However, only employees who have worked for their employers for at least one year are eligible to receive FMLA protection.

State Laws. Many states have their own laws that provide similar leave provisions for employees as the FMLA. However, many of the states may have lower employee thresholds than the FMLA, so an employee that does not qualify for leave protection under the FMLA may still be protected under a state law. Although the FMLA currently does not provide paid leave, certain states, such as New York, do provide paid, protected leave for eligible employees.

Some states also provide leave protection that can supplement leave provided under the FMLA, such as Florida's Family Supportive Work Program (FSWP), which can provide state employees with up to six months of unpaid leave for a family member's health condition. Florida's FSWP also expands leave protection for non-medical reasons, allowing up to 30 days for reasons such as relocating dependent children into schools, caring for aging parents, or visiting family members in places that require extensive travel time. (Rule 60L-34.0051, F.A.C).

Patient Protection and Affordable Healthcare Act of 2010

Federal Law Pertaining to Health Benefits. The Patient Protection and Affordable Care Act of 2010 (PPACA) law contains tax provisions that affect employers. One of the primary provisions that affects covered employers is the requirement to provide affordable health coverage that provides a certain minimum value to all full-time employees and their dependents. If an employer fails to offer such coverage, the employer will be required to pay a shared-responsibility payment.

The requirement to offer affordable health care coverage or pay a shared-responsibility payment only applies to employers with 50 or more full-time employees. Beginning in 2016, covered employers are required to file information returns with the IRS about the health coverage they offered and furnish a statement to employees about the coverage offered. However, the PPACA also contains reporting requirements that can apply regardless of the employer's size. For example, any employer who offers self-insured health coverage to their employees must file an annual return that contains certain information about each employee they cover, as well as notice to each employee about the information sent to the IRS.

To comply with the PPACA, there are certain benefits available to employers depending on the employer's size. Employers with 50 employees or less are eligible to provide health care coverage through the Small Business Health Options Program (SHOP) Marketplace provided they meet certain requirements, such as offering health coverage to all full-time employees, and enrolling at least 70% of the employees who are offered insurance (minimum participation rate).

Additionally, some small businesses may also be eligible for small business healthcare tax credits if they meet certain requirements including, but not limited to, covering at least 50% of their employees' premium costs for a qualified health plan, and having fewer than 25 employees.

State Laws Pertaining to Health Benefits. Some states expand the availability of the SHOP to businesses with up to 100 employees, but may also have different requirements regarding minimum participation rates. For example, according to HealthCare.gov, Mississippi has a 0% minimum participation rate, while several other states such as Iowa and Texas require 75% minimum participation rates. Further information on eligibility for SHOP can be obtained from Healthcare.gov or your state's department of insurance.

Federal Law Pertaining to Nursing Mothers. The PPACA also amended the FLSA by requiring employers to provide additional break time, as well as a private place (other than a bathroom) free from intrusion, for employees who are nursing mothers to express breast milk. Such break time does not have to be paid unless the employer already allows paid breaks for others, and to be considered true break time, one must truly be relieved from job duties at that time.

This provision of the PPACA does not apply to all employees, since the PPACA exempts employees who are also exempt from the FLSA overtime requirements. Additionally, employers with less than 50 employees do not have to comply if doing so would cause an undue hardship.

State Laws Pertaining to Nursing Mothers. According to the United States Department of Labor, many states have their own laws pertaining to protections for nursing mothers. For example, Maine's law goes further than the PPACA in that it applies to all employers and their employees regardless of size. In New York, there is no one-year limitation on an employer's obligations to accommodate nursing mothers.

Genetic Information Nondiscrimination Act of 2008

Federal Law. Title II of the Genetic Information Nondiscrimination Act of 2008 (GINA) prohibits discrimination by employers on the basis of genetic information in any aspect of employment. Genetic information includes an individual's genetic tests and those of the individual's family members, as well as any information about any disease, disorder, or condition of an individual's family members (family medical history). Such information is sometimes obtained by employers when employees apply for FMLA protection or an ADA accommodation and must provide certain medical information.

Employers are also prohibited from requesting, requiring, or purchasing genetic information. However, this does not apply to instances where employees are applying for FMLA protection or ADA accommodations, nor does it apply to inadvertent acquisition of genetic information, such as a manager overhearing someone talking about a family member's illness, or genetic information obtained as a result of a voluntary wellness program offered by an employer.

Regardless of how genetic information may be obtained, GINA requires employers to keep such information confidential and, if in writing, separate from an individual's other personnel information. Also, if an employer does make a lawful request for health-related information to support the employee's request under ADA or FMLA, the employer is obligated to warn the employee and employee's healthcare provider not to provide genetic information.

GINA applies to employers with 15 or more employees and includes state and local government employers.

State Laws. Many states have similar anti-discrimination laws based on genetic information, but some have different thresholds. For example, California prohibits employers with 5 or more employees from employment discrimination based on genetic information.

Human Resource Requirements of Other Governing Bodies

As employers, sports and recreation organizations should also be aware of any applicable bylaws or regulations of governing bodies that oversee the athletic organization (e.g. NCAA, NJCAA, NAIA, etc.) or specific sports in which the athletic organization is engaged (e.g. USA Wrestling, USA Gymnastics, etc.). For example, NCAA's Division I Manual contains bylaws that contain conditions for employing high school, preparatory school, or two-year college coaches, or other individuals associated with prospective student athletes (NCAA, 2018, p. 51), as well as conditions for employing current or prospective student-athletes (NCAA, 2018, pp. 142-143).

Summary

As employers, sports and recreation programs must be aware of all applicable human resource laws, including federal, state and local laws, and any applicable bylaws or regulations of governing bodies that oversee the program or specific sport. Although there are many resources to aid employers in learning and complying with the various laws, human resource law is very complex. Employers should ultimately consult legal counsel to ensure that the employer is meeting all legal obligations and complying with all applicable laws and regulations.

The earliest federal human resource laws (from 1866 to 1989) that affect employers cover areas such as minimum wage, overtime, child labor, social security and medicare, unfair labor practices, workplace safety, employee background checks, retirement packages, continuation of healthcare benefits, and certain types of employee discrimination. More recent laws (1990-present) cover areas of employee disability, employment and reinstatement of military members, unpaid protected leave, employee health benefits, and additional types of employee discrimination. Although many of these federal human resource laws contain exemptions for small employers, often defined as those with under 50 employees, employers can still be subject to state and local laws that cover the same areas yet have different requirements and obligations.

References

California Department of Fair Employment and Housing (n.d.). Ca.gov [website]. State laws prohibit discrimination in the workplace. Retrieved from https://www.dfeh.ca.gov/employment

Child Labor Violations-Civil Money Penalties, 29 U.S.C. § 216(e) and 29 C.F.R. pt. 579.

City of Chicago Office of the Mayor (n.d.). City of Chicago Minimum Wage Orginance. [website]. Retrieved from https://www.cityof-chicago.org/city/en/depts/mayor/supp_info/minimum-wage.html

Discrimination in the Treatment of Persons; Minority Representation, Florida Stat. Section 760.01 (2019).

Employment Regulation and Supervision, State of California, Cal. Lab. Code §§ 1503, 1504

Fair Credit Reporting Act of 2011, 15 U.S.C. §§ 1681-1681x.

Family Supportive Work Program, Florida Ad. Code, Rule 60L-34.0051 (2002).

Federal Trade Commission. (n.d.). Business Center Guidance [website]. Using Consumer Reports: What Employers Need to Know. Retrieved from https://www.ftc.gov/tips-advice/business-center/guidance/using-consumer-reports-what-employers-need-know

Florida Health Insurance Coverage Continuation Act, Florida Stat. Section 627.6692, (2019).

HealthCare.gov (n.d.). How to Enroll in SHOP Insurance [website] See if your small business qualifies for SHOP. Retrieved from https://www.healthcare.gov/small-businesses/choose-and-enroll/qualify-for-shop-marketplace/

Internal Revenue Service. (2015, August 4). Affordable Care Act [website]. What Employers Need to Know about the Affordable Care Act. Retrieved from https://www.irs.gov/affordable-care-act/employers/what-employers-need-to-know-about-the-affordable-care-act

Internal Revenue Service. (2017, July 20). Understanding Employee v. Contractor Understanding. [website]. Retrieved from https://www.irs.gov/newsroom/understanding-employee-vs-contractor-designation

Internal Revenue Service. (n.d.). Determining if an Employer is an Applicable Large Employer. [website] Retrieved from https://www.irs.gov/affordable-care-act/employers/determining-if-an-employer-is-an-applicable-large-employer

Internal Revenue Service. (n.d.). Federal Unemployment Tax [website]. Retrieved from https://www.irs.gov/individuals/international-taxpayers/federal-unemployment-tax

Labor, Employment; Unlawful Discrimination, definitions, Oregon Stat. ORS § 659A.001 (2017).

Labor, Employment; Unlawful Discrimination, because of race, color, religion, sexual orientation, national origin, marital status, age or expunged juvenile record prohibited, Oregon Stat. ORS § 659A.030 (2017).

Maine Revised Statutes Annotated. Title. 5, Section 2423-E(2)

Minority Labor Groups, Florida Stat. Section 450.081(2), (2019).

National Labor Relations Board. (n.d.). Employer/ Union Rights and Obligations [website]. Retrieved from https://www.nlrb.gov/rights-we-protect/rights/employerunion-rights-and-obligations

National Labor Relations Board. (n.d.). Employee Rights [website]. Retrieved from https://www.nlrb.gov/rights-we-protect/rights/employee-rights

New York State. (n.d.). New York State's Minimum Wage. [website] Retrieved from https://www.ny.gov/new-york-states-minimum-wage/new-york-states-minimum-wage

New York State (n.d.). Employees [website]. Paid Family Leave: Information for Employees. Retrieved from https://paidfamilyleave.ny.gov/paid-family-leave-information-employees

OregonLaws.org. (2017). Legal Glossary [website]. 2017 ORS 659A.3201. Discrimination Based on Information in Credit History Prohibited. Retrieved from https://www.oregonlaws.org/ors/659A.320

Public Employees' Rights; Organization and Representation, Florida Stat. Section 447.301 (2018).

Public Employees' Rights; Strikes Prohibited, Florida Stat. Section 447.505 (2018).

Regulations to Implement the Equal Employment Provisions of the Americans with Disabilities Act, 29 C.F.R. § 1630.2(n)

State of Connecticut, Office of the Attorney General. CT.gov [website]. General Guidance Regarding the Rights and Duties of Public-Sector Employers and Employees in the State of Connecticut after *Janus v. AFSCME Council 31*. Retrieved from https://portal.ct.gov/AG/General/Guidance_on_Janus

State of Massachussetts. (n.d.). Mass.Gov, Office of Attorney General [website]. Employment Rights of people with Disabilities. Retrieved from http://www.mass.gov/ago/consumer-resources/your-righs/civil-rights/disability-rights/employment-rights.html

State of Nevada, Department of Business and Industry, Office of the Laborer Commissioner [website] Frequently Asked Questions-Employers. Retrieved from http://labor.nv.gov/uploadedFiles/labornvgov/content/Employer/Frequently%20Asked%20Questions-%20Employers(1).pdf

The Employee Credit Privacy Act, Illinois Stat. 820 ILCS 70/5 (2011).

The Military Forces of the State of California, Privileges and Penalties, Cal. Mil. & Vet. Code §§ 394, 394.5, 395.06

USA.Gov. (n.d.). Labor Laws and Issues, Wrongful Discharge/Termination of Employment. [website]. Retrieved from https://www.usa.gov/labor-laws

U.S. Department of Homeland Security. (n.d.). Citizenship and Immigration Services [website]. Penalties. Retrieved from https://www.uscis.gov/i-9-central/penalties

U.S. Department of Labor. (n.d.). Employee Benefits Security Administration [website]. Fact Sheet: What is ERISA. Retrieved from https://www.dol.gov/agencies/ebsa/about-ebsa/our-activities/resource-center/fact-sheets/what-is-erisa

U.S. Department of Labor. (n.d.). Employee Benefits Security Administration [website] https://www.dol.gov/sites/dolgov/files/EBSA/about-ebsa/our-activities/resource-center/faqs/cobra-continuation-health-coverage-for-employers.pdf

U.S. Department of Labor. (2016, September). Employee Benefits Security Administration [website]. *An Employee's Guide to Health Benefits Under Cobra.* Retrieved from https://www.dol.gov/sites/default/files/ebsa/about-ebsa/our-activities/resource-center/publications/an-employers-guide-to-group-health-continuation-coverage-under-cobra.pdf

U.S. Department of Labor. (2013, August). Employee Benefits Security Administration [website]. *MEWAs Multiple Employer Welfare Arrangements under the Employee Retirement Income Security Act (ERISA): A Guide to Federal and State Regulation.* Retrieved from https://www.dol.gov/sites/dolgov/files/ebsa/about-ebsa/our-activities/resource-center/publications/mewa-under-erisa-a-guide-to-federal-and-state-regulation.pdf

U.S. Department of Labor. (n.d.). Leave Benefits [website]. Family and Medical Leave (FMLA). https://www.dol.gov/general/topic/benefits-leave/fmla

U.S. Department of Labor. (n.d.). Office of the Assistant Secretary for Policy [website]. Frequently Asked Questions, Jobs & Training. Retrieved from https://webapps.dol.gov/dol-faq/go-dol-faq.asp?faqid=127&faqsub=Hiring&faqtop=Jobs+%26+Training&topicid=3&lookfor=userra

U.S. Department of Labor (n.d.). Occupational Safety and Health Administration [website]. Employer Responsibilities. Retrieved from https://www.osha.gov/as/opa/worker/employer-responsibility.html

U.S. Department of Labor (n.d.). Occupational Safety and Health Administration [website]. OSHA Penalties. Retrieved from https://www.osha.gov/penalties/

U.S. Department of Labor (n.d.). Occupational Safety and Health Administration [website]. State Plans. Retrieved from https://www.osha.gov/dcsp/osp/index.html

U.S. Department of Labor. (n.d.). Office of Disability Employment Policy [website]. Employers and the ADA: Myths and Facts. Retrieved from https://www.dol.gov/odep/pubs/fact/ada.htm

U.S. Department of Labor. (n.d.). Wage and Hour Division. [website]. Break Time for Nursing Mothers. Retrieved from https://www.dol.gov/whd/nursingmothers/faqBTNM.htm

U.S. Department of Labor. (n.d.). Wage and Hour Division [website]. State Labor Offices Retrieved from https://www.dol.gov/whd/contacts/state_of.htm

U.S. Department of Labor. (2018, January). Wage and Hour Division [website].Fact Sheet #71: Internship Programs Under the Fair Labor Standards Act. Retrieved from https://www.dol.gov/whd/regs/compliance/whdfs71.htm

U.S. Department of Labor. (n.d.) Wage and Hour Division [website] Classifying Exempt Status. Retrieved from https://www.dol.gov.whd/regs/compliance/hrg.htm#8

U.S. Department of Labor. (2008, July). Wage and Hour Division. [website]. Fact Sheet #32 Youth Minimum Wage – Fair Labor Standards Act. Retrieved from https://www.dol.gov/whd/regs/compliance/whdfs32.pdf

U.S. Department of Labor. (2019, July 1). Wage and Hour Division [website]. Consolidated Minimum Wage Table. [website] Retrieved from https://www.dol.gov/whd/minwage/mw-consolidated.htm

U.S. Department of Labor. Wage and Hour Division [website]. Overtime Pay. Retrieved from https://www.dol.gov/whd/overtime_pay.htm

U.S. Department of Labor. (2009, July). Wage and Hour Division [website] Fact Sheet #53 – The Health Care Industry and Hours Worked. Retrieved from https://www.dol.gov/whd/regs/compliance/whdfs53.htm

U.S. Department of Labor. (2016, November). Wage and Hour Division [website]. *Child Labor Bulletin 101.* Retrieved from https://www.dol.gov/whd/regs/compliance/childlabor101.htm

U.S. Department of Labor. (2018, January 1). Wage and Hour Division [website]. Selected State Child Labor Standards Affecting Minors Under 18 in Non-farm Employment as of January 1, 2018. Retrieved from https://www.dol.gov/whd/state/nonfarm.htm

U.S. Department of Labor. (n.d.). Wage and Hour Division [website]. Employment/Age Certificate Retrieved from https://www.dol.gov/whd/state/certification.htm

U.S. Department of Labor. (n.d.). Women's Bureau [website]. Employment protections for workers who are pregnant or nursing. Retrieved from https://www.dol.gov/wb/maps/

U.S. Department of Labor. (n.d.). Veteran's Employment and Training Service [website]. VETS USERRA Fact Sheet 3. Retrieved from https://www.dol.gov/vets/programs/userra/userra_fs.htm

U.S. Employment Taxes 1964, 26 U.S.C. 3101-3125

U.S. Equal Employment Opportunity Commission. (n.d.). Laws, Regulations & Guidance [website]. The Age Discrimination in Employment Act of 1967. Retrieved from https://www.eeoc.gov/laws/statutes/adea.cfm

U.S. Equal Employment Opportunity Commission (n.d.). Laws, Regulations & Guidance [website]. Age Discrimination. Retrieved from https://www.eeoc.gov/laws/types/age.cfm

U.S. Equal Employment Opportunity Commission. (n.d.). Laws, Regulations & Guidance [website]. Disability Discrimination. Retrieved from https://www.eeoc.gov/laws/types/disability.cfm

U.S. Equal Employment Opportunity Commission. (n.d.). Laws, Regulations & Guidance [website]. Equal Pay/Compensation Discrimination. Retrieved from https://www.eeoc.gov/laws/types/equalcompensation.cfm

U.S. Equal Employment Opportunity Commission. (n.d.). Laws, Regulations & Guidance. [website]. Genetic Information Discrimination. Retrieved from https://www.eeoc.gov/laws/types/genetic.cfm

U.S. Equal Employment Opportunity Commission. (n.d.). Laws, Regulations & Guidance [website]. Laws Enforced by the EEOC Retrieved from https://www.eeoc.gov/laws/statutes/index.cfm

U.S. Equal Employment Opportunity Commission (n.d.). Laws, Regulations & Guidance [website]. Prohibited Employment Policies/Practices. Retrieved from https://www.eeoc.gov/laws/practices/index.cfm

U.S. Equal Employment Opportunity Commission. (n.d.). Publications [website]. Background Checks: What Employers Need to Know. Retrieved from https://www.eeoc.gov/eeoc/publications/background_checks_employers.cfm

U.S. Equal Employment Opportunity Commission. (n.d.). Publications [wesbsite]. Facts about Age Discrimination. Retrieved from https://www.eeoc.gov/eeoc/publications/age.cfm

U.S. Equal Employment Opportunity Commission. (n.d.). Publications [website]. Facts About Sexual Harassment. Retrieved from https://www.eeoc.gov/eeoc/publications/fs-sex.cfm

U.S. Equal Employment Opportunity Commission. (n.d.). Publications [website] The ADA: Questions and Answers. Retrieved from https://www.eeoc.gov/eeoc/publications/adaqa1.cfm

U.S. Equal Employment Opportunity Commission. (n.d.). Small Business FAQs [website]. Who is an "Employee" under Federal Discrimination Laws? Retrieved from https://www.eeoc.gov/employers/smallbusiness/faq/who_is_an_employee.cfm

U.S. Federal Unemployment Tax Act, 26 U.S.C. Sections 3301-3310

Review and Discussion Questions

1. What is the difference(s) between an employee and an independent contractor?

2. What is employment-at-will?

3. Are interns and volunteers considered to be employees?

4. If an employer is subject to more than one minimum wage law (federal, state, and local), which of the minimum wages must the employer pay?

5. Under the Fair Labor Standards Act, are all employees eligible to receive overtime pay?

6. What is FICA tax?

7. Define the term collective bargaining.

8. What is a right-to-work state?

9. Which employers are subject to the Occupational Safety and Health Act?

10. List the three steps that the Fair Credit Reporting Act requires employers to complete prior to using a third-party company to obtain a background check on an applicant or employee.

11. Which federal agency enforces the Employment Retirement Security Act of 1974 (ERISA)?

12. List the protected classes that are protected under the Civil Rights Act of 1964?

13. Describe the difference(s) between disparate treatment and disparate impact discrimination.

14. Which individuals are protected by the Age Discrimination in Employment Act (ADEA)?

15. What is a reasonable accommodation?

16. How does the Uniformed Services Employment and Reemployment Rights Act (USERRA) protect past and present members of the military?

17. What is the maximum amount of unpaid leave employees may be eligible for under the Family Medical Leave Act of 1993?

18. Describe the features of the Small Business Health Options Program (SHOP) Marketplace.

19. Under what circumstances do employers occasionally obtain genetic information of their employees?

Application Exercises

1. From online research, find and identify three methods/programs offered by the EEOC for an employer to use to resolve charges of discrimination that have been against the employer.

2. You are the general manager for a college athletic program. You have a long-time employee who has always performed his job well, but is now reporting that he has been suffering from migraines and is having trouble performing his job effectively. The employee is requesting an accommodation to be able to perform his job, but is unsure of what type of accommodation he needs. However, he thinks his migraines may be triggered by the lighting and noise level in the workplace.

Using the Jobs Accommodation Network online (https://askjan.org/), research migraines under disabilities and accommodations, and answer the following regarding migraines and accommodation ideas:

- Is there more than one type of migraine?

- What are three possible accommodations that could address the employee's sensitivity to light to help the employee perform the essential functions of his job?

- What are three possible accommodations that could address the employee's sensitivity to noise to help the employee perform the essential functions of his job?

- Identify the accommodation(s) that would be the most reasonable for most employers to provide (or that would be the least likely to constitute a hardship most employers).

Human Resource Management Term Project
Individual Written and Oral Presentation

The student will have a final individual project as a part of their course grade. The assignment will be divided into two graded components.

Part 1

The student will present a written paper on a human resource management legal topic. The paper will be 10-15 pages in length and will be written within accepted academic protocols (e.g. APA). All concepts should be well supported with current researched references.

Part 2

The student will present his/her researched findings on the written topic in a formal oral presentation. The presentation will be 15 minutes in length with a 5-10-minute Q&A session. Visual aids/Power point will be utilized to assist with the presentation.

Term Project Topics

Equal Employment Opportunity Commission Laws (Choose One)

    Equal Pay Act (1963)

    Civil Rights Act (1964)

    Age Discrimination Act (1967)

    Disabilities Act (1990)

    Civil Rights Act (1991)

    Family Medical Leave Act (1993)

Employment Court Cases (Choose One)

    Griggs vs Duke Power

    Mc Donald Douglas vs Green

    U.C. Regents vs Bakke

    US Steelworkers vs Weber

    Connecticut vs Teal

    City of Richmond vs J.A. Crosan Company

    Martin vs Wilkes

Legal Aspect of Collective Bargaining

Occupational Safety and Health Act (OSHA)

National Labor Relations Act (Wagner Act)

chapter three

Essentials of Human Resource Planning

Chapter Objectives

- Identify the components and importance of a comprehensive strategic operational plan
- Know and explain the components of a sport or recreation program
- Explain high level program planning concepts
- Define the components of the program plan document
- Define the program's human resource plan
- Understand and apply the operational philosophy of human resources
- Examine the role of human resource goalsetting, internal assessments, execution and monitoring of a human resource plan
- Identify and explain the functional components of a program human resource plan

Key Terms

Program Planning

Vision Statement

Mission Statement

Value Statement

Executive Summary

Goals and Objectives

Organizational Chart

SWOT

Human Resource Planning

Policies and Procedures

Ethical Obligations

Marketing Mix

Financial Planning

Budgeting

Pro-Forma Financial Statements

Operational Philosophy

Human Resource Values

Internal Assessment

Hierarchical Structure

Net Human Resource
   Requirements

Action Plans

Performance Management

Performance Appraisals

Disciplinary Systems

Human Resource Safety and Health
   Reward Systems

Strategic Planning in Sports and Recreation Programs

The all-inclusive strategic operational plan can best be defined as a blueprint, map, or, in the sports vernacular, game plan for the entire sports and recreation program. Accordint to Bateman and Snell (2011), a strategic plan is

the actions or means the managers intend to use to achieve goals. At a minimum, planning should outline alternative actions that may lead to the attainment of each goal, the resources required to reach that goal through those means, and the obstacles that may develop. (p. 128)

Unquestionably, a strategic plan establishes the ultimate direction of the sports or recreation program and "lays the groundwork" for decisions and actions to get there.

Strategic operational plans include high-level, "big picture" elements for a sports and recreation program:

- vision statements
- operational mission statements
- core foundational values
- long-term goals.

Strategic operational plans cover explicit action areas such as:

- Short-term objectives (to reach long-term goals);
- SWOT analyses (which examines the internal strengths and weaknesses and external opportunities and threats of a program);
- Marketing, human resources, and accounting/financial plans (which encompass functional focused disciplines)
- Specific competitive and industry-wide strategies; and
- Current and pro-forma financial data.

What are the Benefits of Strategic Operational Planning?

Before undertaking a sports or recreation program a strategic operational plan, it must be acknowledged that the process and final product will (1) cost significant time, (2) require a concerted effort by all program stakeholders, and (3) necessitate a commitment of organizational resources and money. Without question, these opportunity and real costs must be weighed against the enduring advantages of assembling and utilizing a strategic operational plan to place immediate sacrifices and expenditures in proper context. There are many universal benefits business enterprises (sports and recreation programs included) reap when creating and implementing a strategic operational plan:

- Organizational focus for maximum utilization of resources and capabilities
- Professionalism and a confidence in leadership
- Operational unity among all departments and personnel
- Legal and regulatory compliance
- Strengthened internal motivation and employee retention
- Curtailed reactionary management
- Reduced organizational complacency and stresses continuous improvement
- Core foundation for developing policies and procedures

- Diagonstic measurements/targets to quantify operational success
- Refocused mindset from day-to-day thinking to emphsize future growth
- Tangibility and an atmosphere of goal reality
- Readily available reference for all personnel
- Head-on confrontation of difficult decisions
- Contingencies addressed ahead of rather than responding to after the fact
- Input from a variety of sources
- Organizational learning and adaptability
- Opportunities to analyze industry factors and specific competitors
- Combat operational complacency
- Support for holistic measurements to gage the overall health of the organization

HR Tip

Perhaps the most valuable aspect of developing a strategic operational plan and implementing its strategies is in the way the document can unite all levels of the operation from top ownership and executives to functional employees. The greater this unity, the more of a competitive advantage a sports and recreation program will have over its competition.

A more thorough examination of strategic operational plans, is provided in Chapter 3 Appendix 1

Developing Human Resource Plans – A Critical Focus

The human resource plan is developed within the global strategic operational plan. They are produced and implemented together to accomplish the overall tactical goals and objectives of the sports and recreation program. As an extension of the strategic operational plan, human resource plans precisely reflect the impact and needs of the program's current workforce and impending changes to that workforce in the near and extended future. Because of the indispensable value of the human resources in an organization, human resource plans should be definitive in nature and thoroughly concentrated on the human asset in an organization. Like strategic operational plans, human resource plans have comprehensive configurations, goals and objectives, and decisive strategies for their achievement. Moreover, strong human resource planning prevents a multitude of issues that can threaten the productivity and even the longevity of the sports or recreation program, such as:

- Over- or under-staffing the operation
- Interdepartmental conflicts
- Lag in industry skills and competencies
- Decreased productivity
- Declining employee morale

- Poorly qualified personnel
- Increased turnover
- Wasted organizational resources

Human Resource Plan Breakdown

Table 3.1 provides a comprehensive breakdown of a a typical human resource plan. Within the identified areas of focus for a human resource plan, a successful plan will consider the various related details in the conceptual focus, while still maintaining unity of strategy within the overall vision and goals of the program.

Considering the operational plan's strategies supersede and guide human resource strategies and should never be circumvented or ignored in the human resource plan, it makes sense that the human resource plan should derive and flow seamlessly from the program's operational plan. Any incongruities between the two can have serious implications for the sports or recreation program. Simply stated, the success of the operational plan depends upon unified, coherent agreement with subplans and sections within the overall plan, especially the human resources plan, defined here.

Section 1. Operational Philosophy and Values

The operational philosophy and values of the human resource plan explore central human resource functions within the framework of the sports or recreation program's vision, mission, and values. Established

---

TABLE 3.1 Human Resource Plan Breakdown

Section 1	Operational philosophy and values
Section 2	Overview of laws and regulations
Section 3	Short and long term goals of HR management
Section 4	Human resource internal assessment
Section 5	Current and future operational projections:
	Hierarchical structure
	BOD, administrative, staff job descriptions
	Net human resource requirements and action plan
	Selection and hiring procedures
	HR information system
	Orientation and training
	Performance management
	Reward systems
	Disciplinary system
	Safety and health

---

operational plan vision, mission, and value statements, must be inherent in the human resource operational philosophy and values.

In their textbook, Ivancevich and Konopaste (2013, p. 11) define nine human resource principles that provide a foundation for creating a solid, successful human resource operational plan. These principles

- Help the organization reach its goals.
- Employ the skills and abilities of the workforce efficiently.
- Provide the organization with well-trained and well-motivated employees.
- Increase to the fullest the employee's job satisfaction and self-actualization.
- Develop and maintain a quality of work life that makes employment in the organization desirable.
- Communicate HRM policies to all employees.
- Maintain ethical policies and socially responsible behavior.
- Manage change to the mutual advantage of individuals, groups, the enterprise, and the public.

Manage increased urgency and faster cycle times. These core human resource principles are universal to most (if not all) progressive thinking business enterprises. This is not to say that they should be adopted verbatim. These human resource foundations should be individually studied and deliberately adapted to each sports or recreation program's distinct vision, mission, and values.

HR Tip

The sports or recreation program's operational philosophy and values are the link between the conceptual vision, mission, and values of the organization and the tangible functioning and utilization of its human resource asset. While often motivational, the human resource operational philosophy and values are purposeful and deliver definitive guidance/direction to program employees.

Section 2. Overview of Laws and Regulations

The legal and regulatory compliance and adherence discussed in Chapter 2 should be mapped to the precise impact they will have on the human resource asset. The implication of legal and regulatory directives on essential internal policies, procedures, and reporting requirements, must be included in human resource plan, and should be (1) meticulously developed to avoid any potential irregularities, (2) accessible to all administrators, staff, and coaches, and counselors, (3) linked to all published human resource literature and legal and regulatory resources (e.g. websites, online manuals, etc.), and (4) thorough in defining all protocols and reporting responsibilities within the operation. The clerical administration of the legal and regulatory mandates should be provided, often in the human resource plan's appendix, or a separate comprehensive document. The appendix or compliance manual should contain all relevant paperwork, forms, and human resource templates.

> **HR Tip**
>
> To limit personal and organizational liability, the construction of Laws and Regulations section of the HR plan should be developed in conjunction with legal counsel, as well as internal compliance coordinators and external agency or regulatory approval.

Section 3. Goals of Human Resource Management

Guiding principles for goal development in the operational plan essentially apply to goal and objective formation in the human resource plan. Aswathappa (2013) contends that ,

> HR plans need to be based on organizational objectives. In practice, this implies that the objectives of the HR plan must be derived from organizational objectives... Once the organizational objectives are specified, communicated and understood by all concerned, the HR department [administrators] must specify its objectives with regards to HR utilization in the organization. (p. 109)

The process for creating distinctive goals and objectives in the human resource plan is uncomplicated in theory, but can become problematic in construction and implementation. The step-by-step process is as follows:

1. Identify a long-term goal or objective (3-5 years in length) from the operational plan.
2. Rework goal or objective into a coherent long-term goal or objective for use in the human resource plan.
3. Generate specific short-term actions to accomplish selected long-term goal.

A basic illustration of this process is provided in Figure 3.1. Program adminstrators should provide detailed chronological timelines for posting positions, developing database of candidates, and recruitment; the selection process for each position; search committee criteria and scheduling; and onboarding and orientation calendars and content. The number and detail of each short-term action will depend on the human resource plan's long-term goal. As a general rule, the more depth and clarity in short-term action, the better chance for successful execution. Delineate office and facility usage for new sports program staff, in conjunction with internal and external stakeholders, to create individual goals and success targets for all new personnel, which will become the foundation for performance evaluations through win/loss percentages, budgets, and participant rates and other criteria. Develop specific compliance manuals for the new sports program personnel.

Section 4. Human Resource Internal Assessment

In the operational plan, a significant section is devoted to the SWOT analysis of the organization's venture. For human resource planning, it is important to audit the sports or recreation program's in-house

Long-Term Program Goal (5 Years)

XYZ Athletics will expand and diversify its sports portfolio to include two new sports programs: Women's Competetive Cheer and Men's and Women's Indoor Track & Field

Adaptation to HR Goal

Based on XYZ Athletics long-term goal, the objective is to construct 1) comprehensive HR impact assessments and 2) complete HR development outlines for both new sports programs

HR Short-Term Actions (2/3 Years)

Designate a project manager for each new sports program.

Through research, construct a complete hierarchical chart for each sports program

Develop all-inclusve job descriptions for all positions in each sports program's hierarchical chart

Reconfigure theXYZ Athletics hierarchical structure to include the new sports programs with chain of command and reporting responsibilities

Research and recommend salary ranges, benefits, incentive packages, for all personnel in the new sports programs.

Also provide supplementary expenses associated with the new positions (parking, relocation, meals, merchandise, summer camp facilities)

FIGURE 3.1   Adapting Organizational Goals/Objectives to the Human Resource Plan

human resource elements with a modified SWOT tool known as an *internal assessment*. The internal assessment examines the current state of the sports or recreation program's primary human resource components from a standpoint of strength or weakness. Table 3.2 identifies the primary internal elements of human resources for an internal assessment. Obviously, when reviewing these factors, program administrators should expect to see as many human resource elements as program strengths. Does this mean that one should be complacent about continuing (and even improving) these human resource strengths? No. However, this type of assessment is critical to provide administrators, coaches, counselors, and staff with a true illustration of the human resource component of the operation, similar to what the snapshot of a SWOT analysis achieves for the overall organization.

Scenario 1. Internal Strength. If an element from Table 3.2 is considered a strength of the human resource component, it should be cultivated and exploited to achieve human resource goals and objectives, which, in turn, should achieve organization goals and objectives.

Scenario 2. Internal Weakness. If an element from Table 3.2 is considered a weakness of the human resource component, there are two possible actions. The first would be to commit program resources—time,

---

TABLE 3.2   Internal Assessment of Strength and Weakness

Vision and commitment to program personnel

Operational philosophy statement

Human resource values

Strategic coordination with overall operational plan

Strategy-focused training programs for program personnel

Functional cross-training programs for program administration

Active personnel retention programs

Communication systems

Competitive salaries/pay/incentives/benefits

Proper utilization of the human resource asset for maximum productivity

Position-by-position inventory of competencies and skills

Valid and reliable recruiting systems

Valid and reliable selection processes

Effective orientation and onboarding systems for new hires

Personnel replacement and positional depth charts

Valid and reliable performance evaluation systems

Program-wide teamwork and interpersonal communication systems

User friendly and accurate human resource information systems

High profile personnel (adding to program's branding strength)

Desirable work environment for personnel (facilities, equipment, locations, technology)

Definitive human resource structure (hierarchical charts/matrix, job descriptions)

Career development programs

Health and safety (historical standards and current systems)

Availability of employee assistance programs

Knowledge & communication of, and compliance with program policies and procedures

Human resource personnel/employee hotline

Fair and equitable disciplinary and grievance systems

Absenteeism and tardy rates/percentages

Compliance with governmental regulations (EEOC, IRS, OSHA)

Compliance with governing body regulations

Each of these elements can be:

  An internal strength

  An internal weakness

  Neither an internal strength or weakness (non-applicable element)

  Both an internal strength and weakness

---

money, staff, etc.—to convert the weakness into a human resource strength. The second would be to minimize or eliminate the impact of the weakness on human resources and control or contain the element as much as possible.

Scenario 3. Neither an Internal Strength or Weakness . If an element from Table 3.2 is considered neither a strength or weakness, it is considered a nonapplicable element, but it should be monitored for any possible future impact.

Scenario 4. Both an Internal Strength and Weakness. If an element from Table 3.2 is considered to be multifaceted, with some aspects being considered strengths and others weaknesses, each aspect must be scrutinized for its relevance and impact on the program and determined whether to cultivate/exploit, convert/modify, or minimize.

Section 5. Human Resource Operational Projections

Each of the operational components of the human resource plan listed below should be examined from a current use perspective and, more importantly, for potential future strategic change, if applicable. The most common operational elements listed below are the subject of examination, and fall into one of three general categories

Hierarchical Structure	Orientation and Training
Job Descriptions	Performance Management
Net Human Resource Requirements and Action Plan	Reward Systems
Selection and Hiring Procedures	Disciplinary System
HRIS	Safety and Health

1. The component requires a total strategic overhaul (e.g. replacement with new systems, procedures, tactics, personnel, etc.)

2. The component must be target future modifications, but the core foundations of the operational component remains unaffected.

3. The component remains unchanged over the duration of the human resource plan (typically 3-5 years).

Hierarchical Structure. Organizational charts are visual depictions of the sports or recreation program's professional positions/jobs and where they fall into the operation's chain of command. Thompson, Peteraf, Gamble, & Strickland (2018) define the hierarchical structure of an organization as "the formal and informal arrangement of tasks, responsibilities, lines of authority, and reporting relationships by which the firm is administered" (p. 308). The structure for a sports or recreation program is clearly conveyed through straight-line organizational charts.

If the sports or recreation program is envisioning either growth or reduction in the future, administrators can show the progression of how the hierarchical structure will change by providing multiple organizational charts over a time frame. For example, a sports or recreation program may be planning a major transformation to its organization within the next three years, and then again in five years. In this case, providing comparative organizational charts in the human resource plan that detail (1) the current organizational structure, (2) the three-year projected structure, and (3) the five-year structure would be obligatory.

Job Descriptions. The human resource plan should contain job descriptions for all levels of sports or recreation program personnel, including board of directors, administrators and staff. If new positions are projected in the future, the human resource plan should have a detailed job description for each of these new positions.

HR Tip

Because the planning process is about targeting the future, it is critical that as much of the future changes be identified and delineated in the present. This is especially true of job descriptions.

The operational plan should correspond with all board of director job descriptions, as well as any auxiliary positions that could be critical to the program, such as fundraising personnel, volunteers, and booster club positions. As with job descriptions, any new projected position should be included in the human resource plan. Functional level personnel who are critical in the achievement of program goals should have detailed job descriptions in the human resource plan. The critical assessment of each staff position's job responsibilities should be in concert with any possible future program goals and strategic transformations. Chapter 4 discusses occupational modeling through job analysis, structure, and job descriptions.

Net Human Resource Requirements and Action Plan. If the sports or recreation program is planning major strategic changes to its goals and objectives over the next three to five years, it is necessary to define the human resource requirements to fulfill those goals and objectives. Action planning is needed to increase or modify personnel through new hires, strategically focused training of current personnel, redesigning positions to meet expectations, and developing new performance measures. Chapters 5, 6, and 7 discuss in more detail the acquisition of new personnel, training and development programs, and assessment techniques.

Selection and Hiring Procedures. The three main concerns of a program's selection process are (1) validity, (2) reliability, and (3) equitability. Noe, Hollenbeck, Gerhart, & Wright (2004) state that *validity* is "the extent to which a performance measure (such as test scores) is related to what the measure is designed to assess (such as job performance)" (p. 173), and asks whether the selection process measures what was intended or wanted. *Reliability* signifies "an indicator of a measure's internal consistency" (Zikmund & Babin, 2013, p. 257), and asks whether the program's selection and hiring process measure the same criteria from person-to-person without discrimination or bias. *Equitability* asks if people being treated in a fair, impartial, and objective manner in their interactions with the program.

If the program's selection and hiring process is proven valid, reliable, and equitable to all involved, then the current processes used to select new internal stakeholders/personnel should be clearly described in the human resource plan. If serious flaws are discovered in any area of the selection and hiring processes (application, selection criteria, interview questions, EEOC regulations, etc.), a deliberate change must be immediately implemented and documented in the human resource plan.

Human Resource Information System. Badgi (2012) states that human resource information systems (HRIS) are software programs,

> associated with managing employee data, overall lifecycle of the employee, benefits administration, leave management, talent management, payroll and related HR functions. HRIS is therefore about technology to manage HR functions. (p. 4)

From a planning perspective, basic questions should be answered to determine the need for and appropriate system for use in the program.

- Does the program have a HRIS? If not, would having one be a factor for enhancing operational efficiency and productivity in the future?
- If the program currently has a functioning HRIS, will it be sufficient in the management of projected future growth and/or operational changes (in the 3-5-year goals)?
- Are there more suitable human resource information systems available? If so, what are the changeover or conversion issues associated with their acquisition and adaptation?

The best-case scenario from these fundamental planning questions would be that the program has an appropriate, fully functional HRIS capable of modifications and future growth. However, if this is not the case (and if the size, capabilities, and resources of the program warrant modernization), a new or upgraded HRIS system should be procured and employed. The acquisition and implementation of a new or upgraded system requires the following planning effort: (1) a needs assessment, (2) a market review of systems that would match the needs of the program, (3) a timeline for adoption and information translation, (4) a training itinerary for applicable administrators, coaches, counselors, and staff, and (5) establishing a program-wide launch date.

Orientation and Training. Rue, Ibrahim, and Byars (2016) describe orientation as the introduction of new employees to the organization, work unit, and job.

> The major objectives of company orientation programs are: (1) reducing new employee stress, (2) lowering start-up costs of integrating the new employee into the organization, (3) eventually reducing turnover caused by failure to understand the rules and culture of the organization, (4)

reducing the time required to integrate the employee into the job, and (5) helping the employee adjust to his or her work team or work environment more quickly. (p. 157)

It is easy to see how an orientation system is a salient part of the employee success. If the existing orientation program is meeting all of the criteria described above (and will meet these criteria points in the future), then its inclusion in the human resource plan is a straight-forward utilization of existing orientation policies and procedures. If no orientation program exists for new employees, or the current program needs updated or reengineered, the new program or its modifications should be defined and detailed in the human resource plan.

In any program, training is the primary way the human resource asset is augmented and improved over time, which equips the program with a distinctive advantage over its competition. Training, by its very nature, is futuristic; it should be planned for and designed to be as professional and economical as possible, and the human resource plan should outline a comprehensive, forward-thinking blueprint for all individual, group, and program-wide training programs.

Companies use a wide variety of delivery methods to build worker skills. As with many human resource programs, there is rarely one best way to deliver training. Hands-on approaches, along with technology-based solutions effectively deliver the content, determine the learner's current skill level, and establish targeted learning goals, do so within budget considerations, and many other factors. Each organization tries to obtain the greatest value for its training investment; this approach has led to many innovations and changes in the training area. (Mathis, Jackson, Valentine, & Meglich, 2017, p. 282)

Because training has become so significant with so many state-of-the-art, innovative ways to develop the human resource asset, planning for future training needs is critical in avoiding haphazard, unsystematic training programs that could be a considerable waste of valuable resources and even be counterproductive, all while leaving the program's personnel underdeveloped.

When constructing the training program in a human resource plan, some of the questions to ask include:

- What are the goals of the training programs?
- Are the training goals in-line with the program's long-term goals and objectives?
- What positions will need to have training?
- What information will need to be conveyed?
- What are the best training methods and deliveries?
- What are the costs associated with future training programs?
- Where will the training programs be conducted?
- When will the training programs be conducted?
- Will there be a series of training sessions or one all-inclusive session?
- Who will be conducting the training?
- What technology will be available for the training programs?
- How will the effectiveness of the training be measured?

The concept of training and human resource development will be discussed further in Chapter 6.

Performance Management. Performance management is frequently associated with performance appraisals, which are the final outcome assessments (and documentation) of a sound performance management system. Mathis and Nkomo (2008) state that an effective performance management system should do the following:

- Make clear what the organization expects.
- Provide performance information to employees.
- Identify areas of success and needed development.
- Document performance for personnel records. (p. 275)

In human resource planning, each of these points should be audited for their impact on the program. Performance expectations, performance guidance (written sources or through one-on-one meetings), key positional success factors, and performance evaluations and appraisals should all be organized in the plan for easy access and implementation. Understandably, if there are performance management gaps, administrators should utilize the the human resource planning process to reengineer or restructure the system components for future efficiency. The concept of performance management is discussed further in Chapter 7.

> ### HR Tip
> As with all human resource functions, constructing a performance management system should be in consultation with the organization's legal counsel. The concept of objectivity, fairmindedness, and universal equity among all sports or recreation program members is the foundation of a resilient and impactful performance management system.

Reward Systems. Reward systems are predominantly made-up of compensation (salary, hourly, overtime), supplemental benefits (medical, dental, 401K), pay-for-performance remunerations (incentives, bonuses, piece-rate subsidies), and auxiliary allowances (employee health programs, ancillary services such as parking, merchandise contracts, tickets, external training opportunities, and special program events, meals, and ceremonial occasions). The depth and complexity of these reward system components varies greatly from program to program. For the human resource plan, reward systems should be examined from two principle vantages: the program's reward system philosophy and a market comparison. A sports or recreation program's reward philosophy should, according to Armstrong (2012):

consist of the set of values and beliefs that influence reward strategy and the design and operation of the reward system. An organization's reward philosophy may be defined and set out in the form of guiding principles. But it may be implicit—all organizations have a reward philosophy which governs reward practice even if they do not articulate it. And it may be just a crude understanding of what is done, such as offering competitive rates of pay or paying for performance. Reward philosophies are concerned with the ways in which people are paid, the levels of payment, the extent to which pay should be related to performance, the scale of employee benefits and the adoption of total reward policies which provide both financial and non-financial rewards. They also cover the degree to which reward practices are ethical in the sense that they are fair, equitable and transparent. (p. 7)

Following Armstrong's view, the program's human resource plan, should provide a complete delineation of its strategic philosophy toward rewarding its internal stakeholders to circumvent administrative misunderstandings and organizational confusion. This will authenticate and support the operation's organizational culture and atmosphere for productivity. As with all exemplifying statements that guide a program's functional operation, a disconnect cannot exist between what is professed in the philosophical reward system statement and what is happening in actuality. Simply stated, saying one thing and doing another within a rewards system can have ruinous implications on the sports or recreation program.

Obviously, if the sports or recreation program has a longstanding and progressive reward system philosophy that has produced a healthy organizational culture and elevated levels of productivity, the administration should maintain and monitor these philosophical values for any potential adjustments. If a program is crafting a new philosophical reward system statement or overhauling its previous philosophical position, it is necessary to conduct a position-by-position market analysis to establish a starting/connection point between the sports or recreation program's new foundational values and actual market standards. This discussion of reward systems will be covered in more depth in Chapter 8.

HR Tip

Even if the sports or recreation program has a progressive reward system with strong core values toward internal stakeholders, it is still advisable to conduct periodic market comparisons of reward systems (within similar sports or recreation programs) to stay abreast of new trends and reward packages.

Disciplinary Systems. In many organizations, the disciplinary procedure is considered to be the most sensitive and critical HR activity. Durai (2010) suggests that,

Many managers, as far as possible, avoid involving themselves in the disciplinary action procedure due to the fear of future consequences. Their ignorance of the organizational rules and the legal dimensions of the disciplinary action also discourage them from being strict in upholding discipline and in punishing the undisciplined employee. However, an effective, well publicized and legally sound disciplinary proceeding which protects the manager from undue legal harassment can gain their confidence and willing involvement in the disciplinary procedure. (p. 492)

It is crucial for all internal stakeholders to know and feel comfortable with the sports or recreation program's disciplinary process. Strong disciplinary systems set the tone for employee behavior and expectations. Without strong systems in place, the procedures will be conducted inconsistently and habitually avoided by program administrators.

Furthermore, if the sports or recreation program has a sound disciplinary system which (1) has solid step-by-step procedures, (2) has been reviewed and approved by all relevant parties (including legal counsel), (3) has coherent, user-friendly documentation, and (4) is well established and known throughout the operation, the fundamental components and processes should be a part of the human resource plan. In developing a new disciplinary system, it is advisable for the administrators to:

- benchmark processes from other business enterprises;
- create step-by-step procedures for managing disciplinary issues;
- construct a baseline list of possible infractions and what disciplinary actions are associate with each;
- compose documentation/forms for the disciplinary system;
- have the entire disciplinary system verified and approved by legal counsel; and
- train all relevant parties on disciplinary processes/procedures.

Once again, all of these areas are essential aspects of a discipline system and should be detailed in the human resource plan. The development of a disciplinary system, as well as corrective action processes and employee separation, will be explored in depth in Chapter 9.

Safety and Health. Stakeholder/employee safety and health, from a human resource perspective, is twofold. Employee workplace safety, while interconnected with employee health programs, is a distinct sports or recreation program operational factor.

Employee safety is exceptionally noteworthy for sports or recreation program stakeholders. It is an area that, if not well managed, can be the cause of unthinkable harm to individuals, and could expose the program to enormous liability. In the book, *Workplace Safety: A Guide for Small and Midsized Companies*, Hopwood and Thompson (2006), discuss the four primary areas for managing workplace safety.

- Establish a clear commitment to safety
- Identify unsafe actions and conditions
- Provide resources for safety training (advanced safety training for supervisors)
- Assign someone the task of safety or assume it yourself, and provide the resources (time and money) (p. 2)

These four themes should be the foundation of the human resource plan's safety program. Through the human resource plan, the administrators must also consider a number of other factors:

1. Convey a zealous dedication to workplace safety by constantly creating and modifying safety policies and procedures, establish open lines of communication with all program stakeholders, be proactive in safety matters, and lead by example in all safety situations.

2. Schedule periodic safety audits that (1) pinpoint unsafe or hazardous situations, (2) strategize the elimination or minimization of all safety concerns, (3) report safety issues and concerns to all levels of the organization's hierarchical structure, and (4) develop tracking and reporting documentation for all safety issues and incidences.

3. Schedule periodic safety training seminars for all personnel. These seminars should be focused on specific program safety needs, as well as broad-spectrum safety training (first aid, CPR, fire drills).

4. Designate a point person (by position) for managing the safety program.

Over the past 20 years, progressive employee health programs have gained substantial momentum. Employee health programs can augment the organization's overall wellbeing by offering numerous events and ongoing activities such as company or family gatherings, philanthropic experiences, health fairs, and various wellness/social functions. Organizations may offer ongoing activities such as company teams and sporting interests, employee assistance programs (psychiatric, medical, financial), dieticians, personal trainers and exercise programs, and work/life training programs. If these employee wellness and health programs are being considered for the program, each of these events and activities should be listed, defined, and scheduled in a program-wide calendar and be defined in the human resources plan. Employee safety and health program planning will be discussed in detail in Chapter 10.

Execution of the Human Resource Plan

It has been expressed many times that a plan is only as good as its execution. No matter the quality and concentration of the human resource plan, if it is not followed, it is inconsequential. The X factor that contributes to the plan's acceptance and success is leadership. While management of the plan's execution is vital, stakeholders follow leaders, especially those whom have demonstrated a passion for the plan. This enthusiasm is exhibited from a top-down dedication to the whole plan and all it's aspects. Simply stated, the leader's commitment to the plan must be real and unremittingly communicated to all internal stakeholders. The loyalty and leadership in executing the plan must be more than lip service. Resources and assets must be allocated towards achieving the strategic goals and mission of the human resource plan. This tangible pledge is realized in the form of financial, tactical training, facilities, equipment, and support staff.

Accountability in the execution of the human resource plan is also vital. Each sports or recreation program member must know their assignments and responsibilities and be empowered to perform those duties and obligations. Furthermore, group consensus is essential to program success. The weakest link theory is extremely pertinent when it comes to the execution of the human resource plan, as it can literally take only one program stakeholder to undermine the human resource plan's strategies and goals, and set back progress towards the achievement of short and long term goals and objectives.

Monitoring the Human Resource Plan: A Living Document

As with all strategic plans, human resource plans are documents that must be perpetually evaluated for their significance and applicability. Each component of the program's human resource plan described throughout this chapter can be assessed using one of three different scenarios.

- Scenario 1. The identified goal, strategy, or specific action is meeting expectations and being implemented as anticipated.

- Scenario 2. The identified goal, strategy, or specific action is surpassing expectations and is being accomplished more efficiently than anticipated.

- Scenario 3. The identified goal, strategy, or specific action is deficient or inadequate in the fulfillment of its expectations and lacking in execution efficiencies.

In the Scenario 1, most program administrations will, predictably, continue to monitor the component for variations and maintain the status quo. If the Scenario 2 occurs, analyze the goal to understand why it is exceeding expectations. If the analysis determines that it is a temporary anomaly, then the goal, strategy, or action should be monitored for its return to planned operational expectations. If the analysis shows permanent elevated fulfillment and efficiencies in the goal , adjust the human resource plan to reflect the new improved performance levels. Finally, if the goal, strategy or action is deficient in satisfying expectations or lacks execution efficiencies, program administration should (1) investigate why this goalstrategy action is not meeting anticipated outcomes, (2) take corrective action to enhance its execution, or (3) discuss replacing the goal with other possible alternatives.

Summary

The adage, "failing to plan is planning to fail," is tremendously significant when discussing the resourceful utilization of the sports or recreation program's personnel. Because personnel are the sport and recreation program's most valuable resource, planning its acquisition, development, and utilization creates a decisive competitive advantage. Successful sports and recreation programs competently apply the human resource element to maximize productivity and stakeholder retention. Unfortunately, sports and recreation programs without strategic human resource plans haphazardly squander a precious and uniquely valuable asset which contributes to decline and ultimately failure.

References

Armstrong, M. (2012). *Armstrong's handbook of reward management practice: Improving performance through reward* (4th ed.). London, UK: Kogan Page. Retrieved from http://search.ebscohost.com.research.flagler.edu/login.aspx?direct=true&db=nlebk&AN=1406071&site=eds-live&scope=site

Armstrong, M. (2008). *Strategic human resource management: A guide to action* (4th ed.). London, UK: Kogan Page.

Aswathappa, K. (2013). *Human resource management: Text and cases* (7th ed.). New Delhi, India: McGraw Hill Education India Private Limited.

Badgi, S. M. (2012). *Practical guide to human resource information systems.* New Delhi, India: PHI Learning Private Limited.

Bateman, T. S., & Snell, S. A. (2011). *Management: Leading and collaborating in a competitive world* (9th ed.). New York, NY: McGraw-Hill/Irwin.

Byrd, M. J., & Megginson, L. C. (2009). *Small business management: An entrepreneur's guidebook.* New York, NY: Mc Graw-Hill/Irwin.

Capezio, P. (2010). *Managers guide to business planning.* New York, NY: McGraw-Hill Professional.

Durai, P. (2010). *Human resource management.* Noida, India: Dorling Kindersley/Pearson.

Enz, C. A. (2010). *Hospitality strategic management: Concepts and cases.* Hoboken, NJ: John Wiley & Sons.

Glaser, R. G., & Traynor, R. M. (2014). *Strategic practice management: Business and procedural considerations* (2nd ed.). San Diego, CA: Plural Publishing.

Hopwood, D., & Thompson, S. (2006). *Workplace safety: A guide for small and midsized companies.* Hoboken, NJ: John Wiley and Sons.

Ivancevich, J. M., & Konopaste, R. (2013). *Human resource management* (12th ed.). New York, NY: McGraw-Hill/Irwin.

Mathis, R. L., Jackson, J. H., Valentine, S. R., & Meglich, P. A. (2017). *Human resource management* (15th ed.). Boston, MA: Cengage Learning.

Mathis, R. L., & Nkomo, S. M. (2008). *Applications in Human Resources.* Mason, OH: Cengage Learning.

Noe, R. A., Hollenbeck, J. R., Gerhart, B., & Wright, P. M. (2004). *Fundamentals of human resource management.* New York, NY: McGraw Hill/Irwin.

Olsen, E. G. (2011). *Strategic planning kit for dummies.* Indianapolis, IN: For Dummies.

Reynolds, C. (2010). *Introduction to business architecture.* Boston, MA: Course PTR.

Rouillard L. (2009). *Goals and goal setting: Achieve measurable results.* Rochester, NY: Axzo Press. Retrieved from http://search.ebscohost.com.research.flagler.edu/login.aspx?direct=true&db=nlebk&AN=383340&site=eds-live&scope=site

Rue, L. W., Ibrahim, N. A, & Byars, L. L. (2013). *Management: Skills and applications* (14th ed.). New York, NY: McGraw-Hill/Irwin Higher Education.

Rue, L. W., Ibrahim, N. A, & Byars, L. L. (2016). *Human resource management* (11th ed.). New York, NY: McGraw-Hill/Irwin – Higher Education.

Shim, J. K., & Siegel, J. G. (2009). *Budgeting basics and beyond.* Hoboken, NJ: Wiley and Sons.

Simerson, B. K. (2011). *Strategic planning: A practical guide to strategy formulation and execution.* Santa Barbara, CA: Praeger.

Smith, A., Haimes, G. A., & Stewart, B. K. (2012). *Organizational culture and identity: Sport, symbols and success.* Hauppauge, NY: Nova Science Publishers.

Swayne, L. E., & Dodds, M. (2011). *Encyclopedia of sports management and marketing.* Thousand Oaks, CA: SAGE Publications.

Thompson, A. A., Peteraf, M. A., Gamble, J. E., & Strickland, A. J. (2014). *Crafting and executing strategy: The quest for competitive advantage* (19th ed.). New York, NY: McGraw-Hill/Irwin.

Thompson, A. A., Peteraf, M. A., Gamble, J. E., & Strickland, A. J. (2018). *Crafting and executing strategy: The quest for competitive advantage* (21st ed.). New York, NY: McGraw-Hill/Irwin.

Venugopal, P. (2010). *Marketing management: A decision-making approach.* New Delhi, India: SAGE Publications.

Zikmund, W. G., & Babin, B. J. (2013). *Essentials of marketing research* (5th ed.). Mason, OH: South-Western Cengage Learning.

Review and Discussion Questions

1. List in sequential order the primary sections of a strategic operational plan.
2. What is a vision statement?
3. What is a mission statement?
4. What are values statements?
5. What are some integral parameters and rules on establishing goals?
6. What are potential goal areas for sports or recreation programs?
7. What is a SWOT analysis?
8. Define the term policy. Define the term procedures.
9. What are the four ingredients of the marketing mix?
10. What are the five primary sections of a human resource plan?
11. What is the step-by-step process involved in creating distinct human resource goals/objectives?
12. What is a human resource internal assessment?
13. Name the four scenarios that are possible from an internal human resource assessment.
14. What are organizational charts?
15. What are the three main concerns in a sports or recreation program's selection process?
16. Name the five major objectives of an orientation program.
17. What are the questions to ask when constructing a training program?
18. Name the predominant components of a sports or recreation program's reward system.
19. What are the four aspects of a sound disciplinary system?
20. What are the four foundational themes for a sports or recreation program's safety program?
21. Describe leadership as a salient factor in executing a sports or recreation program's human resource plan.
22. In monitoring a human resource plan, what are the three assessment scenarios?

Application Exercises

1. Choose an actual recreation program in your area and construct for them a (1) human resource operational philosophy statement and (2) five human resource value statements.
2. Through research, construct a current straight-line hierarchical structure for a local recreational program.
3. Construct individual rewards (compensation, benefits, remunerations/incentives, and auxiliary allowance) for the following four athletic program positions and justify your reward choices:
   - NCAA Division I Athletic Director
   - NAIA Softball Head Coach
   - Club Director for AAU Basketball Program
   - High School Assistant Swim Coach

Appendix
Strategic Operational Planning for Sports and Recreation Programs

The following is an abridged structure for creating an operational plan for a sports or recreation program, extrapolated from the textbook, *The Administrative Side of Coaching: Applying Business Concepts to Athletic Program Administration and Coaching* .

It is important for operational plans have everyone's commitment. The document cannot be a single person's perspective but must be the vision of everyone involved with the operation and administration of the sports or recreation program. Enlisting participatory involvement from all appropriate internal and external stakeholders is vital for planning and goal fulfillment.

Table 3.3 is a comprehensive breakdown of a far-reaching operational plan. Observe how Section X: Human Resource Management Plan seamlessly flows from and within the entire sports or recreation overall operational plan.

TABLE 3.3   Operational Plan Breakdown

I. Title Page

    Organization Name (school, university, club)

    Operational Address, Phone Numbers, E-Mails, Web Page

    Organization Logo (as an underlay)

    Page Title – XYZ's Operational Plan

    Date of Plan

    Administrators and Team Members

    Completion/Distribution Date

    Copy Numbers (for tracking)

II. Table of Contents

    Major Sections

    Sub-Sections

    Page Numbers

III. Executive Summary

    One/Two Page Synopsis of:

    Overall Program

    Products and Services

    Human Resource Strategies

        Marketing Program

        Operational Systems

        Management Team

        Financial Status

Continued

TABLE 3.3 (*Continued*)   Operational Plan Breakdown

IV. Vision, Mission, and Value Statements

    All-Encompassing Statements on the Program's

        Future Vision

        Operational Philosophy Values

        Major Goals

V. Program History

    A Synopsis of:

        Operation's History

        Past Program Strategies and Achievements

VI. Long-Term Goals (3-5 years)

    Three to Five Total Long-Term Goals of the Sports or Recreation Program

    Broad and Measurable (if possible)

VII. Short-Term Goals (1-2 years)

    Specific Actions for Each Long-Term Goal (this year or next)

    Precise and Measurable

    Personnel Accountability

    Time Frames for Completion

VIII. SWOT Analysis

    Strengths, Weaknesses, Opportunities, and Threats

    Scenario Analysis

IX. Policies, Procedures, and Ethical Obligations

    Breakdown of the Program's Policies (rules)

    Breakdown of the Program's Procedures (critical operational functions)

    Ethical Guidelines and Ethical Code of Conduct

X. Human Resource Management Plan

    Operational Philosophy and Values

    Overview of HR laws and regulations

    Long and Short term goals HR management goals

    Human Resource Internal Assessment

    Operational projections for Human Resources

    Hierarchical Structure

        Job Descriptions

        Net Human Resource Requirements and Action Plan

        Selection and Hiring Procedures

        HRIS

        Orientation and Training

TABLE 3.3 *(Continued)*   Operational Plan Breakdown

Performance Management

Reward Systems

Disciplinary System

Safety and Health

XI. Marketing and Promotional Plan

Marketing Goals and Objectives

Marketing Mix (product, price, place, promotion)

Product/Service	Life Cycle Position
	Specifications and Features
	Customer Service
	Bundling/Packaging
Price	Pricing Philosophy (cost, market, customer value)
	Projected Demand for Product
	Price Elasticity
Place	Facility Size
	Facility Location
	Facility Accessibility and Parking
	Travel Policies and Procedures
Promotion	Promotional Plan (positioning goals)
	Brand Development Models
	Message Concept
	Promotional Mix (advertising, P.R., sales promotions, personal selling, direct marketing, technology)
	Budget Requirements (projected expenditures for promotional mix)
	Projected Success of Promotional Mix

Segmentation and Target Audience

Market Segmentation

Target Market (size, location, profitability, etc.)

Detailed Customer Profile (demographics, geographic, psychographics, purchasing behavior)

Consumer Buying Habits and Purchasing Power (for target market)

Customer Influences on Product Adoption and Purchasing

XII. Financial Planning and Pro-Forma Financial Statements

Expenditure and Revenue Projections for the Sports or Recreation Program

XIII. Appendix

Note: From The Administrative Side of Coaching, 3rd Ed.© 2018, West Virginia University. Used with permission.

I: Title Page

While the title page, or cover to the operational plan might appear to be inconsequential, it sets the tone for the importance and professionalism of the plan. Its design should reflect the makeup of the sports or recreation program, and should include:

- program name (school, university, club name);
- address, phone, email address, website URL;
- date of plans construction;
- sports or recreation program design logo; and
- copy numbers (indispensable for protecting/tracking).

II: Table of Contents

A table of contents is an obligatory element of a well-organized and functional operation plan. The table of contents, that includes a sectional format and consistent page numbering presents straightforward and organized identifiable program information to the reader and serves as a valuable reference for specific information as needed.

III: Executive Summary

The executive summary is an abridgment of the entire sports or recreation operational plan. This overview accentuates key sections of the operational plan to provide readers with a summation (characteristically one or two pages) of the plan's core components. Byrd and Megginson (2009) even suggest that "The executive summary of your plan must be a real 'grabber;' it must motivate the reader to go on to other sections. Moreover, it must convey a sense of plausibility, credibility, and integrity" (p. 146).

The executive summary is composed of a condensed description of the sports or recreation program's services provided and products produced; an abstract view of the competitive market and proposed marketing tactics; main points of the operational plan; a rundown of the sports or recreation program's management team (program administrators, coaches, and staff); and an encapsulated picture of the financial condition under which the program operates and any new projected budgetary/capital needs.

Because the executive summary is a synopsis of the entire sports or recreation operational plan, it is completed last after all other plan components are finalized.

IV: Vision, Mission, and Value Statements

A sports or recreation program's operational plan originates with three fundamental but essential statements. They are the vision statement, mission statement, and value statements.

Vision Statement. A sports or recreation program's vision—characteristically five to 10 years in the future—is not simply an unrealistic or imaginary view of the program. Constructive vision statements are built with tangibility and coherent foresight. Capezio (2010) asserts that a compelling vision statement is what the company is striving to be and do in the marketplace at a future point in time that everyone in the company can relate to. Focus areas for the vision statement include financial perspective, customer perspective, internal business processes perspective, and people and learning perspective. Other categories for consideration are growth and innovation, as well as core capabilities. (pp. 62–63)

Generally, these universal areas of a vision statement are pertinent components in developing a core strategy for the sports or recreation program's future. If administration is radically altering the direction of an existing program within these primary areas, they should recognize that particular stakeholders may be unwilling or unable to envision these operational changes. To get internal and external stakeholders enthusiastic about the new vision, program administration should:

1. Discuss the proposed vision changes within the context of the advantages/benefits each stakeholder will receive if implemented and achieved.

2. Solicit each stakeholder's input when crafting the sports or recreation program's new vision.

3. Take advantage of opportunities to reinforce the new vision through convincing and unremitting communication.

4. Show an unconditional commitment toward the new vision.

Undeniably, administrators must guide the sports or recreation program toward its new vision. Without unqualified devotion, the vision will be minimized or completely ignored to the detriment and ultimately the failure of the entire program.

Mission Statement. Because the future is uncertain, vision statements are, to a certain degree, speculative in their makeup. However, sports and recreation program mission statements have well-defined relationships to perceptible objectives and strategies. According to Olsen (2011) a mission statement is

the company's purpose or its fundamental reason for existing. The statement spotlights what business a company is presently in and the customer needs it presently strives to meet. To build a solid foundation for a successful business, having a written, clear, concise, and consistent mission statement is essential. The statement should simply explain who you are and why you exist. (p. 93)

The language employed in a mission statement is dependent upon the sports and recreation program administrator's subjective preferred writing style. However, a properly formulated and worded mission statement:

- defines the nature, focus, and intent of the organization.
- provides boundaries within which the organization will operate, potentially including opportunities or threats the organization will address, needs or expectations the organization will fulfill, services and/or products the organization will provide, the market or geographic area

the organization will target, and the impression the organization hopes to make on its clients, customers, and community.

- sets expectations on how all members of the organization should behave and perform and inspires them to do the right thing for the right reasons when making decisions and conducting business (whatever that business might be).

- helps employees (at all levels) understand why they are being asked to do what they do on a daily basis and how what they do on a daily basis helps the organization achieve its mission.

- helps customers and clients know what to expect from the organization, in terms of how they are to be treated when speaking to or meeting with members of the organization and the services and products they are likely to receive from the organization or what needs or requirements the organization is likely to fulfill.

- sends a clear and concise message about the organization's intention to various stakeholders (such as board members, investors, and prospective employees).

- helps establish mutual understanding of an organization's function and intention in regulatory filings, organizational charters, and partnership agreements.

- helps guide decision making and actions (relating to, for example, how monies are allocated—especially when money is scarce and programs, imperatives, and initiatives must be prioritized).

(Simerson, 2011, pp. 120–121)

Depending on the operation, a sports or recreation program's mission statement can be as transitory as a few direct statements or pages of extensively elucidated statements, based on Simerson's points above . A succinct, abbreviated mission statement could be beneficial for sports and recreation program operational plans constructed for outside funding and sponsorship. By delivering a comprehensive groundwork and strategic progression, an in-depth sports and recreation program mission statement could be more internally applicable to guide in-house administrators, coaches, and staff.

Value Statements. Sports and recreation program administration must appreciate the magnitude of instituting germane, lucid value statements. They serve as the foundation of the operation's culture. In other words, clear-cut value statements are the cultural basis of the sports or recreation program. Smith, Haimes, and Stewart (2012) assert that culture drives the performance of its workforce, and this is true of the culture in sports or recreation programs; they

drive performance, leverage powerful histories and change quickly in turbulent conditions. Sport organizations with great cultures find ways of winning because drive and ambition lie at the heart of their identities...sport cultures can be reinvented, rebuilt and redesigned so that they create a productive, high performance environment. Organizational culture and identity provide an understanding of how and why an organization does things, the way the people within the organization behave, and the perceptions held sovereign by stakeholders. Put another way, culture provides a means by which an organization's members interpret the way things are done, and what happens in daily working life. It governs individual actions and behavior including how others, both inside and outside the organization, regard individuals. (p. 2)

A variety of conceivable value statement factors can be the basis for the sports or recreation program's culture. Value themes for sports and recreation program cultural development include: fans, internal stakeholders and program administrators.

Fan or customer program interaction. Where there is an unqualified dedication to ethical conduct concerning fans or customers, unmatched commitment to superior sports and recreation program activities and sporting events where, "no fan or customer left behind" attitude in which all individuals are valued, and ease of sports or recreation program access for all.

Internal stakeholders. Where there is a critical respect in the workplace for all internal stakeholders, positional empowerment in sports and recreation program positions, unconditional assistance when needed… servant leadership concept, 100% commitment for internal program stakeholder safety, and enlistment in the long-term strategic future of the sports or recreation program.

Sports and recreation program administrators. Where there is a leadership-first attitude, encouragement of interaction and accessible communication, development and enforcement of sound policies and procedures, establishment of a family atmosphere, and challenging but achievable expectations.

V: Program History

Developing a program history section for an operational plan might seem unproductive to some administrators. In actuality, this section furnishes internal and external stakeholders, who are fundamentally defined as people who have any type of existing or future interest in the program (internal: administrators, coaches, and staff; external: outside administrators and future sponsors, customers, fans), with a point of reference and a progressive framework that they can follow. In other words, for program stakeholders to know where the operation is going in the future, a significant starting point is with the program's past. The

TABLE 3.4 Potential Value Areas for Sports and Recreation Programs

Supporters Customers Fans	*Employees*	*Administration*
The program experience is everything	Sincerely treated as the most valuable resource in the program	Lead by example – Walk the talk
Unconditional commitment to ethical treatment of supporters/customers/fans	Authorized to make decisions	Open communication and trust
	Trust and support	Established sound policies and procedures
Providing the highest quality activities, sporting events, and programs	Unconditional commitment to employee safety	Goal focused leadership
	Every person, no matter what the position, is a valuable asset	Total quality management philosophy in all aspects of the sports or recreation program's operation
100% participation philosophy for all supporters/customers/fans	Vested interest and contribution in program development and implementation	
Promotion of self-esteem, citizenship, and enthusiasm for all		

program's history can be constructed as a detailed narrative or a year-by-year timeline. No matter what the sports and recreation program's history, it should be written in optimistic, positive language.

VI and VII: Long- and Short-Term Goals and Objectives

These two sections of the operational plan are regarded as the core components for laying the program's future strategic foundation and focusing direct and immediate assignments and actions for the entire sports or recreation program. Long-term goals are the program's strategic targets (two, or three to five years in length), while individual short-term goals andobjectives are the immediate, identifiable, and unambiguous actions that will be utilized to achieve each specific long-term goal and objective.

From a global perspective, the goals and objectives of any business, sports and recreation programs included

- Will inform how the business wants to fit in with the world around it.
- Shape the communications of the business.
- Guide the process the business needs to put in place in order to be effective.
- Help in understanding the entities that will matter to the business.

(Reynolds, 2010, p. 26)

The actual writing of objectives can be SMART: specific, measurable, attainable, relevant, and timely. According to Capezio (2010), the SMART criteria for writing objectives "may be overused, but it bears reference as a standard to measure well-written objectives." The SMART test that objectives must pass to be effective is as follows:

- *Specific.* Stated in precise, not vague terms. Objectives are quantified.
- *Measurable.* Measurements are included to provide targets for the objectives.
- *Attainable.* Objectives are realistic but challenging and provide "stretch" to be attained.
- *Relevant.* Objectives must link to the business and functional objectives.
- *Timely.* Dates for completion are included in the objectives.

(Capezio, 2010, p. 42)

Finally, to determine priorities in positioning goals and objectives within the operational plan as a guiding element for all internal and external stakeholders, program administrators should categorize each long-term and short-term goal and objective. Rouillard (2009) states the classification of goals and objectives requires a review of each goal statement to determine whether its outcome is:

- *Essential.* Required for the operation of the business or for personal improvement; it must be done.
- *Problem-solving.* Proposes a more appropriate or desired condition or ways around obstacles.
- *Innovative.* An activity that will result in something better, faster, cheaper, easier, or safer.

(Rouillard, 2009, p. 60)

When classifying and prioritizing goals and objectives, utilize all sports or recreation program administrators, coaches, and staff. Their institutional knowledge is crucial in determining which statements are essential, problem-solving, and innovative. Because misclassifying a goal or objective can have serious consequences at all levels of the program, use as many intellectual capital sources as possible to focus the program's strategic long-term and short-term goals and objectives.

Goal Parameters in Operational Planning. The actual makeup of each unique goal is up to the sports or recreation program administration. However, there are some integral parameters and rules that should guide the establishment of goals.

1. All goals should ultimately emanate from the vision, mission, and value statements.
2. When formulating goals, long-term objectives should be defined first. Subsequently, short-term actions should work toward accomplishing each long-term goal.
3. It is critical to base all goals in reality. It is necessary to ask the following questions:
   - Do we currently have the resources and funds to achieve our projected goals?
   - Do we have the future potential to acquire the essential resources and funds to accomplish goals?
   - Do we have the staff or the likelihood of acquiring the staff to attain goals?
   - Is the timeframe for the execution of the goals practical?
   - Will there be any internal or external confrontation or resistance to the goals?
4. Goals should be easily comprehensible by everyone in the organization. They should be straightforward, concise, and in common language.
5. Each goal should be distinctive and salient. In other words, are the goals repetitive or are they unique in origin?
6. Each goal should have the absolute endorsement and focus of everyone in the organization. In the sports or recreation program setting, the coaches, counselor, staff, and administrators should be involved in the goal-setting process. Without everyone's input, key internal stakeholders might not take an active interest in operations, which, in turn, may leave goals unattained.
7. Each goal and program objective should be as precise and measurable as possible. The advantage of quantifying goals is to supply program administration with concrete numbers so that they can compare projected goals with actual results.
8. Goals should be challenging but realistic. Setting goals beyond the reach of current resources and capabilities could be profoundly discouraging. Conversely, setting goals that are too easily achieved will depreciate the critical value of goal setting and goal achievement. Sports and recreation program administration must balance these two factors to maximize the program's potential.
9. To be effective, goals need individual and group accountability. Simply put, a sports or recreation program goal without individual and group accountability will fail because assumptions will be made on who is expected to work on and accomplish the goal.

10. Goals need to be time precise. While the word "deadline" has a negative connotation in our society, in goal setting and achievement it is tremendously appropriate. Once again, the time frame to achieve a particular goal must be challenging but realistic.

In their text *Management: Skills and Applications*, Rue, Ibrahim, and Byars (2013) outline ten possible goal areas that are universal to most businesses. These 10 areas can be adapted to sports and recreation organizations. The following list is a summation of their concepts.

1. **Profitability**. Measures the degree to which the firm is attaining an acceptable level of profits.
2. **Markets**. Reflects the firm's position in the marketplace.
3. **Productivity**. Measures the efficiency of internal operations.
4. **Product**. Describes the introduction or elimination of products or services.
5. **Financial resources**. Reflects goals relating to the funding needs of the firm.
6. **Physical facilities**. Describes the physical facilities of the firm.
7. **Research and innovation**. Reflects the research, development, or innovation aspirations of the firm.
8. **Organizational structure**. Describes objectives relating to changes in the organizational structure and related activities.
9. **Human resources**. Describes the human resource assets of the organization.
10. **Social responsibility**. Refers to the commitments of the firm regarding society and the environment.

(Rue, Ibrahim, & Byars, 2013, p. 153)

It is frequently asked, how many long-term goals should our program develop and implement? Because of the generalized nature and enormity of long-term goals, as well as the limited resources of most sports or recreation programs, no more than four or five long-term goals should be attempted. How many short-term actions should be devised for each long-term goal? As many as it takes to accomplish that long-term goal. Simply put, it may take a few short-term and immediate actions or it could take dozens. It all depends on the long-term goal.

VIII: SWOT Analysis

A SWOT analysis, which is the evaluation of an organization's strengths, weaknesses, opportunities and threats, is an essential part of establishing the future direction of the sports or recreation program. The analysis supplies a comprehensive, contemporary snapshot of the organization. Enz (2010) describes how tstrategists evaluate SWOT analyses as part of operational planning:

Strengths are company resources and capabilities that can lead to a competitive advantage. Weaknesses are resources and capabilities that a company does not possess, to the extent that

TABLE 3.5   Potential Goal Areas for Sports and Recreation Programs

Profitability	• Maximizing and diversifying revenue sources • Minimizing and controlling expenses • Creating strong, adept budgeting • Adopting fiscal responsibility philosophy
Market	• Creating a sustainable competitive advantage over similar sports and recreation programs with: • Superior operational planning • Stronger organizational configuration • Competent and motivated internal stakeholders • Sound leadership • Clear and valid control systems
Productivity	• Internal systems design in areas such as recruiting, travel, training, general administration • More efficient use of resources to produce quality outputs
Production	• Addition/deletion of: • programs, teams, activities, and events • Merchandise • Summer instructional camps • Fundraising events and activities
Financial Resource	• Increasing: • Ticket sales (season and individual events) • Merchandise sales • TV, radio, and media revenue • Fundraising events, activities, and programs
Physical Facility	• New facilities • Renovation of current facilities • Capacity utilization of facilities to maximize revenue • Facility cost controls
Research & Innovation	• Researching: • New personnel training • New administrative procedures • New legislative issues • New technological advances

Continued

TABLE 3.5 (*Continued*) Potential Goal Areas for Sports and Recreation Programs

Organizational Structure	• Objectives to assist in facilitating: • Effective communication throughout the sports or recreation program • Resource utilization and focus • Orderly working environment with clear lines of authority
Human Resource	• Objectives to improve: • Recruiting systems (for acquiring personnel) • Staffing systems (for acquiring administrators, coaches, and staff) • Orientation programs • Skill, knowledge, and attitudinal training • Performance evaluation systems • Disciplinary systems
Social Responsibility	• Community involvement and improvement • Increasing public awareness of sports or recreation program through social responsibility • Developing a sense of community within and around the sports or recreation organization

their absence places the firm at a competitive disadvantage. Opportunities are conditions in the broad and operating environments that allow a firm to take advantage of organizational strengths, overcome organizational weaknesses, and/or neutralize environmental threats. Threats are conditions in the broad and operating environments that may impede organizational competitiveness or the achievement of stakeholder satisfaction. (p. 16)

The SWOT analysis should answer the following questions:

• What are the attractive aspects of the [program's] situation?

• What aspects are of the most concern?

• Are the [program's] internal strengths and competitive assets sufficiently strong to enable it to compete successfully?

• Are the [program's] weaknesses and competitive deficiencies of small consequence and readily correctable, or could they prove fatal if not remedied soon?

• Do the [program's] strengths outweigh its weaknesses by an attractive margin?

• Does the [program] have attractive market opportunities that are well suited to its internal strengths? Does the [program] lack the competitive assets to pursue the most attractive opportunities?

- All things considered, where on a 1 to 10 (where 1 is alarmingly weak and 10 is exceptionally strong) do the [program's] overall situation and future prospects rank?

(Thompson, Peteraf, Gamble, & Strictland, 2014, p. 96)

From the above questions, one can see how strategically important it is for program administrators to develop and continuously revisit the operation's SWOT analysis. For this reason, SWOT is a salient component of the operation plan.

IX: Policies, Procedures, and Ethical Obligations

In *Strategic Practice Management: Business and Procedural Considerations*, Glaser and Traynor, (2014) underscore the magnitude of creating and implementing a sports or recreation program's policies and procedures manual by stating that

> the Policy and Procedures Manual (P&P Manual) may serve as the informational source developed for a specific individual or group of employees and as the basis for employee manuals or handbooks, but that it may also be reserved solely for the use of specific managers or directors within an organization. (p. 335)

While policies and procedures are generally discussed collectively, they are two independent operational areas that contribute to an organization's success. Policies are associated with sports or recreation program regulations and rules that influence internal and external stakeholder actions (people focused), while procedures are methodologies that elucidate how to achieve program duties and responsibilities (task focused).

Typically, policy and procedural manuals are distinct, comprehensive documents that have substantial depth. For this reason, in the operational plan, program administration should provide an outline or an overview of the manual rather than the entire manual. The concentration and range of policy items within an operational plan are determined by the operation's philosophy, position, environment, ethical history, and traditions. Some areas may be more accentuated than others. Procedures are step-by-step actions taken to perform specific tasks. Sports or recreation program administration should establish straightforward procedures in areas of travel, purchasing, budgeting, cash handling, registration, and other administrative functions. The biggest dividend in determining procedures for administrative functions is uniformity. This saves time, coordinates activities, and minimizes frustration that may arise from disorganization.

HR Tip
Policy and procedure manuals are only beneficial if they are acknowledged, established, and applied. Continuously emphasize the sports or recreation program's commitment to its policies and procedures.

X: Human Resource Plan

The human resource (HR) element of an operational plan should be looked at as an vital sub-plan within the overall plan. Human resource management can best be interpreted as "a strategic and coherent approach to the management of an organization's most valued asset—the people working there, who individually and collectively contribute to the achievement of its objectives" (Armstrong, 2008, p. 5).

XI: Marketing and Promotional Plan

The leading misnomer concerning the term *marketing* deals with the limited perception that it is only concerned with the sole promotional communication topic of advertising. Marketing goes far beyond that basic assumption. It is the wide-ranging operational function that "develop solutions that address consumer needs…. [Marketing] must educate prospects about how their products and services will meet these needs better/faster/cheaper than the existing products in the market" (Venugopal, 2010, p. 15).

The principal theory for marketing is broken down into four factors known as the 4Ps of marketing, otherwise known as the marketing mix. In *Encyclopedia of Sports Management and Marketing*, Swayne and Dodds (2011) describe the marketing mix for sports or recreation organizations as

> gathered information that serves to help an organization to make appropriate product and service, pricing, delivery, and promotional decisions…. The product includes the total tangible or intangible outputs of an organization…. Price is the value a consumer equates to a good or service or the amount of money or goods asked for in exchange for something else…. Place deals with the methods of distributing the product to consumers…. Promotion represents how information about the product is communicated to customers, with a goal of receiving positive response from the consumer, and results in product sales. (pp. 848–849)

XII: Financial Planning and Pro-Forma Financial Statements

Financial planning is also known as budgeting. Budgets are

> the formal expression of plans, goals, and objectives of management that covers all aspects of operations for a designated time period and a tool to provide targets and direction that emphasizes the importance of evaluating alternative actions before decisions actually are implemented. (Shim & Siegel, 2009, p. 1).

The question is, what items can a sports or recreation program administrators budget? While core budgets are interested in the financial forecasts of the sports or recreation program (projected revenues generated and expenses distributed), any asset that contributes to the achievement of goals and objectives can and often should be budgeted. Sports or recreation program administrators can budget: facility usage (gyms, fields, weight rooms, parking); manpower (administrators, staff, coaches); equipment and uniforms; transportation (buses, vans, flights); office space; and any asset line-item.

The development and employment of budgets leads to sports or recreation program proficiency. Accurate budgeting is paramount if a program is to achieve maximum efficiencies. Efficiency is the use of fewer inputs and assets to create the best quality output. All organizations (sports and recreation program included) have limited resources and assets. Being more resourceful with those inputs and resources is a way to achieve a competitive advantage over one's competition, and budgets assist in that aspiration.

chapter four

Modeling Human Resources: Job Analysis, Structure, and Descriptions

Chapter Objectives

- Understand occupational modeling concepts for sports and recreation programs
- Understand and apply the job analysis process and scenarios
- Examine the four principle methods for gathering job analysis data
- Understand the potential concerns with conducting a job analysis
- Understand the development process of job designing for sports and recreation programs
- Understand the aspects of the scope enrichment, expansion, rotation and simplification of job design
- Examine job analysis and job design scenarios
- Understand the fundamental construction of job descriptions
- Understand and evaluate, section-by-section, the components of sports and recreation program job descriptions
- Understand and construct all-inclusive hierarchical/organizational charts

Key Terms

Occupational Modeling
Job Analysis
Job Design
Strategic Initiatives
Job Analysis Methods
Interviews
Benchmarking Research
Job Analysis Data
Fixed Response Questions
Open-Ended Questions
Position Analysis Questionnaire (PAQ)
Overt Observation
Covert Observation

Department of Labor
   Occupational Information
   Network (O*NET)
External Research
Embellishment
Holistic Viewpoint
Job Scope
Job Enrichment
Job Enlargement
Job Rotation
Job Simplification
Self-Managed Work Group
Flextime
Condensed Work Week

Virtual Work
Job Descriptions
Position Title
Position Synopsis
Essential Responsibilities
Job Qualifications
Position Rewards and Benefits
Organizational Structure
Hierarchical/Organizational
   Charts
Outsourcing
Strategic Alliances

Occupational Modeling

Occupational modeling is conceptualizing and crafting employment positions to maximize human resource productivity. Fundamentally, an occupation is "made up of the daily tasks and activities in which people engage coupled with the meaning or personal, subjective value these tasks and activities provide" (Hinojosa, Kramer, & Royeen, 2017, p. 28). The key for sports or recreation program success is to (1) model and construct job position responsibilities that achieve organizational goals while (2) furnishing the individuals who execute those tasks and jobs with a feeling of worthwhile contribution and accomplishment. These two elements are not mutually exclusive. For example, constructing a program position with exceptional intrinsic value to the employee, but with little or no relevance to organizational objectives is an unqualified waste of program resources (especially its human capital). Conversely, to model a position focused solely on accomplishing organizational objectives without regard to the employee's personal satisfaction would often lead to reduced productivity, diminished morale, and decreased employee retention. The ultimate goal in occupational modeling is to have a win-win with decidedly goal-focused positions that are personally rewarding to employees.

Why Develop an Occupational Modeling System?

Financial and labor costs for establishing an occupational modeling system are considerable and must be taken into account prior to committing the organization's resources and capabilities. Nonetheless, the constructive impact on an organization listed below more than justify the monetary outlay and collective effort needed to institute and maintain an occupational modeling system.

1. Eradication of organizational counter-productivity, disorganization, and employee frustration. Occupational modeling systems organize a program's workload to reduce (if not totally eliminate) (1) doubling of work, (2) overlooking critical responsibilities, and/or (3) not completing tasks appropriately. Moreover, occupational modeling systems will minimize employee frustration with their employment situation (due to confusion about assignments orduties), as well as positively amplify their attitude toward the overall sports or recreation program.

2. Increasing operational efficiency. Effectual occupation modeling systems can have a measureable increase on the macro and global productivity of the entire sports or recreation program. This productivity relates to the efficacious use of the program's human resource asset, which is the most vital and typically the most expensive element of the operation. Simply stated, definitive job designs, descriptions, and organizational structures assist sports and recreation administrators in directing and capitalizing on individual and organizational performance.

3. Delineated accountability. Having sound "watertight" job descriptions leads to a new level of individual accountability. Two side benefits of having this increased employee-initiated accountability are (1) the program members have a more vested interest in the success of the program and (2) program administration can transfer its energy from day-to-day monitoring of individuals to long-term organizational strategic improvements.

4. Advancement of a high performance culture. Through occupational modeling systems, having a well-defined labor force can generate or modify a program's culture from a characterless ornondescript culture to a high performance, adaptable culture. This transformation is achieved through better workflow, unified and goal concentrated interactions, and newly formed cooperative synergies and relationships.

5. Increasing organizational safety. By focusing job responsibilities through definitive job descriptions, a sports or recreation program can experience an enhanced emphasis on task expertise and task safety. By comprehending exactly what duties they are undertaking, program members can become more proficient and safe in accomplishing them.

6. Fostering a team attitude. By focusing program members on individual jobs, the sports or recreation program will experience a more "team-like" atmosphere. While this last statement seems counterintuitive, in actuality, it is true. "Within an organization, units and individuals must cooperate to create outputs. Ideally, the organization's structure brings together the people who must collaborate in order to efficiently produce the desired outputs" (Noe, Hollenbeck, Gerhart, & Wright, 2004, p. 104).

7. Understanding market forces. By forming an occupational modeling system, a sports or recreation program can continually scrutinize internal positions as to their external relevance in the marketplace. Items such as new job task innovations, evolving job responsibilities, removal of antiquated or irrelevant tasks, changing job qualification requirements, and understanding the market value of positions (compensation = salaries and benefits) can all be researched and kept up-to-date.

8. Increasing customer focus. Because customer demands endlessly fluctuate, an occupational modeling system can help a program adapt its human resource asset to customers' changing needs by focusing occupational modeling on new value-added activities and customer responsiveness.

9. Special assignments. Having precisely specified job descriptions to operate from, program administrators can have conclusive information on which organizational positions are ideal for special assignments and work groups. Instead of indiscriminately "throwing" program members into special assignments or workgroups, administrators can examine which positions can add the most cross-functionality and value to the unique circumstance, activity, or assignment.

Timeline for Developing a Structured Occupational Modeling System

Table 4.1 provides (1) operational phases, (2) step-by-step processes, and (3) wide-ranging timelines for developing a structured occupational modeling system in a sports or recreation program.

1. This is a comprehensive template that can be "scaled back" to suit the size, number of positions, and complexity of the organization.

2. The time ranges provided can vary greatly based on the organization, number of positions, number of research participants, resources and personnel commitment to "working" the project, and specific time constraints. While the phases and individual steps are standardized, the execution must be customized for each distinct operation.

TABLE 4.1   Phases of Development for an Occupational Modeling System

Item	*Estimated Time Range*
Phase I Administrative Preparation	**2 weeks to 1 ½ months**
Delineation of all current and future sports or recreation positions (based on strategic operational plan and human resource plan	1 week
Organization-wide notification of impending occupational	1 Week
Modeling system work (verbal, electronic, hardcopy, etc.)	
Data collection scheduling	1 Week
• Methods to be utilized	
• Number of participant per method	
• Review work schedules for participants	
• Final participant schedules for involvement in system	
Finalizing data collection instruments (designing or purchasing data collection instruments for each data collection method)	2 – 4 Weeks
Phase II Data Collection	**2 Weeks to 2 Months**
Interviews	2 Weeks
• Option #1 Three, 30 minute one-on-one interviews for each position	
• Option #2 One collective/group interview for all individuals in each program position	
Questionnaires (distribution and collection of instruments for all personnel in all positions)	2 Weeks
Observations	2 Weeks
• Option #1 – Overt shadowing and recording	
• Option #2 – Covert surveillance and recording	
Benchmarking (external research required for all new program positions)	1 – 2 Weeks
Phase III Data Analysis	**2 Weeks to 2 Months**
Positional analysis (position-by-position analysis of primary job duties, secondary job duties, and auxiliary job duties)	1 – 2 Weeks
Job design (tangible structuring of data into coherent positions)	1 – 2 Weeks
Job description creation (comprehensive and uniform for each program position)	2 – 4 Weeks
Organizational chart (hierarchical chart with positions, divisions, reporting relationships, etc.)	1 Week
Phase IV Post Administrative Work	**1 – 2 Weeks**
Collective administrative review of job descriptions and organizational chart	1 week
Department meetings to review and fine-tune occupational modeling	1 week
Individual meetings (at need) to review specific job descriptions implementation	1 – 2 weeks
	Daily

Job Analysis

The first step in job modeling is to conduct a job analysis. Whether it is for a new program position, or for restructuring an existing program position, the

> purpose of a job analysis is to provide an in-depth understanding of the competencies required for success in order to select appropriate candidates. A job competency is a behavior, or set of behaviors, necessary to accomplish a specific work task or achieve a specific goal. (Prien, Goodstein, Goodstein, & Gamble, 2009, p. 5)

A pertinent factor for job analysis success relates to the commitment of time, energy, and resources to perform these critical investigations. Without an organizational-wide dedication to the job analysis process, the subsequent job designs and final job descriptions would, at best, be irrelevant and, at worst, be cause for counterproductivity and profound operational chaos.

HR Tip

For new positions, undertaking job analysis research is an obvious obligation. The question to then ask is: why does a sports or recreation program need to conduct a job analysis for a position(s) that already exists? The answer is to improve human resource efficiencies which, in turn, give the sports or recreation program a distinct competitive advantage. The more up-to-date a position, the more impact it will contribute to the program.

When Should a Job Analysis be Conducted?

There are four primary circumstances in which job analyses should be conducted.

1. Periodically. In every business enterprise, job positions transform or evolve over time. New responsibilities need to be added while obsolete tasks need to be removed. As discussed, the prevailing goal for reevaluating positions is to capitalize on internal efficiencies. Because of the composition of sports and recreation, annual job analyses (based on competitive seasons) are recommended.

2. Strategic initiatives. Before undertaking new, overhauled, or altered strategic initiatives, it is prudent to conduct either detailed or abbreviated job analyses, depending on the initatives in question. It is very rare when an organization's strategic objectives have little or no impact on jobs and the people in them; it is more likely strategic objectives will have an acute influence on the jobs and employees.

3. New position. When a new position is added to a sport or recreation program, a job analysis review is needed for other current program positions to reveal the potential cascading impact the new position will have on the operation. Impact factors such as additional assignments, eliminated responsibilities, altered duties, and supervisory changes are all elements to be examined.

4. Elimination of positions. If positions are eliminated in a sports or recreation program, conceivably from strategic downsizing or occupational obsolescence, administration should conduct job analyses to assess the outcome those removals have on the remaining program positions. Eliminating positions will often necessitate redistribution of essential activities and responsibilities to other jobs.

How to Conduct a Job Analysis: Methodologies and Tactics

The book *Staffing the Contemporary Organization: A Guide to Planning, Recruiting and Selecting Human Resource Professionals* simplifies the job analysis process into five primary components (in order):

1. Identification of each job in the organization;
2. Collection of information about duties, responsibilities, and working conditions of each job;
3. Delineation of essential job functions and marginal or nonessential job functions;
4. Determination of the human qualifications needed to perform the job; and
5. Preparation of the job descriptions and job specifications. (Caruth, Caruth, & Pane, 2008, p. 97)

Straightforward applications can be utilized from job analysis components for sports and recreation programs.

Identification of each job in the organization. When initiating the job analysis process, administrators should identify all of the existing program positions as well as any future positions based on the vision and long-term goals of the organization. Additionally, all sports or recreation program positions and stakeholders, from the executive level (athletic directors, owners, executive administrators, board of directors, etc.) to the operational level (coaches, clinician, counselors, administration, medical staff, student interns, etc.), should be distinguished.

Collection of information about duties, responsibilities, and working conditions of each job. The next section of this chapter discusses the need for program administration to evaluate and employ the best possible method for accumulating requisite data for identified program positions. Job analysis data collection methods can encompass interviews, questionnaires, observations, and benchmarking.

Delineation of essential job functions and marginal or nonessential job functions. Administrators should collect all of the relevant information on each position, then create a prioritized list of job functions in descending order of importance. The list could be subsectioned into essential job responsibilities and duties and marginal, nonessential job responsibilities and duties.

Determination of the human qualifications needed to perform the job. There is no easy way to accomplish this element of a job analysis. Each essential job responsibility must be examined for its optimum human resource qualification. In other words, to accomplish each vital job responsibility, program administrators should examine cognitive requirements, physical constraints, experience obligations, and special circumstances of that task. If the position being constructed is new to the organization, but not new to the world, it is critical to research standard qualifications, as well as adjusting those qualifications for the specific program. If the position is a long-standing job in a sports or recreation program, an historical review of past success factors should be available to determine qualifications.

HR Tip

The key factor in solidifying qualifications for particular job responsibilities is in the word justification. After a qualification has been determined administors must objectively justify its assessment and inclusion for the position.

Preparation of the job descriptions and job specifications. The final step in the job analysis process is in developing job descriptions. Please see Table 4.2 for a standardized template for developing a job description.

Job Analysis Data Collection Methods.
There are four principal approaches for gathering job analysis data on program positions: interviews, questionnaires, observations, and benchmarking. "The method you choose depends on the amount of time you have, your access to performers or subject matter experts (SME's), and the level of detail you need" (Franklin, 2005, p. 2). Additionally, cost is an often-critical influence in selecting a job analysis method. Regrettably for programs with restricted resources, this consideration is predictably the first one taken into account.

While each program position is distinctive (some drastically so), it is important to examine universal areas that encompass all types of jobs, in all types of professions. No matter which data gathering method one chooses, administrators should collect job analysis data based on these general, but comprehensive areas:

1. Knowledge required
2. Skills required
3. Abilities required
4. Physical activities involved
5. Any special environmental conditions
6. Typical worker incidents
7. Worker interest areas (Sims, 2002, p. 95)

Additionally, items such as the position's (1) contribution to the program's goals and objectives; (2) regulatory mandates, such as education, certifications, licenses, or CEU requirements; (3) how the position interacts with other program stakeholders; (4) decision-making and empowerment in the position; and (5) supervisory authority inherent in the position are supplementary areas to investigate. By basing job analysis examinations in these and the above areas, one should be able to gather focused data on the jobs being examined.

Each of the primary methods have numerous advantages and various disadvantages to consider.

Interview Types

Job analysis interviews are leader-structured, supervised dialogues that ask and answer diagnostic or investigative questions based on the position being examined.

> Interviews typically involve group or individual interviews with incumbents and supervisors… Large groups (15-20) of incumbents can participate when it is certain that all incumbents are performing the same major activities. In a separate meeting apart from employees, supervisors often verify incumbent information and provide information unavailable to employees in the job. (Gatewood, Field, & Barrick, 2016, p. 55)

Sports or recreation program administration conduct interviews with uniform, open-ended questions that allow for interviewee elaboration, fixed response questions that provide standardized answers that can be quantified, or a combination of both (strongly recommended). If at all feasible, and with the permission of participating interviewees, consider recording interview sessions to store and reference information long after a job analysis is completed.

Discernible drawbacks to conducting interviews relate to the logistics of setting-up sessions and the time needed to conduct interviews. When setting-up interview sessions, program administration should always consider the productivity impact and potential program stakeholder safety of "pulling personnel off the floor" to participate in the conference. Along the same lines, one should also consider the length of the interview, as well as the costs associated with the lack of actual on-the-job productivity. The business adage, "Time is money" applies to managing the job analysis process.

HR Tip

As with many human resource functions, to maximize the effectiveness and cost of a job analysis interview, administrators should have (1) pre-established objectives, (2) authenticated, legal, and logically ordered questions based on those objectives, and (3) a mind-set of meticulous documentation of the results.

Types of Questionnaires

Basic, but precisely designed job analysis questionnaires are uncomplicated and fairly easy to construct and validate. Universal areas to investigate should provide program administrators with a core list of questions directed toward specific responsibilities, knowledge requirements, skills and ability needed, and special circumstances or work environment parameters for any program position. Intricate, internal development of a comprehensive job analysis questionnaire is far beyond the scope of typical program administration. These instruments are "fine-tuned" after many years of use and can be applied to a large number of professions. Fortunately, there is a standardized questionnaire that could be utilized for sports or recreation program job analysis. It is well tested and has been universal applied for over 40 years… it is named the Position Analysis Questionnaire (PAQ). PAQ's are available online and the results are accessible immediately.

The position analysis questionnaire is a structured job analysis questionnaire that uses a checklist approach to identify elements of a job. It focuses on general worker behaviors instead of individual tasks. Worker behaviors refer to the everyday actions, reactions and behaviors of the employee working the organization, with specific reference to specific skills, abilities, attitudes, and personal traits and characteristics (e.g. friendliness, punctuality), and which of these are needed to perform the job. (Kleynhans, Markham, Meyer, van Aswegen, & Pilbeam, 2006, p. 54)

The questionnaire methodology for conducting a job analysis presents "a major advantage in that information on a large number of jobs can be collected inexpensively in a relatively short period of time. However, the questionnaire method assumes that employees can accurately analyze and communicate information about their jobs" (Mathis & Jackson, 2011, p. 130). Moreover, besides misinterpreting questions, program applicants could provide answers they think the administrator wants, rather than giving their honest assessment of the position.

Observation (Overt and Covert)

The observation method of gathering job analysis data is just that—watching a job holder perform the functions and recording all relevant activities being observed.

Direct observation is used for jobs that require manual, standardized, and short job cycle activities. Observation will be especially useful in jobs that demand few skills, where work is controlled mechanically, which involve physical activities, and where the work cycle is short… In contrast, observation is not appropriate for jobs that involve significant amounts of mental activity… Jobs involving intangible factors, such as judgement, computations and decision-making present few opportunities for supplying information to the observer. (Cooper & Rothman, 2013, p. 126)

If the position is suitable for job analysis observations, tasks and activities must be meticulously recorded for (1) their importance to the overall position, (2) the amount of time allotted to complete the function, (3) the frequency of the task and activity, (4) the steps to complete the element, and (5) any distinct circumstances involved with the job duty.

Another consideration is determining if the best results will be derived from overt or covert observation. Overt observation is unconcealed surveillance where the job holder knows they are being watched. The key to this tactic is to "stay out of the way" of the job holder and allow them to complete their tasks and activities normally. The obvious disadvantage to this approach is often times job holders who are aware of being observed will not perform the task or activity as they routinely would. In essence, they put on an artificial performance for the observer. Covert observation is a disguised, hidden, or veiled reconnaissance to gather job and operational information (e.g. individuals covertly observing job functions and operations are called spotters in the restaurant industry and secret shoppers in the retail industry). The unmistakable key to success for covert observation is never let the job holder know that they're being monitored. Whichever method one chooses, it should be noted that the observation method for job analysis, while extraordinarily insightful, is time consuming, labor intensive, and requires a "skilled eye" to accumulate the precise information needed.

Benchmarking (Research)

When conducting a job analysis for a position that is new to the sports or recreation program or new to the world, conducting germane external research into the position is vital. A significant external resource is the Department of Labor Occupational Information Network (O*NET System). The O*NET

> contains comprehensive information about the tasks, tools and technology, KSAs, education, interests, work styles, wages, and the employment outlook associated with jobs. As a result, it is a good tool for matching the interests and abilities of job seekers with occupations and can serve as a starting point for a person doing a job analysis.... Free-job analysis questionnaires can also be downloaded from the O*NET website. Although they are generic, they can be customized and used as a starting point to collect occupational data from job holders and their managers. (Snell & Bohlander, 2013, p. 150)

Publicly posted job vacancy announcements from similar sports or recreation programs can be enormously illuminating when conducting a job analysis. They can frequently provide the foundation for the position's responsibilities, authority and reporting status in the hierarchical structure, contract periods, wages and salaries, and basic qualifications. If possible, once the foundational information has been collected from various governmental andonline sources, administrators should augment that data with benchmarking positions directly from other sports or recreation organizations.

HR Tip

While it is exceedingly rare to conduct a job analysis for a program position that is entirely new to the world, it is a contingency that necessitates mentioning. The key to constructing the new and/or unique job is to go from and scrutinize "big picture" ambitions and objectives for the position and work backwards toward "small picture" targets. If possible, sports or recreation program administrators should conduct occupational research into other similar positions to create a working foundation, then address program specific needs the position should encompass. It goes without saying that the new position should be adjusted and persistently monitored until it is deemed stable.

The conspicuous advantages of external research and benchmarking are reduced costs and limited time commitments. The cost outlays associated with conducting this type of research are often reduced to the price of a laptop and internet connection. The time requirement can vary greatly on the position being researched. If the position is a "mainstream" sports or recreation program position, information accessibility should be immediate and easily collected. If the position is, to a certain degree, obscure or unusual for sports or recreation programs, the time commitment could be considerably more. The clear disadvantage to external research and benchmarking is in the generic nature of the information available and the problem of fitting that information into the sports or recreation program's unique circumstances.

> **HR Tip**
>
> After reviewing all of the possible data gathering techniques, the question then becomes, which one is appropriate for the position administrators are evaluating? If time, resources, and applicability allow, all of them in a combined strategy will provide the greatest accuracy and detailed job information. In other words, the more data points utilized, the better the information gathered.

Basic Concerns with Conducting Job Analyses

There are some final considerations that should be noted when organizing and conducting program job analyses.

Legal issues. "The legal system does not require organizations to conduct job analyses. However, conducting thorough job analyses increases the likelihood that employment decisions are based on job-related criteria, resulting in a reduction in the organization's exposure to employment-related lawsuits" (Hernandez & O'Connor, 2010, p. 155). Once again, a central factor in minimizing liability issues is determining which job functions are essential to the position and which ones would be considered tangential.

Selection of organizational sources. If the program structure does not allow input from all job holders in a position, due to time, financial, or logistical constraints, the selection of the most competent and talented job holders based on past performance evaluations and administrative consensus should be prioritized. Simply stated, getting participation and input from the correct internal sources for job analyses is critical. Rather than arbitrarily choosing individuals, program administrators should enlist people who have the most institutional job knowledge and experience in their selection of appropriate sources.

Embellishment. In dealing with people, administrators must be cognizant of human nature, especially the psychological defense mechanism that protects one's ego. For some, conducting a job analysis for their job position is very personal, almost an invasion of their individual privacy. Whether intentionally or unintentionally, as a defense mechanism, people could aggrandize, enlarge, or simply fabricate additional job responsibilities and activities for their program position. This is not always the case, however, be mindful when dealing with people and the job analysis process.

Let's get it over with attitude. Frequently, sports or recreation program positions are incredibly demanding and hectic. Asking one to participate in a job analysis process can seem to intensify this situation, resulting in the attitude of "Let's get this over with." To avoid this situation, two factors must be unconditionally emphasized. First, communicate as clearly as possible the importance of conducting job analyses for the program's success. Second, any additional responsibilities associated with participating in the job analysis process should not impact the employee's current job responsibilities and their work schedule.

Holistic viewpoint. While the concept of job analysis is for individual positions, the overall construction of job analyses for the sports or recreation program should be viewed from a holistically. Not only should job positions be analyzed from their individual tasks and activities, they should be analyzed for their place within the larger organization.

Job Structuring and Design

From the information and in-depth understanding of sports or recreation program positions derived in the job analysis process, administrators should design positions to exploit internal efficiencies and maximize productivity for the sports or recreation program's strategic future goals. Job designing is best described as,

> the process of deciding on the content of the job in the terms of its duties and responsibilities; on the methods to be used in carrying out the job, in terms of techniques, systems and procedures and on the relationships that should exist between the job holder and his superiors, subordinates and colleagues. It integrates work content (task, functions, relationships), the rewards (extrinsic or intrinsic) and the qualifications required (skills, knowledge, abilities) for each job in a way that meets the needs of employees and the organization. (Zaidi, 2008, p. 70)

In actuality, job designing is crafting job positions to amplify internal stakeholder satisfaction, while exclusively focusing each position on the strategic long-term goals and operational objectives in the strategic operational plan and subsequent human resource plan. Unquestionably, when designing job analysis data into definitive job positions, program administrators should consider items such as work flow, measurable quantity of output desired, independence and decision-making responsibilities, optimal work hours, repetitive tasks, as well as unique assignments, integral social interactions, flexibility and adaptability, and quality of the work desired by the organization. There are some generic (but meaningful) considerations that should be taken into account when designing program positions.

Job scope. The first and most crucial aspect of crafting a job design is to determine the comprehensive job scope, which

> relates to how many different activities or operations a person performs and how often. As you might expect, a job with few activities and with a high rate of repetition has little scope; the reverse is true for wide-scope jobs. There is also a strong relationship between job scope and where the job appears on an organizational chart. Low-scope jobs tend to be first line and near the lower part of the chart... jobs of high depth and wide scope call for more knowledge, skill, and experience than do jobs with lower degrees of these factors. (Evans & Alire, 2013, p. 397)

In essence, job scope is at the heart of job design and must have cogent and reasoned plausibility for both the organization and employee's benefit. From an organizational viewpoint, providing a position with unrealistically high job scope could cascade throughout the operation when critical tasks are not accomplished (or partially or incorrectly fulfilled). Conversely, providing a position with an insignificant job scope is wasting the program's human capital. From the vantage of the individual whom is working the position, having unachievably high job scope could cause enormous stress and could ultimately lead to worker exhaustion and burnout. Conversely, crafting a position with little or no diversity, depth, and challenge will lead to boredom and reduced retention.

Job enrichment. Job enrichment, as a component of job design, is building into positions the elasticity to enhance productivity and job satisfaction through new and challenging tasks. Durai (2010) constructs a list of job enrichment guidelines that can be adapted to all types of business enterprise positions. The following are a summation of these guidelines:

- Encouraging employees to involve themselves in goal setting and accomplishment activities.
- Enhancing the scope of the job to utilize the diverse skills of the employees.
- Allowing the employees to do the whole job, from beginning until the end, so that they could develop a sense of achievement.
- Providing necessary autonomy to the employees on matters relating to the method, speed, and order of doing the job.
- Encourage the employees to know the significance of their work in terms of its contribution to the accomplishment of the overall goal of the organization.
- Constantly challenging the employees to adopt innovation in job by acquiring new knowledge and skills.
- Improving the information sharing process by strengthening the existing communication channels and by introducing new communication channels.
- Ensuring that the employees get timely and adequate recognition and appreciation for their effective performance and successful completion of the job.
- Enabling the employees to get constant feedback of their own performance by communicating the results of the work they do.
- Making employees believe that the present job is not an end but only a means for better prospects in the organization. (Durai, 2010, p. 93)

While it may not be conceivable to integrate all of these recommendationsinto all job designs, consider each and employ them, if possible.

Job enlargement. Job enlargement is best described as increasing "task variety by combining into one job two or more tasks previously done by separate workers" (Schermerhorn, 2011, p. 375). If a position is enlarged with responsibilities that amplify job motivation and satisfaction, then these additions are a formidable use of the job enlargement concept. Regrettably, arbitrary task "add-ons" to a position without regard to improving motivation and job satisfaction appear—and rightfully so—as a way to increase a position's workload without concern for the person(s) in the position.

Job rotation. Job rotation "systematically moves employees from one job to another, thereby increasing the number of different tasks an employee performs without increasing the complexity of any one job… it provides variety and stimulation for employees" (Daft & Marcic, 2011, p. 419). When designing job positions, look collectively at a group of positions possibly being a part of a scheduled rotation system. The ancillary advantage of having a job rotation system for job positions is in the fact the program will have a multi-skill workforce that can adapt to various foreseen and unforeseen circumstances (e.g., an employee could substitute for another employee on sick leave, vacation, sabbaticals, etc.).

Job simplification. In designing the job, the concept of simplification directly relates to increasing a position's efficiency. When reviewing the job analysis data, ask the question, Can efficiencies be found that could be apart of the new positional design? Three areas to consider:

- Eliminate. Does the task have to be done at all? If not, don't waste time doing it.
- Combine. Doing similar things together often saves time.
- Change Sequence. Often a change in the order of doing things results in a lower total time.

(Lussier, 2009, p. 180)

HR Tip

While the concept of job simplification is ostensibly and rationally apparent for increasing the contribution of the human element in a sports or recreation program, it is often overlooked because frozen systems and long-held methods of work are not challenged to increase efficiency. The statement, "this is the way we have always done that," is a major cause of inefficiencies. An auxiliary, but valuable, outcome of job analysis and design is the opportunity to increase a position's efficiency. It should be noted that simplifying a small task that is continually repeated can have huge long-term efficiency benefits.

Other possible scenarios when designing program positions should be considered.

- *Self-managed work group.* Can the position be a part of a self-managed work group?
- *Flextime or condensed work week.* Can the position have a flexible schedule, cooperatively arranged by all parties in the program, or could a condensed work week be an option (e.g., 4 days at 10 hours per day)?
- *Virtual work possibilities.* Can the position have telecommuting/virtual workplace possibilities?
- *Job sharing.* Can the position be accomplished by two separate individuals (e.g., two part-time employees making-up one full-time position)?

Detailed Job Descriptions

The ultimate goal of sound job analysis and design is to construct comprehensive job descriptions that define position titles, fundamental overviews, tasks, qualifications, and rewards. In the book *The Jobs Description Handbook*, Mader-Clark summarizes the benefits of developing job descriptions by stating,

having job descriptions will make the task of finding, interviewing, and hiring the right person much easier. However, job descriptions serve a number of other important purposes as well. Job descriptions communicate your expectations and let employees know what it takes to excel in their jobs. Done properly, descriptions can: enhance communication between you and your employees, measure future performance, set the stage to fairly and legally discipline and terminate employees who don't meet your expectations, improve your ability to retain stellar employees, help you plan for the future, and improve employee morale (Mader-Clark, 2013, p. 4).

> ## HR Tip
> A safe, pragmatic tactic in developing and/or modifying job descriptions is to think of them as contracts/agreements between the organization and current or potential sports or recreation program members. Prior to publishing them, descriptions should be reviewed by legal counsel to avoid any inadvertent legal issues.

Constructing a Detailed Job Description. Job descriptions are formal organizational documents that illustrate the functional aspect of program positions. They answer questions related to the overall job, its specific duties, the qualification for the position, and rewards and benefits of the position. Table 4.2 provides a template for the construction of job descriptions.

> ## HR Tip
> If possible when describing the position's essential responsibilities, include estimated percentages of time for each task, responsibility, and function as they relate to the overall position (totaling 100%). Remember, the more detail in developing the essential responsibilities, the less ambiguity and the better execution of tasks for the position.

There are some general considerations for constructing each of the components of the job description outlined in Table 4.2.

Position title. There are three conceivable ways to title a position in a job description: (1) stay with the position's existing designation currently being used within the sports or recreation program, (2) benchmark or copy the position's title from designations used in other sports or recreation programs, or (3) create a new designation that purposely reflects the specialization of the position.

Position synopsis. Provide a comprehensive understanding of (or "feel" for) the central functions and purpose of the position. The summation should be concise, factually relevant, contemporary, and easily comprehensible.

Essential responsibilities. Because of its critical importance, commit time and resources to get each responsibility correct and not to overlook any crucial tasks for the position. Additionally, it is important to acknowledge that this component of the job description will need continuous review and maintenance as the position evolves to meet new and challenging organizational goals and objectives.

Job qualifications. The criteria delineated in job qualifications cannot be arbitrary and must be proven ***valid and reliable*** to avoid possible systemic discrimination. Sports or recreation program administrators should perform positional research and analysis to avoid prerequisite qualifications that are incongruous or unsuitable for the position. Simply stated, job qualifications must be in-line with essential responsibilities component of the job description.

Positional rewards and benefits. Rewards and benefits should reflect the importance of the position in the sports or recreation program. The concept of rewards and benefits are discussed in more detail in Chapter 8.

TABLE 4.2 Fundamental Assembly of a Job Description

Position Title	Elements include: • Position's Designation/Name • Position Number (if applicable) • Full- or Part-Time Status • Department • Date of Job Description (or updated/redesigned date) • Reporting Accountability (to whom does the position report)
Position Synopsis	Overview description (or big picture aspect) of the position, significance of the position in the program, main duties, empowerment, and supervisory functions associated with the position. Completed in paragraph form.
Essential Responsibilities	Delineate all the critical tasks of the position typically in a bullet list in descending order of importance, and include a sub-section of marginal/nonessential job functions.
Job Qualifications	Defines mandatory characteristics of the individual in the position. Major subcategories defined by minimum prerequisites and/or preferred requirements include: • Physicality requirements (if applicable) • Mental cognitive abilities (formal education degrees, certifications, and valid/reliable internal testing instruments) • Years of experience desired • Special skills necessary
Positional Rewards and Benefits	Rewards and benefits associated with the position encompass: • Compensation (salary, hourly, overtime, paid time off, etc.) • Supplemental benefits (medical, dental, 401K, etc.) • Pay-for-performance remuneration (incentives/bonuses, piece-rate subsidies, etc.) • Auxiliary allowances (employee health programs, parking, merchandise contracts, tickets, external training opportunities, special program events, meals, and ceremonial occasions, etc.)

Organizational Structure and Hierarchical Charts

Sports or recreation program administrators must structure the operation to maximize each and every position's potential and productivity.

Organizational structure is the organization's formal system of task, power, and reporting relationships. Organizational structure coordinates, controls, and motivates employees to cooperate in attaining organizational goals… Organizational structures influence employee behavior by enabling or restricting communication, teamwork, and cooperation, as well as inter-group relationships. (Phillips & Gully, 2014, p. 127)

The most straightforward tool for displaying and managing the operation's structure is a hierarchical chart (also known as an organizational chart). Hierarchical charts are graphic depictions of the structure of an organization that provide stakeholders with a visual construct of the program and organization. There are numerous types of hierarchical charts. Matrix/projected based, departmental or functional, product type, and geographic are just a few of the chart structures that businesses use. Sports or recreation programs generally utilize a simple straight-line chart with direct lines of accountability, top-down reporting, and communication. Figure 4.1 is an illustration of a possible sports or recreation program hierarchical chart.

Constructing Hierarchical Charts. Construct (and/or modification) organizational or hierarchical charts with these tips in mind.

1. Assemble hierarchical charts electronically for swift updates and changes, as well as uncomplicated distribution throughout the organization. Microsoft Word and Power Point templates can be effortlessly altered and adapted to match most sports or recreation programs.
2. Under no circumstances should hierarchical charts be based on the current people in the organization. Construct hierarchical charts solely on the positions in the organization. Simply stated, people will come and go in a sports or recreation program. Positions are stable and structural.
3. Always remember to emphasize organizational and human resource goals when building or modifying hierarchical charts.

> ### HR Tip
> The sports or recreation program's strategies must be facilitated through job descriptions, hierarchical charts, and overall organizational structure of the operation. If strategies and structure are not interdependent and symbiotic, then goals will most likely remain unfulfilled.

4. The hierarchical chart should be designed to amplify the human resource asset in a program while curtailing bureaucratic "slow-downs" and decisionmaking bottlenecks.
5. Outsourced elements that are significant for organizational goal attainment should be incorporated into the hierarchical chart. For example, if the day-to-day bookkeeping and year-end accounting are outsourced to an independent accounting firm, this should be noted in the hierarchical chart.
6. Meticulously consider the reporting connections and networks between positions to make sure that the right subordinate position is reporting to the right supervisory position.

As with outsourced elements, long-term strategic alliances should be accounted for in the hierarchical chart.

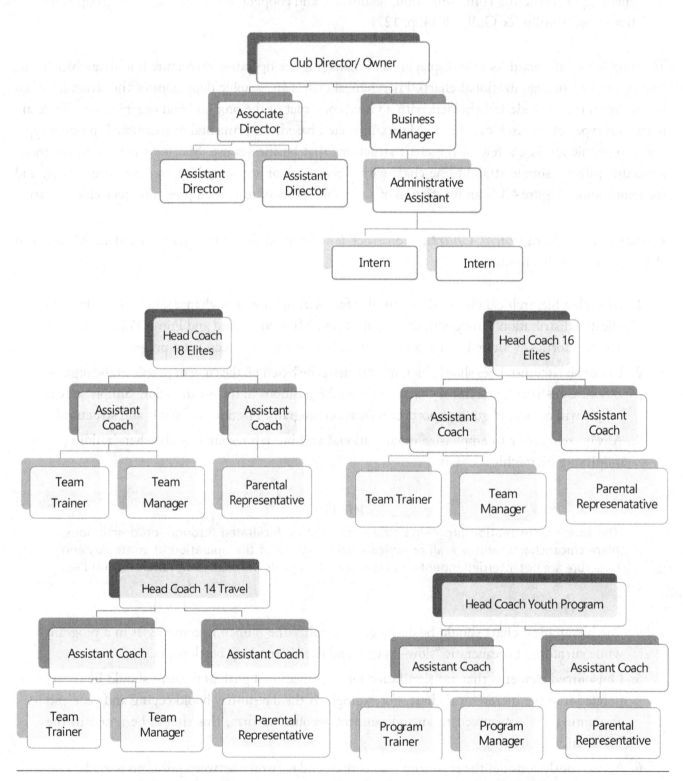

FIGURE 4.1   Sports or Recreation Program Hierarchical Chart

> **HR Tip**
>
> The connection between job descriptions and the hierarchical chart's organizational structure is direct and impactful. If job descriptions are meticulously "spelled-out" for each position, the hierarchical chart will flow. Unfortunately, ambiguity in job descriptions will promote dysfunction and inefficiencies in the sports or recreation program.

Summary

By conducting a job analysis, designing or redesigning job positions, developing definitive job descriptions, and constructing hierarchical or organizational charts, a program can increase its internal operational efficacy while providing all stakeholders with a sense of professionalism and administrative confidence. By completing all stages of occupational modeling, a program can develop a sustainable competitive advantage over its competition while promoting a cooperative and highly functional work environment. The ultimate goal of occupational modeling is to exploit the program's most important resource: its people.

References

Caruth, D. L., Caruth, G. D., & Pane, S. S. (2008). *Staffing the contemporary organization: A guide to planning, recruiting and selecting human resource professionals* (3rd ed.). Westport, CT: Praeger.

Cooper, C., & Rothman, I. (2013). *Organizational and work psychology: Topics in applied psychology.* New York, NY: Routledge.

Daft, R. L., & Marcic, D. (2011). *Understanding management* (7th ed.). Mason, OH: South-Western/Cengage.

Durai, P. (2010). *Human resource management.* Noida, India: Dorling Kindersley/Pearson.

Evans, G. E., & Alire, C. A. (2013). *Management basics for information professionals* (3rd ed.). Chicago, IL: American Library Association.

Franklin, M. (June, 2005). *A guide to job analysis.* American Society for Training and Development Press, 0506, 2.

Gatewood, R.D., Field, H. S., & Barrick, M. R. (2016). *Human resource selection* (8th ed.). Boston, MA: Cengage Learning.

Hernandez, S. R., & O'Connor, S. J. (2010). *Strategic human resource management in health service organizations* (3rd ed.), Clifton Park, NY: Delmar/Cengage.

Hinojosa, J., Kramer, P., & Royeen, C. B. (2017). *Perspectives on human occupation: Theories underlying practice* (2nd ed.). Philadelphia, PA: F. A. Davis.

Kleynhans, R., Markham, L., Meyer, W., van Aswegen, S., & Pilbeam, E. (2006). *Human resource management: Fresh perspectives.* Cape Town, South Africa: Pearson/Prentice Hall.

Lussier, R. N. (2009). *Management fundamentals: Concepts, applications, skill development* (4th ed.). Mason, OH: South-Western/Cengage.

Mader-Clark, M. (2013). *The job description handbook: Everything you need to write effective job descriptions – and avoid legal pitfalls* (3rd ed.). Berkeley, CA: Nolo Publishing.

Mathis, R. L., & Jackson, J. H. (2011). *Human resource management* (13th ed.). Mason, OH: South-Western/Cengage.

Noe, R. A., Hollenbeck, J. R., Gerhart, B., & Wright, P. M. (2004). *Fundamentals of human resource management*. New York, NY: McGraw-Hill/Irwin.

Phillips, J. M., & Gully, S. M. (2014). *Human resource management*. Mason, OH: South-Western/Cengage.

Prien, E. P., Goodstein, L. D., Goodstein, J., & Gamble, L. G. (2009). *A practical guide to job analysis*. San Francisco, CA: Pfeiffer/Wiley.

Schermerhorn, J. R. (2011). *Introduction to management: International student version* (11th ed.). Hoboken, NJ: John Wiley and Sons.

Sims, R. R. (2002). *Organizational success through effective human resource management*. Westport, CT: Quorum Books.

Snell, S. A., & Bohlander, G. W. (2013). *Managing human resources* (16th ed.). Mason, OH: South-Western/Cengage.

Zaidi, M. L. S. Q. (2008). *Human resource management*. New Delhi, India: Excel Books.

Review and Discussion Questions

1. Define occupational modeling.
2. What is the purpose of a job analysis?
3. When should a job analysis be conducted?
4. What are the five steps in the job analysis process?
5. What are job analysis interviews?
6. What are open-ended questions? What are fixed response questions?
7. What are the drawbacks of conducting job analysis interviews?
8. What are positional analysis questionnaires (PAQs)?
9. Define overt observation. Define covert observation.
10. What is the Department of Labors Occupational Information Network (O*NET)?
11. Why are job postings a valuable source in job analysis research?
12. Describe job analysis embellishment.
13. What is job designing?
14. Define job scope.
15. What is job rotation? What is an ancillary benefit of job rotation?
16. What are the three considerations in job simplification?
17. What are the foundational components of a job description? Describe each component.

Application Exercises

1. Develop five open-ended questions and five fixed response questions for a job analysis interview for the athletic program position of External Development Director/Fundraising Administrator.
2. From online research, find three city-based recreational program job postings. From each posting, delineate any and all information that could be used to develop core job analysis data.
3. From online research, find three general recreation program job descriptions. Based on Table 4.2, critique each job description and make any relevant suggestions for their improvement.

Term Project
Individual/Group Oral Presentation

You and your group are the new athletic program administrators for a mid-sized NCAA Division I athletic program. The athletic program is growing rapidly and has no formalized job analysis system or job descriptions in its operation. Design, from the ground up, three job positions (group's preference) and complete a job analysis, job design, and job description for each.

Elements:

- Discuss the job analysis procedures that the group will use to gather data on the selected positions. Justify your choices of methods to be used.

- Discuss the process for designing each position. Elaborate on relevant considerations while designing positions.

- From Table 4.2, construct and discuss the detailed job descriptions for each position. Justify your rationale for each job description point.

Criteria:

- Develop a 30-minute presentation that details the athletic program's job modeling process for the three selected positions.

- Prepare for a 15-minute Q & A session after main presentation.

- Create Power Point slides and visual aids to supplement the presentation (hard copy to be submitted prior to presentation).

- Conduct extensive external research to justify your selections.

chapter five

Recruiting, Selecting, and Onboarding New Personnel

Chapter Objectives

- Examine the concepts of recruitment and selection and how they impact sports and recreation programs
- Understand various internal and external recruiting sources
- Recognize the advantages and disadvantages of internal and external recruiting
- To describe human resource selection
- Understand a comprehensive four phase, ten step selection process
- Further examine job analysis, job design, and job descriptions as a function of the selection process
- Develop a framework for constructing a job posting
- Understand the importance of applicant screening
- Examine the two critical aspects of job screening interviews
- Understand the possible job testing areas in the selection process
- Examine the divergent types of job interviews and questions
- Examine a universal list of interview guidelines and tips
- Understand the three types of reference checks
- Understand the process of an employment background check
- Examine tentative selection decisions, negotiations, and final employment offers
- Explain the concepts of onboarding and new employment orientation
- Examine the benefits of new employee orientation systems
- Review various organizational and departmental orientation strategies and actions
- Understand a new employee's first day and needs

Key Terms

Recruitment	Extrinsic Rewards	Candidate Pool
Selection	Internal Recruiting Sources	Selection Process
Intrinsic Rewards	External Recruiting Sources	Job Analysis

Continued

Job Design	Work Sample Tests	Background Checks
Job Description	Personality Tests	Tentative Selection
Job Posting	Objective Tests	Physical Exams
Applicant Screening	Situational Tests	Negotiation
Resumes/CV/Applications	Final Interview	Official Offer of Employment
Job Testing	General Screening	Letters of Agreement
Aptitude Tests	Open-ended Questions	Employment Contracts
Interest Tests	Fixed Response Questions	Onboarding
Intelligence Tests	Reference Checks	Organizational Orientation
Job Knowledge Tests	Consent Forms	Departmental Orientation

Recruitment & Selection

Recruitment and selection goes beyond obtaining competent employees that can accomplish program responsibilities and tasks. It is a systemized process that matches the sports or recreation program's goals and objectives, and subsequent work requirements, with consummate professionals, who have exceptional, proven characteristics, qualities, and expertise. The recruitment and selection process parallels two primary suppositions: (1) there is a direct correlation between accomplishing pre-established long-term goals and short-term objectives in a sports or recreation program with the quality of its internal stakeholders, and (2) the greatest asset in a sports or recreation program is its human resource asset.

The Impact of Recruitment and Selection Systems in Sports and Recreation Programs

Prior to examining recruitment and selection systems and their explicit processes, it is significant to appreciate the long-term consequences of having, or unfortunately not having, them in a sports and recreation program. Table 5.1 illustrates the consequences on a sports and recreation program can be drastic.

Recruitment and Selection Systems

According to Gatewood, Field, and Barrick (2016) recruitment and selection is

> the process of collecting and evaluating information about an individual in order to extend an offer of employment. Such employment could be either a first position for a new employee or a different position for a current employee. The selection process is performed under legal and market constraints and addresses the future interests of the organization and of the individual. (p. 3)

This definition can be expanded to include the following critical, but far-reaching, aspects and general guidelines for recruiting and selecting employees among a pool of candidates.

TABLE 5.1   The Impact of Recruitment and Selection Systems

Recruitment With Systems	*Recruitment Without Systems*
• The quantity and quality of prospective candidates increases	• The pool of prospective candidates is diminished in quantity and quality
• Potential program members are recruited and selected on their capacity to accomplish strategic goals as well as day-to-day functions	• Potential program members are typically chosen solely on their functional day-to-day capabilities
• Conveys professionalism throughout the entire operation	• Conveys general disorganization and lack of coherent leadership
• Is equitable to all current and future program members	• Due to the absence of structure, it can be seen as inequitable and bias
• Can decrease/curtail employee turnover by screening out unacceptable and unqualified candidates	• Has a "hit-or-miss" methodology which can contribute to unqualified program members and increased turnover
• Furnish statistical data on various aspects of the recruiting and selecting system (for current and future decision making)	• Has little or no quantitative data (to make recruiting and selection system decisions)
• Job candidates can be analyzed for their training needs and future potential professional growth	• Job candidates are an "unknown" and can only be assessed for training needs and future professional growth after being hired
• Supplies job candidates with full-disclosure information on the specialized position and overall organization	• Job candidates will have partial knowledge/information on the specialized position and overall organization
• Delivers core information for new hires personnel documentation	• All new hire data must be accumulated posthumously
• For contributing members of hiring committees, recruiting and selecting new personnel can be motivational and team building	• Due to centralized decisions, the team concept in hiring will be marginalized, discounted, or ignored
• Renewed and accentuated focus on legal compliance and the limiting of potential hiring litigations	• Legal compliance in hiring could be overlooked, opening the program to various lawsuits and legal actions
• Reference and background checks are underscored and mandated	• Reference and background checks could be sporadically completed (or entirely overlooked) opening the program to considerable long-term issues

1. When recruiting and selecting sports or recreation program personnel, a premium should be placed on individuals who cognitively evaluate situations, are action-oriented, and can make independent decisions within their purview of responsibilities.

2. In the recruiting and selection process, emphasize people with passion and intrinsic motivation. This excitement and enthusiasm can be, but does not necessarily have to be, about the position being hired. It can be for any activity, interest, or hobby. Be circumspect of individuals whom are focused solely on the extrinsic aspect of the sports or recreation program position. While extrinsic rewards of the position are important (money, benefits, incentives, etc.), people who have a single-minded concentration on these items typically lack the zeal needed to "go over and above" their compensated job duties for the sports or recreation program and its distinct objectives and targeted actions.

3. In recruiting and selecting, always appreciate the significance of interpersonal and communication skills. In the people-centered service industry of sports and recreation, being able to communicate effectively with a wide variety of individuals is an important dexterity in which the sports or recreation program should highly value.

4. Always remember that recruiting and selection miscalculations can be catastrophic to any program. Hiring one poorly or hastily selected candidate can have devastating consequences on a sports or recreation program. To minimize recruiting and selection errors, administration should always follow the recruitment and selection processes. Short-cutting personnel decisions, while possibly deemed acceptable in the present moment, in the long-term can be irreparable.

5. In recruiting and selection, greatly value teamwork and the demonstrable ability to work with others (also known as organizational citizenship). Throughout the entire recruiting and selection process, examine the entire person, not just their quantifiable education and work experiences. Activities, sports teams, clubs, volunteerism, and social groups are all viable and concrete examples of proficiency in group dynamics.

6. Exponentially accelerating environmental changes in areas such as technological advances, economic volatility, demographic changes, societal perceptions, global impact, legal and regulatory additions and amendments, and competitive pressures, demand employees with demonstrated skills in adaptability. Having flexible personnel can help a sports or recreation program adapt to the external environmental factors quicker, which, in turn can provide a sustainable competitive advantage.

7. In recruiting and selecting new personnel, recognize the importance of one's hiring experience and intuition. While the systemized procedures should be followed precisely, the X factors in many hiring decisions is intuition. The best method for confirming one's intuition regarding candidates is to enlist other sports or recreation program personnel's insightful opinions into candidates.

HR Tip

Reviewing recruiting sources and procedures in the selection process, is in no way a guarantee for 100% successful hiring. In business (and sports and recreation programs are businesses), there are no guarantees for success in any operational area, human resource management included. Then why go through the arduous work of recruiting and selecting personnel? Simply stated, administrators must do everything within their power to minimize selection errors and bad hires. The statement, "Front-side recruiting and selection diligence can eliminate backside personnel issues and problems," applies directly to minimizing personnel hiring mistakes.

It is essential to have legal counsel review all recruiting and selection procedures. Not only will it emphasize equitable treatment for all potential program members, it will limit the program's legal compliance liability/exposure.

Carbery and Cross (2013) define recruitment as

searching for and obtaining job candidates in sufficient numbers and quality, so that they feed the selection process. Once the pool of candidates has been collected, it is over to the selection process to filter these candidates further, shortlist them until agreement is reached on which candidate(s) should be offered the position(s). An organization may have an excellent system for evaluating and selecting candidates, but if the pool of candidates that come through the recruitment process is insufficient or of low standard/quality, the resulting choice will not be optimum. (pp. 23-24)

Salient factors that go into cultivating a pool of superior candidates include (1) creating a well-worded and specific job advertisement that can encourage qualified candidates to apply, while setting definitive parameters andcriteria for the position based on the job analysisand job design (which eliminates unqualified candidates while eliminating any unintentional disparate impact on certain protected classes), (2) making the application process as user friendly and welcoming as possible, (3) employing the most worthwhile and suitable sources of recruiting (see Table 5.2), (4) having the most up-to-date database system that accumulates and preserves the pool of candidates with easy accessibility for administrators, and (5) following all laws and regulations and established internal policies and procedures for recruitment.

HR Tip

Often times in developing a pool of candidates, a sports or recreation program must utilize as many sources of recruits as possible, both internally and externally. The limiting factors in this approach are available time and financial resources. However, once a sports or recreation program has gone through numerous recruitment cycles, administrators typically get an idea of which internal and external sources provide the greatest number of qualified candidates. However, just because a sports or recreation program has success with certain recruiting sources, it is not a guarantee that another program will have the same success.

TABLE 5.2   Internal and External Sources for Personnel

Internal	*External*
• Electronic in-house job posting boards	• Traditional media sources (e.g. newspapers, trade publications, radio, tv, governing bodies, etc.)
• Internal stakeholders already employed/participating in program	• University interns and graduates
• Referrals by current program personnel	• Networking sources from current and past internal stakeholders
• Departmental transfers	• Web sources (generic or specific job posting web sites)
• Re-hirable former program stakeholders	• Walk-ins
• Previous applicants maintained in data base	• Headhunters and employment agencies
	• Job fairs

Sources of Recruitment: Internal and External. There are two primary areas for acquiring sports and recreation program personnel: internal sources are known as promotion from within, and external sources are new hires. Table 5.2 delineates the sources for each.

The source program administrators select hinges upon the recruiting situation, as well as the benefits and drawbacks of each method. Table 5.3 itemizes the benefits and drawbacks of internal and external recruitment.

TABLE 5.3   Advantages and Disadvantages of Internal and External Recruits

Internal Recruits/Promotion Within

Advantages	*Disadvantages*
• Motivational for existing internal stakeholders	• Inbreedng of concepts; lack of a fresh perspective (innovations)
• Less uncertain; current employee is a known quantity	• Encourages a competitive work environment; possible team breakdown
• No organizational earning curve	• "Bad feelings" for non-promoted individuals
• Cascading impact; new positions open	• Limited talent pool
• Cost and time effective	

External Recruits/New Hires

Advantages	*Disadvantages*
• New/innovative program thinking	• "Stepping over" internal candidates
• High profile hire adds to program image	• More expensive and time consuming
• New hire is not part of internal political/ bureaucratic environment	• Organizational learning curve
	• Job position learning curve

Human Resource Selection

Once administrators have accumulated a suitable qualified pool of candidates, a sequence of activities begins on selecting the right person for the position. The right person can be defined as someone who:

- matches the requirements identified by the qualifications, experience, skills and competencies set out in the job specifications

- has had satisfactory references, where future predictions indicate their success in the position

- has expressed sufficient interest in the position at interview to indicate that they wished to be offered the position.

(Stredwick, 2014, p. 90)

In theory, finding a "right fit" (the most suitable person for the program position at the precise time in the organization's lifecycle) is simple to understand. In practice, human resource selection can be a demanding and frequently stressful process that has no assurance of success. However, by following a step-by-step process, administrators can diminish or eliminate some of the guesswork and apprehension associated with filling program positions. Table 5.4 provides a phase-by-phase and step-by-step selection process. Certain administrators may feel that various steps in this process are superfluous or beyond the program's financial resources and time constraints. As long as administration can demonstrate that an abbreviated selection process is legitimate and non-discriminatory, while producing strong personnel choices, they can

---

TABLE 5.4 The Selection Process

Phase 1 Development and Preparation

Step 1   Internal review of job analysis data, job design, and job description

Step 2   Developing and publishing job posting

Phase 2 Applicant Screening

Step 3   Collection and screening of resumes, curriculum vitae, applications
in candidate pool

Step 4   Preliminary screening interview

Step 5   Job testing (if applicable)

Phase 3 Focused Candidacy Review

Step 6   Final interview(s)

Step 7   Verifying reference checks and independent background screening

Phase 4 Selection, Negotiation, and Offer

Step 8   Tentative selection decision

Step 9   Physical exam (if applicable)

Step 10 Negotiation and official offer of employment

---

adjust the phases and steps to fit their situation or the position(s) being hired. As with all human resource program operations, a review of the selection process by legal counsel is a prudent precaution.

HR Tip

Some administrators consider a step-by-step selection process as a sequence of barriers the candidate needs to successfully overcome to be chosen for the position. Similarly, candidates can often feel these obstacles are difficulties they must conquer to be considered for the job. A more advantageous way for all parties to look at the selection process is to view it as a two-way street. Not only is the organization selecting a new and valued member of its team, but the candidate is deciding throughout the process whether they want to be a member of that particular sports or recreation program's team. This mutually reciprocal attitude by all parties involved in the selection process will provide the best result for everyone.

Phase One: Development and Preparation

Step 1. Internal review of job analysis data, job design, and job description. The often-used adage, "preparation is key," is enormously important when it comes to starting the selection process. The first step in the process is to collectively review, with all pertinent stakeholders, the key success factors for the position, as specified in the job analysis, job design, and job description (as discussed in Chapter 4). The noteworthy phrase is *collectively review*. Administration should analyze the position with as many "voices" as possible, especially current and former job holders of that position. These individuals can impart critical insight into indispensable performance elements of the position. In essence, by enlisting the feedback of program members knowledgeable in the position, administrators can often (1) authenticate and update the written elements of the job design and description and (2) develop those perceptions into key selection factors. Once the position's key success factors are defined, qualifications defined in the job analysis can be also confirmed and emphasized.

As discussed in Chapter 4, job analysis and design are a continual human resource management activities. Not only should they be done periodically to keep the position current, Arthur (2012) states that,

> job analysts [administrators] should review duties and responsibilities of a job each time a position becomes available. Even if an opening was filled six months ago and is now vacant again, assessing its current status will ensure that no major changes have occurred in the interim. This, in turn, will guarantee up-to-date information and accuracy when discussing the position with potential employees. (p. 72)

HR Tip

The selection process will be completely derailed if the first step of Phase #1 is not completed correctly. All other subsequent steps in the process will be incorrectly focused and, subsequently, the person being hired will likely be the wrong fit for the position.

Step 2. Developing and publishing job postings. In the book *Fundamentals of Human Resource Management*, DeCenzo, Robbins, and Verhulst (2016) present four key elements of writing acumen necessary for a solid, attractive job posting.

1. Tell enough about the job. Job seekers barely spend 30 seconds reading job postings. Keep it brief, but provide enough information so that potential applicants can determine whether they are interested or qualified. Use an engaging writing style and explain why they will love the job and company.

2. Include the job title and keywords. Include important essential functions and specifications. If you're posting online, keywords will help job seekers find your job posting in an online search.

3. Set clear expectations. Does the job require extensive travel? What will it take to succeed in the position? Is the compensation competitive? Are there requirements that need to be communicated to comply with ADA requirements? You better say so.

4. Make sure it's attractive and correct. Candidates give more attention to attractive, branded ads. Make sure the layout is pleasing and there are no grammatical or punctuation errors. Include logos, videos, or any other graphics that help tell your story. (p. 133)

After crafting an effective job posting announcement, the problematic question then becomes, where does the program publish the job posting to get the most exposure to the best qualified candidates? The volume of publicizing possibilities is vast. For example, in online postings alone, athletic program positions could be circulated externally throughout governing body websites (e.g. NCAA, NJCAA, NAIA, State High School Athletic Associations, etc.), sport specific websites (USA Soccer, Wrestling, Softball, etc.), or conventional public websites (Indeed, ZipRecruiter, Monster, etc.). Over time, the solution in choosing the best potential strategy for advertising a program position is by developing measurement systems for each possible advertising strategy, then tracking, not only the volume of response, but the quality of the applicants from each source.

HR Tip

The quality of candidates produced from a job posting is far more important than quantity. Getting five quality candidates from a job posting is far superior to getting 50 unqualified candidates from another.

Phase Two: Applicant Screening

Step 3. Collection and screening of applications in candidate pool. Collection of resumes, CVs and application materials for potential candidates' must follow four main criteria. First, the collection method should be as well-organized and disciplined as possible, with a single point person collecting all resumes, CVs, applications (in any format: hard copy or online submissions). Second, all submitted information should be regarded with the upmost discretion, confidentiality, and data security. Third, it should be a standard policy that each individual who submits a materials, regardless of their qualifications and background, receives a response email or general correspondence (letter or post card) that acknowledges their submission and interest in the position and thanks the applicant for their interest in the program. Finally, all application materials should be securely stored for a period of at least 6 months to one year after the position's closing date, depending on program human resource data retention policy. For time saving, utilization of space, and ease of retrieval, hard copy documentation can be scanned to a secure electronic hard drive database.

When starting the initial screen stage in the selection process, Deb (2006) recommends that application materials should be screened

> using a checklist of essential qualifications to quickly and accurately identify how well each applicant meets all the job's requirements. A written record of each screening decision will then be available for review or applicant feedback. This highly organized, yet straightforward, process significantly reduces screening time and makes application-screening decisions accurate and easy. (p. 167)

Construct this form is in two sections. The first section could be an itemized checklist of the minimum qualifications specified in the position's job design and description. The primary areas to concentrated on could be educational minimums, as well as years of professional experience. For example, an NCAA signatory institution is hiring an Assistant Athletic Director for NCAA Compliance. The minimum requirements for this position, as determined in the job analysis, job design, and final job description, should be a BA or BS in business administration, sport management/administration, or pre-law and professional experience of at least three years working in athletic administration. From these two minimum categories alone (and there may be several more minimum qualifications), administrators could feasibly eliminate one half, or even more, of the applicants.

Once the first section's minimum qualification analysis is completed, all remaining *qualified* applications should be examined a second time. This second evaluation is for part two of the form - preferred qualifications. From the example above, the preferred qualifications for an assistant athletic director for NCAA compliance could be educationally a Masters degree in business administration, sports management, law degree (juris doctorate) with five years working in athletic administration NCAA compliance (once again, there may be other preferred qualifications as specified in the job analysis, job design, and final job description). Section two of the form should leave ample space for assessors to make remarks and amplifications about the qualifications of an individual. These critical notations are the differentiating factors that separate individual applicants. For instance, in the above example, a significant element could be that an individual has 15 years of athletic administration, with 10 of those years being exclusively in NCAA compliance. This would be a noteworthy annotation to make.

HR Tip

If a sports or recreation program uses job applications as the data source for candidates, there are some customary components of most applications. These are (1) contact data, (2) education, (3) professional work history, (4) military experience, (5) specialized training (job specific), (6) skills and job-related abilities, (7) honors, activities, and interests, and (8) miscellaneous information (job specific). The final component of an all-inclusive job application is the certification statement and signature, which affirms that the information presented by the applicant is accurate and correct.

Step 4. Preliminary interview screening. Before moving further into the selection process, many organizations prefer to complete a screening interview of those applicants who appear qualified based on information submitted on their resume and applications. Yakkaldevi and Dubey (2015) recommend administrators conduct screening interviews by telephone. The interviewer asks a few straightforward questions to determine the candidate's job qualifications and appropriateness for the position. If it is determined that the applicant is not appropriate for the position, the interviewer may refer the candidate to another open position within the organization, if something is available that matches the applicant's skills. If there is nothing else available and the candidate is obviously unqualified for the position, the process ends there, saving both the candidate and organization the time and expense going further into the selection process. (p. 32)

The screening interview has two primary purposes. The first, as stated above, is to confirm the individual's qualifications submitted in the application materials. The interviewer could employ the same form utilized in the submission screening process described in Step 3. The second purpose is to gauge the individual's continued interest in the position and program. Capable people, who are actively searching for a job, characteristically do not "stay on the market" for very long. In the time it takes a sports or recreation program to post the position, collect application materials, and conduct preliminary screening for qualifications, a highly credentialed applicants could already have accepted a position at another organization.

Step 5. Job testing (if applicable). Job testing can be another viable way to identify and vet the ideal candidate. Kumar describes five types of employment tests that could be utilized for job screening candidates. A summation of the testing instruments are as follows:

1. *Aptitude tests* or potential ability tests are widely used to measure the talent and ability of a candidate to learn a new job or skill. Aptitude tests measure ability and skills.

2. *Interest tests* are used to find out the type of work in which the candidate has an interest. An interest test only indicates the interest of a candidate for a particular job. It does not reveal his ability to perform the job. Interest tests aim to learn the types of work in which a candidate is interested. They are inventories of the likes and dislikes of the people in some occupations.

3. *Intelligence tests* are used to find out the candidate's intelligence. By using this test, the candidate's mental alertness, reasoning ability, power of understanding, etc., are judged. Word fluency, memory, inductive reasoning and speed of perception are tested.

4. *Performance tests* are also called an achievement test. This test is used to measure the candidate's level of knowledge and skill in the particular trade or occupation in which he will be appointed, ifselected. Achievement test are of two kinds:
   - Test for measuring job knowledge
   - Work sample tests

5. *Personality tests* are used to measure those characteristics of a candidate which constitute his personality. They assess a candidate's motivation, interest, his ability to adjust himself to the stress of everyday life and his capacity for interpersonal relations and self-image. Personality tests are three types:
   - Objective tests measure self-sufficiency and self-confidence.

- Personality tests assess a candidate's interpretation for certain standard stimulus situations. They test a candidate's values – motives and personality.

- Situation tests measures a candidate's reaction when he is placed in a particular situation.

(Kumar, 2011, pp. 112-113)

Whatever testing instrument is used, and through whatever means (either purchasing an external instrument or creating one in-house), sports or recreation administrators must show a direct, unequivocal connection between the open position and the testing instrument applied in evaluating candidates for that position. Administrators must also demonstrate that the instrument is valid and reliable to avoid any systemic discrimination.

Reviewing processes and practices, at a minimum, must determine that job related tests used to select candidates exhibit both statistical validity and reliability. Job-related validity refers to the accuracy of a test (in this case, any hiring practice used as a part of the selection process) to identify correctly what it intends to measure. Job-related reliability indicates consistency of the measurement (test) results over time. Both validity and reliability are critical in determining whether or not job-related discrimination is present when selection decisions are made. (Daly, 2012, p. 47)

HR Tip

In any form, discrimination in the selection process opens up the program to (1) potential damaging litigation and (2) negative public perception. Whether it is deliberate discrimination (through human conduct) or unintentional discrimination (through system processes such as invalid testing instruments), the sports or recreation program must be cognizant of all possible inequitable practices and should eradicate them immediately from the selection process and operation.

Phase Three: Focused Candidacy Review

Step 6. Final Interview(s). In the selection process, the final interview consists of performing in-depth discussions (and for the lack of a better term—interrogations) with a designated short list of candidates. The types of interviews and varieties of question can range greatly for each program position. Some of the typical categories of interviews and question varieties can encompass the following provided in Table 5.5.

Interview Tips. In conducting interviews, there are some straightforward guidelines and suggestions one can employ. They are as follows:

- To become a competent interviewer, it takes practice and repetition. Simply stated, to develop proficiency at interviewing, one needs to develop their own tactics, understand their own comfort level, and find their own overall interview style.

TABLE 5.5 Interview and Question Types

Interview Types		*Question Types*	
Individual	One-on-one	General Screening	Base level position constructed questions
Panel	Group interviews	Specific Informational	Advance level position specific
Sequential	One interviewer after another	Open-ended	Free flowing questions withing preestablished framework
Stress	High pressure rapid fire interviews	Fixed response	Predetermined questions and inflexible answers
Tryout	Demonstrations		
Scenario	Situation and response		
Online	Remote virtual interviewing		

- An excellent approach to increase effectiveness at interviewing is to benchmark (observe) other strong interviewers and duplicate and adapt their interview strategies.

- Environmental management for an interview is a meaningful factor in its success or failure. Beforehand, arrange for room preparations, emphasize comfort and privacy. If possible, changing the interview environment can decrease the potential for day-to-day distractions while enhancing interview productivity.

- Small talk at the beginning of the interview session can establish a calm, friendly atmosphere that puts the candidate at ease. For effective small talk, discuss topics outside the job being interviewed (e.g. honors, activities, and interests provided by the candidate on their application). An approachable and social ambiance in an interview will get more honest, detailed responses from the interviewee. However, it is critical to keep the discussion or small talk focused on work related topics. At no time should an interviewer ask or engage in personal questions.

- During the interview, record relevant information immediately, without taking excessive notes. Find a balance between active listening and writing.

- If possible, have an outline of subjects to be reviewed during interview. Refer to this list to keep the interview on topic.

- Prior to the interview, conduct due diligence research on the qualifications and exceptionalities of the candidate, and utilize the data in the selection process (to this point). Administrators should not research an individual's background through social media (e.g. Facebook, Twitter, etc.) or a general Internet search (e.g. Google, Yahoo, etc.), as results may lead to information one is not allowed to ask about and, therefore, better not to have. (See Chapter 2 for additional information on employment discrimination).

- Have full detailed disclosure and open dialog about the position being interviewed. It is essential that the candidate knows all aspects of the position (both desirable and difficult).

- Do not stop the interview until you get the information you need. Allocate sufficient time to conduct the interview. In other words, do not rush its progress. Remember, the final interview is a significant screening step. Sprinting through it could have long-term repercussions on the sports or recreation program.

HR Tip

One of the most difficult aspects of interviewing and hiring is summed up in the statement, "One needs to hire the person who can do the best, not necessarily the person one likes the best." Even though an administrator may have conducted a pleasant and enjoyable interview, they should not lose sight of the candidate's suitability and success factors for the position.

Step 7. Verifying reference checks and independent background screening. An important validating action in the selection process is conducting reference checks. Typically, there are three kinds of reference checks for a job candidate. The first is job confirmation from the candidate's professional history section of the resume, CV or application, the second is contacting professional references, and the third is contacting personal references.

When overseeing job confirmation checks, *it is essential to* **get permission** *from the candidate sanctioning a job confirmation check with their* **current employer**. Most professional job confirmation checks are bound by the internal policies of their particular organization. Generally, current and former employers are permitted to (1) confirm the candidate's employment, (2) validate their position title(s), and (3) verify their dates of employment. In the past, inquiries on whether the candidate was eligible for rehire were typically included in a job confirmation check. However, most organizations have eliminated answering this particular inquiry.

The second type of reference check is a professional reference. These are individuals the candidate has voluntarily submitted on their application materials that are in the same or related professional field. These reference checks are meaningful for their confirmation of the professional qualifications of the candidate. Simply stated, professional references can authenticate the skills, competencies, and specialized proficiencies the candidate has claimed throughout their application materials and interviews.

Finally, personal references are used to check the candidate's personality and psychological disposition. Inquiries into the candidate's integrity, work ethic, temperament, and general characteristics are investigated.

Background Checks. Background checks have become a necessary reality. (Chapter 2 discusses legal issues related to the use of background checks). To be considered for a sports or recreation program position, candidates could go through the following four step background check:

1. The candidate completes a detailed consent form. Administrators should make clear to the candidate that all employment offers and agreements are contingent upon successful completion of the program's background check.

2. Administrators send the consent form, (either electronically or by traditional mail) to an independent, authorized third party. At this point, fingerprint checks are also a prudent background safeguard.

3. The candidate, through an autonomous and sanctioned third party, submits to a drug screening test. Any anomalies in the screening outcomes must be explained and have a physician's accompanying clarifying documentation.

4. If required by internal program policies or external governing regulatory bodies, administrators must conduct any subsequent background checks to verify a candidate's clearance information.

At no time should a candidate be hired for a sports or recreation program position until their background check obligations are satisfied, and screening information has been cleared. A customary processing time for background checks and drug screening by independent agencies is normally between 48–72 hours. As discussed in Chapter 2, prior to launching a background check program (as a part of the selection process), all practices should be analyzed and approved by the organization's legal counsel.

Phase Four: Selection, Negotiation, and Offer

Step 8. Tentative selection decision. In this stage of the selection process, all the data has been accumulated, the sports or recreation program administrators have made their hiring recommendation, and the position is to be tentatively offered to the best qualified candidate. It is critically important "for the supervisor of the position makes the final selection. Often, the supervisor will have a ranked list from a search committee for professional or competitive positions. Supervisors should not overturn search committee recommendations lightly" (Berman, Bowman, West, & Van Wart, 2013, p. 161). Because the direct supervior is accountable for the position and individual, the final hiring decision should belong solely to the direct supervisor.

Prior to contacting the candidate to officially negotiate and offer the job, all internal stakeholders should be in agreement when it comes to the program position regarding the salary, benefits, job responsibilities (as specified in the job description), reporting responsibilities, supervisory empowerment, work hours, etc. to avoid complications later on.

Step 9. Physical exam (if applicable). Certain positions may request that the candidate submit to a physical exam, prior to the official job offer. As with other requirements in the selection process, administrators must show an irrefutable connection between the physicality of the position and the need for the candidate to pass a physical exam. In other words, a physical exam cannot be a precluding or disqualifying factor for employment if the position does not have a substantial physical element in its undertaking.

In addition, even if physical exams are required, reasonable accommodation may still need to be given (if practical).

Step 10. Negotiation and official offer of employment. The negotiation and offer of employment concludes the selection process. Negotiations frequently impact salary, benefits, and auxiliary work items—everything from parking, courtesy cars, phones, computer equipment, health club memberships, merchandise contracts, to summer camps. It is vital for administratiors to enter into a negotiation with a candidate knowing which employment aspects are completely flexible, which have ranges, and which employment stipulations are "in stone" (also known as deal breakers).

After the particulars of the position have been agreed upon between both parties, an offer of employment is made. It is customary for the offer to have an acceptance or rejection time frame, customarily two-to-five days. There are two obvious outcomes from the offer of employment: Acceptance or rejection of the offer. If the candidate declines the offer, administrators can either (1) attempt to renegotiate the offer with the same candidate, (2) offer the position to another candidate, or (3) start the selection process all over. If the offer of employment is accepted, especially a verbal acceptance, while legally binding, a letter of agreement or official contract should be developed that details all of the settled upon negotiated job elements (with legal council's approval). The letter of agreement or contract should (1) have the job description attached, (2) designate the official start date, and (3) be signed by all parties.

After the acceptance of the position by the candidate and the letter of agreement or contract has been signed and received, the onboarding process begins.

Recruiting and Selecting: A Team Perspective

Although it may appear that the hiring process for a sports or recreation program is intricate, somewhat problematic to complete, and, to a certain degree, imprecise, it can also be regarded as an opportunity to bring new talent into the operation while creating a team culture and operational philosophy within the organization. Unquestionably, the recruiting and selection process does not have to be one person's responsibility. It can be accomplished through crossfunctional teams (sometimes known as ad hoc committees) as a way to (1) produce multiple perspectives on job candidates, (2) have diverse program members work together who might not normally interact, and (3) cultivate a culture of social and task oriented teams.

It should be noted that teams are different from groups.

> A team is characterized by a common commitment, whereas the commitment within a group might not be as strong. A team accomplishes many collective work products, whereas group members sometimes work slightly more independently. A team has shared leadership roles, whereas members of a group have a strong leader. In a team there is individual and mutual accountability; in contrast, a group emphasizes individual accountability. Team members produce a collective work product, whereas group members sometimes produce individual work products. (Dubrin, 2007, p. 261)

Strong human resource hiring recruiting and selection teams can be invaluable in five out of the 10 critical selection process steps. The steps in which a hiring team could be most beneficial:

Step 3 – Collection and screening of resumes/curriculum vitae/applications in candidate pool

Step 4 – Preliminary interview (screening)

Step 6 – Final interview(s)

Step 7 – Verifying reference checks and independent background screening

Step 8 – Tentative selection decision

HR Tip

In most cases, a sports or recreation program's hiring team will necessitate administrative guidance and control procedures. However, with suitable direction and clear delineation of protocols, a hiring team can have extremely good results.

Onboarding New Employees

According to Westwood and Johnson (2011), onboarding is the process in which an organization transitions and assimilates new hires into the organization and their roles. The process navigates through HR policies, cultural norms, industry knowledge, and role success factors. The cost to hire and train new employees is very high. It is also becoming apparent in the fast-paced, do-more-with-less, post-recession environment that the speed at which someone becomes fully functional in their role is becoming more critical to the success of the business. (p. 1)

The sports or recreation program has just exerted considerable effort and time to hire the right person to join the operation. The subsequent onboarding is designed to get that individual "up and running" as smoothly and as promptly as possible. This is the primary intention of onboarding new personnel.

Orientation – A Key Impression

Orientation is the central means to achieving the objective of onboarding. It is the key component in onboarding which can have a prolonged, if not permanent, impact on the new program member. Some of the benefits of having a compelling, well-structured orientation system are:

- Transforming trepidation to comfortability to long-term retention. Starting a new position can be exhilarating, as well as slightly frightening. A sound orientation program can convert an individual's anxiety into feelings of comfort, which influence that individual's continuing job retention and productivity with the organization.
- Socialization, engagement, and group bonding. Socialization, engagement, and group bonding are extremely significant in creating an optimistic attitude toward the sports or recreation program and fellow program members. Orientation programs are social experiences. These experiences can generate a core philosophy of teamwork that can remain with a new employee throughout their tenure with the sports or recreation program.
- Sets the tone. The first interaction many new hires have is the orientation program. An effectual orientation system demonstrates a culture of professionalism, which amplifies the new employee's confidence in the leadership of the operation.
- Locks in the visions, mission, and values of the sports or recreation program. A central theme of any orientation program is to "lock in" the vision, mission, and values of the organization with new employees. While each position will have distinct accountabilities toward

organization-wide goals and objectives, the vision, mission, and values of the program are universal and at the core of the operation for everyone.

- Promotes the program's policies and procedures. Policies are aligned with the rules of the operation; procedures are associated with standardized ways to accomplish tasks in the operation. Strong orientation programs underscore the sports or recreation program's universal rules and functional aspects.

Each sports or recreation program, due to time limitations, financial constraints, and philosophical attitude toward onboarding, will have its own distinct and diverse orientation system. Table 5.6 presents orientation stages and elements that can be (1) included, (2) adopted and modified, or (3) disregarded in a program's orientation system.

The New Employee's First Day

As an extension of onboarding, a new employee's first day with the sport and recreational program is critical in developing a bond with the position as well as their coworkers. In an effort to make the individual's first day memorable (and industrious), the sports or recreation program should have the following items "ready and waiting" for the person's arrival.

- Personal access codes to the program's website, intranet system, and email
- Personal access codes to the program's phone system (local and long-distance codes)
- Program cell phone (to be encrypted by new employee upon arrival)
- Program ID card(s) and lanyard
- Keys and/or swipe cards for access to all pertinent program facilities (offices, supplies, storage, athletic facilities, etc.)
- Parking cards, window stickers, and space designations
- Security clearances and security cards
- Desk set-up, including supplies (paper, pens, stapler, filing cabinet, flash drives, etc.), computer, mouse, and appropriate software, phone, copier access codes, and video equipment
- Program merchandise

By having these items present at the new program member's arrival, the new employee will know that they (1) made "the right decision" in choosing this job and (2) feel immediately valued and a part of the team.

Summary

To achieve a sustained competitive advantage over other sports or recreation programs, recruiting, selecting, and constructively onboarding new personnel is paramount. By identifying applicable recruiting sources, programs can develop suitable candidate pools to hand-pick new personnel. By following a well-structured,

TABLE 5.6   Stages of Organizational and Departmental Orientation

Stage 1 Pre-Orientation

Distribution of Relevant Documentation (reviewed during orientation)

- Employee handbook
- Policy and procedure manuals (with all relevant forms)
- Final pre-employment paperwork (with explanations for completion)
- Confirmation of compensation, benefits, contracts, etc.
- Select components of the program plan, vision, mission, and value statements, long-term goals, heirarchal charts, etc.

Safety and Emergency Protocols

Orientation Packet

- Agenda for orientation
- Contact list (internal only)
- Facility/building maps
- Annual calendar of events and holidays

Online Video Welcome from Executive Administrator(s)

Stage 2 Introduction and Greetings

Welcome from Human Resource

- Overview of Sports or Recreation Program History

Overview from Department Heads (e.g. General Administration, Compliance, Medical, External Development, etc.)

Stage 3 Organizational Orientation

Broad Review of:

- Relevant program plan items
- Employee handbook
- Policy and procedure manual
- Safety and emergency protocols
- Other orientation pre-distributed items

Overview from Benefits Specialist

Tour of Facility and Meal

Teambuilding Activity/Outing

Stage 4 Departmental Job Orientation

One-on-One with Direct Supervisor Reviews of:

- Detailed job description
- Individual goal setting and performance expectations
- Departmental hierarchical structure
- Unique departmental policies and procedures
- Specific departmental safety and emergency protocols

Office and Work Area Tour

Departmental Personnel Introduction and Group Social Event or Activity

logically modeled selection process, administrators can minimize the chance of acquiring ill-suited or unqualified employees. Once hired, having a competent, proficient onboarding system, consisting of organizational and departmental orientations, along with focused first day preparations, is the key to retaining personnel and establishing a tone of professionalism throughout the entire sports or recreation program.

References

Arthur, D. (2012). *Recruiting, interviewing, selecting, and orienting new employees* (5th ed.). New York, NY: American Management Association.

Berman, E. M., Bowman, J. S., West, J. P., & Van Wart, M. R. (2013). *Human resource management in public service: Paradoxes, processes, and problems* (4th ed.). Thousand Oaks, CA: Sage.

Carbery, R., & Cross, C. (2013). *Human resource management: A concise introduction.* Hampshire, England: Palgrave Macmillan.

Daly, J. L. (2012). *Human resource management in the public sector: Policies and practices.* Armonk, NY: M. E. Sharp.

Deb, T. (2006). *Strategic approach to human resource management: Concept, tools and application.* New Delhi, India. Atlantic Publishers.

DeCenzo, D. A., Robbins, S. P., & Verhulst, S. L. (2016). *Fundamentals of human resource management* (12th ed.). Hoboken, NJ: John Wiley and Sons.

Dubrin, A. J. (2007). *Leadership: Research findings, practice, and skills* (5th ed.). Boston, MA: Houghton Mifflin.

Gatewood, R. D., Field, H. S., & Barrick, M. R. (2016). *Human resource selection* (8th ed.). Boston, MA: Cengage Learning.

Kumar, R. (2011). *Human resource management: Strategic analysis text and cases.* New Delhi, India: I.K. International Publishing House.

Stredwick, J. (2014). *An introduction to human resource management* (3rd ed.). New York, NY: Routledge.

Westwood, R., & Johnson, L. (2011). *Onboarding for managers.* Alexandria, VA: ASTD Press.

Yakkaldevi, A., & Dubey, P. (2015). *Human resource management.* Maharashtra, India: Laxmi Book Publications.

Review and Discussion Questions

1. Define recruiting and selection.
2. Why is passion important in recruiting and selecting sports or recreation program members?
3. Why go through the arduous work of systematized recruiting and selection?
4. Name all of the internal recruiting sources for sports or recreation program members.
5. Name all of the external recruiting sources for sports or recreation program members.
6. What are three possible disadvantages of internal recruiting?
7. What are three possible advantages of external recruiting?
8. What are the four phases in the selection process?
9. What are the ten steps in the selection process?
10. Why review job analysis data, job designs, and job descriptions in the selection process?
11. What are the four acumens of writing a job posting?
12. What are the four main criteria for collecting and screening resumes, CVs, and applications?
13. What is the value in using a checklist in the screening of resumes, CVs, and applications?
14. What are preliminary screening interviews?
15. Name the possible employment testing categories that could be used by sports or recreation programs.
16. What are the different types of final interviews that could be used by sports or recreation programs?
17. Choose an interview guideline or tip and describe why it is important.
18. Name and explain each of the three types of reference checks.
19. What are the two outcomes in offering a sports or recreation program position? What could happen in each?
20. What are the benefits of a sound orientation system in sports or recreation programs?
21. What are some items that could be available on a new employee's first day?

Application Exercises

1. Research three athletic program job postings online. Critique each one from the acumens of writing a solid, attractive job posting.
2. Design a checklist of preliminary interview questions for the following positions:
    *   Head Summer Camp Counselor
    *   Head Lacrosse Coach
    *   Recreation Department Intern
3. Research employment tests for personality, aptitude, and intelligence online. Critique each one for its sports and recreation program use.

Human Resource Management Term Project
Individual/Group Oral Presentation

You and your group are the new executive administrators for a public recreational organization (group's choice). The organization is growing rapidly and has no formalized orientation program in its operation. New employees are simply "on the floor" their first day. Design from the ground up (1) an orientation program agenda based on the elements in Table 5.6 as well as (2) any/all accompanying new employee documentation relevant to the program agenda.

Elements:

- Research human resource orientation programs that can be used by the operation. Use HR sources (online and journals) to conduct your research.

- Justify each component of the orientation program and why it would be appropriate for the operation.

- Develop a program timetable, and an orientation agenda.

- Elaborate on the cost factors of the orientation program.

- Discuss new software and hardware requirements, costs, and benefits of the orientation program.

Criteria:

- Develop a 30-minute presentation that details the orientation system for this organization.

- Prepare for a 15-minute Q & A session after main presentation.

- Create PowerPoint slides and visual aids to supplement the presentation (hard copy to be submitted prior to presentation).

- Conduct extensive external research to justify your selections.

Human Resource Management Term Project
Individual/Group Oral Presentation

You (and your group) will be evaluating athletic programs from the vantage point of how they recruit and select athletic personnel. Go to the NCAA web site at www.ncaa.org and choose from any program the following advertised positions:

- 1 Administrative Position (Athletic Director, Assistant Athletic Director, etc.)
- 1 Coaching Position (Any sport)
- 1 Support Position (Trainer, Academic Support, etc.)
- 1 Graduate/Intern Position

Contact the athletic department's human resource manager. Discuss with them their process in the recruitment and selection of the current opening.

Project Conditions:

1. Download the actual posted advertisements from the NCAA web site.
2. Obtain a copy of the organizations employment application.
3. Construct (through discussions/interviews with the athletic department human resource manager) a detailed step-by-step diagram of each organization's hiring process.
4. Critique each organization's positional hiring process for:
   - Efficiency
   - Timeliness
   - Thoroughness
   - Compensation Package Offered
   - Legal and Ethical Hiring Practices
   - Referencing Processes
   - Employment Retention Success and Turnover Rate

Criteria:

Develop a 30-minute presentation that details the hiring process.

Prepare for a 15-minute Q & A session after main presentation.

Create PowerPoint slides and visual aids to supplement the presentation (hard copy to be submitted prior to presentation).

Conduct extensive external research to justify your selections.

chapter six

Human Resource Development and Training

Chapter Objectives

- Understand the benefit of participation in training programs
- Understand the operational areas in which training consideration are necessary
- Name and understand the three phase of specific training needs assessments
- Name and understand individual and group training methodologies
- Know and apply definitive training implementation strategies
- Know and apply the four areas of training evaluation

Key Terms

Program Training
Human Resource Asset
Content Delivery
Target Project-Based Training
Departmental Training
Position Training
Individual Program Member
    Training
Organizational Analysis
Task Analysis

Person Analysis
On-the-Job Training (OJT)
    Program
Internships or Apprenticeships
Understudy Training
Online/e-Learning
Video/CD/DVD Asynchronous
    (library resource)
Outsourced Training
Personal Coaching

Job Rotation/Cross Training
Online/Synchronous Virtual
    Classrooms
Dynamic Discussion
Lecturer/Subject Expert Speaker
Onsite Demonstrations and
    Participants Engagement
Team Building Challenges

The Importance of Investing in Personnel Training

The fundamental principle behind sports and recreation program member training is apparent. Within resource constraints, the primary purpose of a sports and recreation program training is to capitalize on the human resource asset so it can maintain and positively advance the operation's sustainable advantage over its competition. To that end, sports and recreation program training:

- Is a profound statement to all internal stakeholders that the organization's culture is employee centered;
- Emphasizes formal training versus informal learning, which promotes consistency and efficiency;

127

- Can have a quantifiable return on investment;
- Can concentrate on knowledge, skills, and attitude improvements;
- Is focused strategically on the future; and
- Can enhance a team atmosphere.

Content delivery is based totally on program needs and the individuals in training. In other words, based on the program's operational plan and subsequent human resource plan, it is a "win-win" outcome for the operation and the employees being trained. The program's benefit through successful training programs is palpable. A more trained human resource asset augments productivity, morale, group cohesiveness, and wide-ranging competitive advantages. According to Lall and Zaidi (2008) the new program employees win:

1. Increased job satisfaction and recognition.
2. Movement towards personal goals while improving interactive skills.
3. Help in eliminating fear of attempting new tasks.
4. An avenue for growth.
5. Internalized and operationalized motivational variables of recognition, achievement, growth, responsibility and advancement.
6. Information for improving leadership, communication skills and attitudes.
7. Help in handling stress, tension, frustration and conflict. (p. 115)

HR Tip

To promote training programs to sports or recreation program employees, the concept of career development should be communicated. Through series of training platforms, program employees can increase their value to the operation, thus increasing their promotability and professional status.

Assessing Needs

High level operational areas in sports or recreation programs should be examined to determine which of the following types of training is required: (1) broad organization-wide training, (2) target project-based training, (3) specific departmental training, (4) position training, and/or (5) individual program member training. Table 6.1 presents universal operational areas that should be considered when evaluating sports or recreation program training needs.

If the administrators conclude from Table 6.1 that there is an identifiable and significant operational component that is new, profoundly changing, or lacking to provide a competitive advantage, then a specific training needs assessment should be conducted.

TABLE 6.1   Operational Training Areas

Area 1   Modifications in or additions to program core values

Area 2   New or changing strategic mission, goals, and objectives
           (based on the operational program plan and human resource plan)

Area 3   Low performances and poor operational efficiencies (supported by quantitative data)

Area 4   Positional changes and rearranging personnel in hierarchical structure

Area 5   Evolving individual program positions

Area 6   New program policies and procedures

Area 7   New sports or recreation program governing body regulatory addendums and additions

Area 8   Structural changes toward individual and group self-management
           (a reduction in administrative supervision)

Area 9   New attitudes required among program members (as determined by the collective
           performance evaluations of all program members)

Area 10   Identifiable sports or recreation organization weaknesses compared to competition

Area 11   Acquisition of new sports or recreation program assets and resources
           (equipment, facilities, sport specific athletic/recreation supplies, etc.)

Area 12   Impactful external environmental force alterations
           (technology, competition, legal, nature, demographic, economic, social changes)

Area 13   Development of new programs, products, and services

Area 14   Developing or reestablishing a social team environment

Area 15   Adoption of new HRIS or communication system

Area 16   Safety issues and concerns

HR Tip

The urgency in training needs can fluctuate greatly among operational areas. For example, if operational staff and administrators recognize substantial safety issues and concerns, this operational area would mandate an immediate and comprehensive effort to develop and implement a training program.

Training Needs Assessments

To conduct a training needs assessment for a program component, Bohlander and Snell (2010) have developed a straightforward, three phase training needs assessment process: organization analysis, task analysis, and person analysis.

- Organizational Analysis of environment, strategies, and resources to determine where to emphasize training.

- Task Analysis of the activities to be performed in order to determine the KSA's [Key Success Actions] needed.

- Person Analysis of performance, knowledge, and skills in order to determine who needs training. (p. 309)

This process is easy for sports or recreation programs to adopt; administrators can apply the three types of analyses above to the areas identified in Table 6.1, to more easily recognize a training need. So, for an impactful external environmental force alteration in technology an administrator discovered that there is a new and innovative operational software that will significantly augment the sports or recreation program's output and efficiency.

From an organizational analysis, administrators should research the all-inclusive impact of the new software innovation on the operating environment, the goals and objectives, and the financial resources of the sports or recreation program. Questions to be asked could include: What divisions or departments need to utilize the new software? How will the new software impact each division or department? What positions in each division or department need to utilize the new software? What will be the organizational commitment needed to purchase and train all relevant program members on the new software?

From a task analysis, the software will need to be dissected for all of its functions and capabilities. A question could encompass: What functions will be utilized by (1) the entire sports or recreation program, (2) each department, (3) each position, and (4) each individual person?

Finally, from an individual or personal analysis, each person who will benefit from the new software innovation must be evaluated for their aptitude and familiarity with the software. If it is a "new to the world" computer software program, everyone using the software will need comprehensive instruction or training. If it is a variation of a prevailing software, a person-by-person assessment will be required to determine who should be trained from the "ground-up" and whom should be "fast tracked" trained.

There are a few distinct notations from this example. First, this scenario is not uncommon for any business, sports or recreation programs included. Software advances and innovations are constantly emerging. Second, because of the intricacy of different operational elements in software packages, a tiered, level-by-level training method could be a viable option. For instance, administration could be trained on the all-inclusive software package while coaches, counselors, and functional staff could have selective training on elements of the software program that directly affect them. Lastly, unless the sports or recreation program has a resident expert in the software's functionality, it is ardently recommended that the software instruction be conducted by a proficient, software company instructor. With their expertise in the complexity of the software, they can determine (from Table 6.2) which training methods are the most effective for instructing program personnel.

Performing a Personalized SWOT Analysis. A SWOT analysis is a "tried and true" business tool for evaluating an organization's internal strengths, weaknesses, external opportunities, and threats. This mechanism can be easily modified and employed for dissecting a single program member's professional strengths, weakness, opportunities, and threats, which can serve as the foundation for constructing that member's short- and long-term training platform. In other words, the customized SWOT analysis will be an indispensable mechanism for establishing the current and future growth of the individual within the sports or recreation program--in essence, a core element of the individual's professional development "game plan." From a sports or recreation program perspective, the individualized SWOT analysis supplies a (1) comprehensive picture of the employee's existing and potential value to the operation, which, in turn, can (2) assist administration in developing customized training to capitalize on the program member's current and potential contributions to the organization.

The initial phase of the individual SWOT breakdown is to evaluate the employee's professional circumstances via an internal assessment. A strength and weakness evaluation analytically examines the individual's proficiencies and competences and judges if each item is a professional strength/asset or a professional weakness/liability. It is logical to start the assessment process by prioritizing (from most critical to least consequential) the employee's specific positional responsibilities. Hopefully, when the internal assessment is concluded, the most notable and significant elements will be principally deemed as strengths. In converting the internal strength and weakness analysis to training needs, administration should always focus on augmenting one's professional strengths and converting professional weaknesses into competencies, or ultimately, strengths.

The second step is a personalized external analysis or an opportunity/threat study. This progression principally audits all of the external environmental factors that affect the employee's position to determine if there are external opportunities for growth and competitive advantage, or professional threats to the individual and their position. Once again, prioritize the environmental elements (from the most significant to the least notable) in relation to the employee's specific position. If one is fortunate, an individual's professional opportunities will outweigh their threats. The administration's philosophy in this individualized external analysis should be to exploit opportunities and to professionally fortify the program member against any current or future career threats.

HR Tip

A simple way to conceptualize an individualized professional SWOT analysis to determine training needs is to (1) maximize the individual's internal strengths, (2) minimize the internal weaknesses, (3) exploit external professional opportunities, and (4) defend against the external professional threats.

The individual professional SWOT analysis should answer the following questions:

- What are the attractive aspects of the company's [individual's] situation?

- What aspects are of the most concern?

- Are the company's [individual's] internal strengths and competitive assets sufficiently strong to enable it [them] to compete successfully?

- Are the company's [individual's] weaknesses and competitive deficiencies of small consequence and readily correctable, or could they prove fatal if not remedied soon?

- Do the company's [individual's] strengths outweigh its weaknesses by an attractive margin?

- Does the company [individual] have attractive market opportunities that are well suited to its [their] internal strengths? Does the company [individual] lack the competitive assets to pursue the most attractive opportunities?All things considered, where on a 1 to 10 (where 1 is alarmingly weak and 10 is exceptionally strong) do the company's [individual's] overall situation and future prospects rank?

(Thompson, Peteraf, Gamble, & Strictland, 2014, p. 96)

Thanks to questions like these, an individualized professional SWOT analysis will provide a durable basis for administration to tailor its professional training platform now and in the future.

Overview of Established Training Methodologies

Table 6.2 provides a comprehensive list of standardized training methodologies which could be utilized by sports and recreation programs.

Individualized Methods

On-the-Job Training (OJT) Program. On-the-job training involves learning through watching and observing someone with greater experience performing a task. On-the-job training is a very popular method of training when new skills and methods are being taught to employees. The advantages of on-the-job training are that it is cheap; the trainees get the opportunity to practice immediately; trainees get immediate feedback; and it can also help in integrating trainees into existing teams (Nickson, 2013, p. 162).

The pertinent key to this type of training is two-fold. First, and most importantly, the on-the-job training program should be structured with agendas and instructional blueprints, itemized task lists (base on job descriptions), completion time frames, performance expectations for each task and job category, and records of completion (to be maintained in employees' human resource file). A serious miscalculation in adopting this form of training program would be to indiscriminately "throw together" the training system without a cogent configuration and organized structure. Secondly, the selection of whom will do the training is vital in the success of the on-the-job training system. The sports or recreation program administrator or employee/mentor (or a combination of both) should be proficient in the accurate workings, as well as all the policies and procedure associated with the position. The wrong selection of trainer could mean that the trainee is being provided with substandard or inadequate instruction, which, in turn, could be "setting them up for failure" even before they formally undertake the position's tasks and responsibilities.

HR Tip

If financially feasible, a sports or recreation program member, who is being utilized as a mentor/trainer in an on-the-job training system should be compensated for their extra work. Even a small incentive could loudly communicate the importance of the assignment.

TABLE 6.2   Training Methodologies for Program Personnel

Individualized	*Group or Program-Wide*
Structured on-the-job training (OJT) program	Online/synchronous virtual classrooms
Internships/apprenticeships	Traditional classroom (dynamic discussion/ workshop format)
Understudy/stand-in training	
Online/e-learning (asynchronous self-regulated)	Traditional classroom (lecture/subject expert speaker format)
Video/cd/dvd asynchronous (library resource)	
Outsourced training through college/university CEUs/certifications/degrees	Onsite demonstrations and participants engagement
Personal one-on-one coaching	Team building challenges
Job rotation/cross training	

Internships/Apprenticeships. Internships and apprenticeships, while autonomous in concept, have similar functional components. Typically, internships are connected with college and university academic programs while apprenticeships are associated with post-education training (often times leading to diverse levels of trade or professional certifications). Both internships and apprenticeships have an extreme concentration of real-world involvement from the intern or apprentice. In other words, the intern or apprentice is regularly engaged by the program for a protracted period of time, working the position designated by their internship or apprenticeship agreements.

From an intern's perspective, the benefits of having a real-world training opportunity are immeasurable.

> Since employers are more likely to hire college candidates with related employment experience, internships can critically enhance resumes. Internship experience is very important to employers, candidates, and college/university efforts. Internships give college students the opportunity to work for different companies and gain important career exposure…These work arrangements often lead to full-time employment after graduation, benefiting both the intern and the hiring corporation. (Mathis, Jackson, Valentine, & Meglich, 2017, p. 227)

It is ciritical to discuss paid versus non-paid internships prior to launching the program. Administrators should consult with legal counsel on all relevant local, state, and national labor laws concerning internship compensation prior to the program's inception.

Appendix C, on page 235, provides an all-purpose template for the development and operation of a college or university sports management internship program.

Understudy or Stand-In Training. This training approach is customarily for managerial or administration positions but can be applied to other jobs in a sports or recreation program as well. Sims (2006) best describes it as:

a form of management modeling that assigns a current or future manager to work with another manager for a certain time frame. If the organization is grooming the person for a specific management position, the individual may understudy one particular manager. For a broader foundation, understudies may rotate among several managers. Using either method, the individual sees the day-to-day leadership duties, while the manager acts as coach and appraiser. The advantage of understudy assignments is that the heir realizes the purpose of the training and can learn in a practical and realistic situation without being directly responsible for operating results. On the negative side, the understudy learns the bad as well as the good practices of the incumbent. (p. 258)

HR Tip

As with actors in theater, an understudy is a person who can take over the performance of a position at a moment's notice, because they have worked the position with the current and/ or previous job holder. It is a huge advantage for sports and recreation programs to have this type of human resource contingency apparatus in-place.

Online Training (Asynchronous Self-Regulated). Sports and recreation programs can exploit online instruction (also called e-learning) in numerous ways for individual, group or unit, or program-wide training. Whether training is delivered within the program's human resource information system (learning management system, or LMS), through a separate, dedicated training website, or from an independent third-party training consultant, online training has become an accepted and prevalent way to deliver information and to enhance individual skills and abilities. Online training benefits to sports or recreation program training embody:

- delivery of training programs 24 hours a day, 7 days a week, 365 days a year;

- permanency, ease of storage, and continued reusability of training modules;

- a self-paced training methodology for all sports or recreation program members, regardless of their expertise and knowledge base;

- adaptability for individual training as well as group-based learning;

- distance learning opportunities when program personnel are away from the physical locale of the operation;

- enhanced learning by utilizing visual and dynamic instruction techniques (video, illustrative aids, graphics, web links, etc.);

- immediate feedback through online quizzes, exams, and certification completions;

- cost efficient and fiscal responsibity by utilizing less sports or recreation program resources for comparable (and even upgraded) results;

- controlled opportunity costs associated with travel, time off-the-clock, etc.;

- incorporated results and training completion instantaneously into human resource documentation;
- expedited completion/fulfillment of organization compliance requirements from governing bodies;
- immediate training feedback for administrators;
- adaptablity with different languages and cultural identities; and
- capability to be revised immediately.

From an individual training perspective, an online training program can be asynchronous and self-regulated. In other words, establish a training program that can be accessed and completed by sports or recreation program members at their convenience.

Video Asynchronous (Library Resource). A somewhat out-of-date, but still viable, training method is the production and deployment of training videos. Once produced, they can be duplicated and delivered to individual employees or centrally retained and cataloged for reference in the sports and recreation program's training library. With innovative and user-friendly computer and software advancements, these multimedia components could be downloaded into an HRIS learning management system, backed up in cloud-based storage, and remotely accessed from any computer at any time.

Outsourced Training. An exceptional, readily accessible training resource for comprehensive instruction is through traditional in-class, hybrid, or online college courses. Whether the topic is business administration, management, kinesiology, sports management, or other related academic fields, sports and recreation programs can utilize already established and extensively developed, authenticated, and regulated college and university courses. Coursework can be through continuing education units, intensive seminars, certification programs, and if warranted, undergraduate and graduate degrees.

Personal One-on-One Coaching. Whitmore (2009), in his book *Coaching for Performance: Growing Human Performance and Potential*, describes the training concept of coaching with the following passages:

> Coaching delivers results in large measure because of the supportive relationship between the coach and the coachee, and the means and style of communication used. The coachee does acquire the facts, not from the coach but from within himself, stimulated by the coach. (p. 9)

Whitmore goes on to say: "Coaching is unlocking people's potential to maximize their own performance" (p. 11).

In essence, one-on-one coaching is the activity of guiding an individual to realize and improve their aptitudes and abilities. It can be employed to advance leadership capabilities, decision making skills, interpersonal communication abilities, as well as to become proficient in targeted job responsibilities and tasks.

The cooperative technique teaches the trainee that their training and professional development is within their own control.

> **HR Tip**
>
> Whether coaching is performed through formal prearranged assignments or through casual discussions, it is not a short-term developmental method. The dedication needed by both parties is considerable. The administrator, acting as coach/trainer, must recognize critical inflexion points in their coaching interactions and "steer" the program member through those junctures. The program member must commit to the reality that, while the coach/trainer is present to guide their progress, the bulk of the learning responsibility is theirs. At its core, training through coaching is a student-based approach that necessitates a high level of long-term dedication and personal responsibility from all parties involved in the process.

Job Rotation and Cross-Training. The job rotation and cross-training model has enormous potential benefits for both the program and the employees, is directly associated with the on-the-job training concept, which rotates, teaches, and prepares employees for a series of program positions. As a training method, job rotation and cross-training creates a more well-rounded workforce that comprehends and appreciates the global workings of the entire sports or recreation program.

> Not only does cross-training allow a business to adapt during employee vacations and sick time, but it give employees a sense of security and versatility. Cross-training also allows managers to redeploy employees away from traditional assignments, allowing others to step into the gaps. A lack of or poorly executed cross-training can be a serious contributor to dissatisfaction, as employees feel ill-equipped to perform new tasks, and work is left undone. (Wiley & Kowske, 2012, p. 109)

As with all on-the-job related training activities, organization and consistency are crucial to the training methodology's success. Each position of the program should have detailed learning objectives, task lists, completion time tables, administrative checkpoints, etc., so that the program member can easily rotate into new responsibilities with an understanding of what that position entails.

Group and Program-Wide Training Methods

Online or Virtual Classrooms. While there are numerous variations for virtual classrooms, as well as exceptionally user-friendly software platforms, their fundamental premise is simple. Program employees can remotely access, partake, and substantially contribute to a virtual classroom session from any location, from any computer, with minimal hardware requirements to support the software platform. Christopher (2015), from his book *The Successful Virtual Classroom: How to Design and Facilitate Interactive and Engaging Live Online Learning*, clarifies the essential workings of this dynamic group instructional mechanism:

The virtual classroom facilitator controls the screen and participants watch as the facilitator demonstrates how to perform specific tasks online. Screen sharing is useful to show a web site or other content to participants on the facilitator's computer instead of through static screen shots. Each participant's screen follows in real time as the facilitator clicks and scrolls through pages... A facilitator might also choose to toggle between the content and screen sharing features... Since facilitators and participants are physically separated, a virtual classroom must obviously support voice communication... The chat feature allows participants and facilitators to send text messages in real time to each other in a virtual classroom... Just as ongoing question-and-answer sessions help keep training interaction in a traditional classroom lively, the chat feature serves the same purpose to connect and engage the participants with the content of the virtual classroom. (pp. 22-25)

In essence, a virtual classroom has all of the same capabilities of traditional face-to-face classroom training while being a more accommodating and cost-effective presentation.

Traditional Classroom. The *dynamic discussion or workshop format* of traditional classroom training is precisely what one might envision: a classroom or conference room where program employees congregate to train in diverse operational elements. While the thought of this group training method might evoke uncomfortable, even painful memories, this technique, which can incorporate fresh and imaginative delivery strategies is still a primary approach in training large groups of people. Some of the inventive ways to enhance in-class training include:

- adopting a back-and-forth dialog where the Socratic training method of questions and answers is applied;
- structuring breakout sessions with roundtable discussions on pertinent subtopics;
- employing a "flipped" classroom model where program members review training materials (videos, documentation, projects, etc.) prior to the actual training session. Instead of reviewing these materials during the training session, individual and group assignments are given, and the session becomes an active practicum format;
- engaging interactive games that teach relevant sports or recreation program content;
- incorporating interactive technology such as YouTube videos, websites, online research articles and literature, etc.;
- utilizing case studies and real-world simulations; and
- implementing role-playing activities.

HR Tip
Producing an energetic in-class traditional training session is only limited by creative ingenuity and effort expended. New and untested face-to-face training enhancements should be well thought-out and, if possible, tested prior to implementation.

Another form of traditional classroom training is the *lecture, or subject expert speaker format*. This approach is a one-way communication technique that often has little or no in interactions during the lecture portion of the session (most have open question and answer time after lecture presentation). This approach begs the question, "Without active involvement from sports or recreation program members, can this be a worthwhile training technique?" The response is yes, with one major caveat. The quality and characteristics of the expert speaker is everything. If the speaker is lively, humorous, entertaining, and exudes energy, this group training approach can be enormously impactful. Unfortunately, if an expert speaker demonstrates none of those qualities, the session will have little or no influence on the program members in attendance.

Onsite Demonstrations and Participant Engagement. If the skill to be trained is primarily a physical activity (from small motor skills to large physical movements), then a demonstration format, which utilizes observation and participant engagement, is extremely effectual and has high learning retention. Sometimes referred to as the direct instructional approach, it can be systemized in a simple, four-phase process for maximizing skill acquisition.

1. *Modeling.* The skill is modeled by the teacher, who thinks aloud while performing the skill.
2. *Direct practice.* The teacher uses questions to lead students through the steps and to help them understand the reasoning behind the steps.
3. *Guided practice.* Students generate their own leading questions while working through the steps; the teacher observes, coaches, and provides feedback.
4. *Independent practice.* Finally, students work through more examples on their own.

(Silver, Strong, & Perini, 2007, p. 35)

HR Tip

For whatever reason, if a sports or recreation program administrator or trainer deems their capacity to demonstrate a skill inadequate, utilizing a "proxy" demonstrator is a significant component of the training. In spite of this, the supervising trainer should direct the training by regulating the demonstrator with verbal cues and instructional comments.

Team Building Challenges. DeCenzo, Robbins, and Verhulst (2016) provide a good basis for understanding trends in group training or efforts to engage and enhance working relationships among employees in an organization:

A recent trend in employee development has been the use of adventure (sometimes known as outdoor, wilderness, or survival) training. The primary focus of such training is to teach trainees the importance of working together or coming together as a team. Adventure training typically involves a major emotional and physical challenge…. The purpose is to see how employees react to the difficulties that nature presents to them. Do they face these dangers alone? Do they freak out? Or are they controlled and successful in achieving their goal? How cooperative are they under harsh circumstances? The reality is that today's business environment does not permit employees to stand alone. This has reinforced the importance of working closely with one another, building trusting relationships, and succeeding as a member of a group. (p. 187)

While this approach to group training has no immediate correlation to a particular function or duty in a sports or recreation program (such as learning new policies and procedures or complying with new regulatory requirements), it can have a vast influence on altering attitudes and cultivating teamwork. By getting employees "out of the office" and into challenging adventure training, operational elements such as: changing core values; improving performances and efficiencies; transforming mindsets and behaviors; reestablishing teamwork and a social environment; and improving program communication are just a small number of program improvements associated with this type of training.

HR Tip

There is a reflective question resulting from reviewing of all of the training methods described. Can a combination of training methods be utilized? Certainly. In fact, if a sports or recreation program can afford unified training, it is strongly recommended that all relevant training methods be combined into a comprehensive training package.

Implementation Strategies for Training Programs

There are essential strategies to consider when planning and implementing sports or recreation program training, identified in Table 6.3.

Evaluating and Improving Training Programs

Evaluation of training can be broken down into four areas:

1. Reaction: How much did the trainees like the program?
2. Learning: What principles, facts, and concepts were learned in the training program?
3. Behavior: Did the job behavior of trainees change because of the program?
4. Results: What were the results of the program in terms of factors such as reduced costs or reduction in turnover? (Rue, Ibrahim, & Byars, 2016, p. 167)

Reaction is a valuable evaluation measure because of the explicit connection between the participant's enjoyment during training with their retention of information. Through post training surveys, administrators can make future training adjustments and improvements. These surveys, either through conventional hand written or electronic instruments, should be circulated and collected directly after the training

TABLE 6.3   Training Implementation Strategies

Timing	The timing of program training should be: • Related to the importance of training issue • The least impactful on regular program operations • The most convenient for program members
Location and Facility (if applicable)	The location and facility for sports and recreation program training should be: • Appropriate for the type of training • Comfortable (seating, environmental elements, etc.) • Accessible and centrally located for all participants • All inclusive with suitable amenities (food and auxiliary services) and proper technology
Efficiency	The training should be: • Professional • Organized (objectives, agendas, timetables, etc.) • Completely supplied with all appropriate materials (hard copy and/or e-copies)
Training Session Execution	Phase 1 Introduction and Training Ground Rules • Roll call (if required) • Facilitate staff introductions (e.g. host, secretary, etc.) • Demarcate training goals and length (projected) • Describe training topics • Review training agenda and special circumstances Phase 2 Body of Training Session • Keep moving training topics along • Introduce presenters (and not steal the show from them) • Avoid tangents; lead group back onto original training topic • Resolve conflict (quickly and truthfully); maintain order and professional standards • Encourage participation from all training session members • Reiterate solutions to open training topics Phase 3 Training Session Termination • Keep on schedule • Provide a summation of the training main points • Set time for next/follow-up training session (if pertinent) • Thank participants for their time and contribution to training session • Have follow-up training information sent to participants ASAP

program has concluded. The rationale for this is clear. First, for an improved response rate, which correlates to more accurate evaluation results, having training participants complete surveys immediately after training will exploit the "captive audience" situation to obtain a 100% response rate. In other words, to conclude the training program, all trainees should be required to complete the survey. Secondly, for more precise responses, the trainees should complete the survey immediately after the final session while the training experience is fresh in their minds (also known as the recency theory).

Learning is a critical evaluation measure because the fundamental objective for any training program is to enhance knowledge. If possible, a pre-test/post-test model could be applied for this evaluation measurement. The concept behind pre- and post-testing is valid and reliable. Prior to participation, the trainee completes a knowledge, skill, or aptitude test centered on the major concepts to be conveyed during the upcoming training session. After the session has concluded, the same test is administered again, under the same conditions. Hopefully, if the training program is impactful, there should be a discernable improvement in the test score and knowledge attained.

Behavior is more problematic to measure after training. Because of its subjective nature, each trainee should be empirically observed over an elongated time period to examine if an attitudinal/behavioral change has occurred, due to the training. Hopefully, targeted attitudinal/behavior training will be imbedded into the work psyche of the individual to the point were there is a marked transformation.

Results, are often the training evaluation criteria that executive administration uses to judge the effectiveness of a training program. Administration wants a return on its investment through (1) measurable improvements in job performance and productivity, (2) the tangible fulfillment of strategic objectives, and (3) increased sports or recreation program competitive advantage. From the administration's perspective, training is only valuable if it can be applied in the context of the position and the sports or recreation program's operations.

HR Tip

There is a clear tenet when it comes to sports or recreation program training: If the program is training for training's sake (so they can pronounce that they have employee development and training programs), it is squandering valuable program resource and wasting everyone's time. If the primary objective for training is strategy execution, then the program will see immediate and long-term competency proliferation, a more contented workforce, and operational longevity.

Personnel Training: A Continuous Imperative

The professional training of sports and recreation program members should never be thought of as a onetime endeavor, but one that is a continuous competitive advantage activity that requires the entire organization's commitment. It necessitates an all-inclusive cooperative attitude that emphasizes a "professional development" atmosphere for everyone in the program. For training to be successful, organizational administrators must maintain a top-down commitment of both resources and energy. Administrators should consider training as an investment rather than a general expense. In other words, the sports or recreation program's commitment to ongoing personnel training should be focused on returns rather than costs. Furthermore, training should not wait until the organization has problems. It should proactively target each position and individual contribution to the strategic goals of the operation.

Employees should appreciate the fact that professional development is a lifetime process (especially in volatile sport and recreation job markets and be ready to commit, at any moment in their career, to professional development. The range of training requirements can be straightforward (training personnel on new equipment procedures)or multifaceted (major positional shifts in responsibilities). Training should not wait until an employee is having issues with their position; a preemptive attitude is essential. Additionally, the more individualized the training program, the better the expected outcomes. Generic training can leave gaps, while direct training objectives, known by everyone, can produce substantially more definitive results.

> **HR Tip**
>
> Do not fail to include everyone in training. Even the best employees (who can get overlooked because they are productive and happy). While some program members should be prioritized, even the best employees should be considered for practical improvement training.

Summary

Progressive programs approach training as a long-term investment that will reap critical, permanent benefits for both the organization and individual. Once an operational area has been diagnosed as necessitating improvement, program administrators should design, through the most suitable training methodologies, a comprehensive training program. By exploiting sound training implementation strategies, an effectual training program can be both cost efficient, bottom-line oriented, and inspirational. Because employee training is an unremitting process, for continuous improvement, training programs should be constantly evaluated and improved.

References

Bohlander, G., & Snell, S. (2010). *Managing human resources* (15th ed.). Mason, OH: South-Western/ Cengage.

Christopher, D. (2015). *The successful virtual classroom: How to design and facilitate interactive and engaging live online learning.* New York, NY: AMACOM.

DeCenzo, D. A., Robbins, S. P., & Verhulst, S. L. (2016). *Fundamentals of human resource management* (12th ed.). Hoboken, NJ: John Wiley and Sons.

Lall, M., & Zaidi, S. Q. (2008). *Human resource management.* New Delhi, India: Excel Books.

Mathis, R. L., Jackson, J. H., Valentine, S. R., & Meglich, P. A. (2017). *Human resource management* (15th ed.). Boston, MA: Cengage Learning.

Nickson, D. (2013). *Human resource management for the hospitality and tourism industries* (2nd ed.). New York, NY: Routledge.

Rue, L. W., Ibrahim, N. A., & Byars, L. L. (2016). *Human resource management* (11th ed.). New York, NY: McGraw-Hill.

Silver, H., Strong, R., & Perini, M. (2007). *The strategic teacher: Selecting the right research-based strategy for every lesson.* Upper Saddle River, NJ: Pearson.

Sims, R. R. (2006). *Human resource development: Today and tomorrow.* Greenwich, CT: Information Age Publishing.

Thompson, A. A., Peteraf, M. A., Gamble, J. E., & Strickland, A. J. (2014). *Crafting and executing strategy: The quest for competitive advantage* (19th ed.). New York, NY: McGraw-Hill/Irwin.

Whitmore, J. (2009). *Coaching for performance: Growing human performance and potential.* Boston, MA: Nicholas Brealey Publishing.

Wiley, J., & Kowske, B. (2012). *Respect: Delivering results by giving employees what they really want.* San Francisco, CA: John Wiley and Sons.

Review and Discussion Questions

1. What statement is made to internal stakeholder when sports or recreation program commits to training?

2. List the sports or recreation program member benefits or "wins" when participating in training.

3. What are the five levels of sports and recreation program training?

4. Name three operational areas that (in your opinion) would necessitate immediate sports or recreation program training consideration. Justify your selections.

5. What are the three need assessment components? Describe each.

6. What are the two keys to on-the-job training? Describe each.

7. What is the difference between an internship and an apprenticeship?

8. For an intern, what are the benefits of participating in an internship?

9. What is asynchronous, self-regulating online/e-leaning?

10. What are the advantages of outsource training through college or university courses?

11. What is the essence of one-on-one coach training?

12. Describe cross-training/job rotation.

13. What are virtual classrooms? How do they work?

14. What ways can traditional classroom training be enhanced?

15. What is the most critical aspect of lecture/subject expert training?

16. What are demonstrations?

17. What are the benefits of team building challenges?

18. What are the three training implementation strategies related to timing?

19. What are the three phases in training session execution and describe each?

20. What are the four training evaluation areas? Describe each.

Application Exercises

1. Research any city park and recreation program position online. From its job description, structure an on-the-job training program. Include:
   - Agendas for instruction
   - Task lists
   - Time frames
   - Performance expectations
   - Relevant documentation

2. Outline a program-wide certification training session on workplace sexual harassment. The framework should include:

   • PowerPoint slides

   • Point-by-point comprehensive coverage of the topic

   • A short, post-completion certification exam

3. Research three technology companies that could be used to facilitate a virtual classroom session. Critique each for:

   • Capabilities

   • Costs

   • User friendliness

   • General system requirements

chapter seven

Human Resource Performance Management and Evaluations

Chapter Objectives

- Know and explain performance management and performance evaluations
- Explain the interconnection between performance management and performance evaluations
- Explain the advantages and disadvantages for establishing and operating a performance management system and performance evaluations
- Identify an analytical phase-by-phase, step-by-step progression for performance management
- Understand and explain the approaches for conducting final performance reviews
- To explain the four major performance evaluation instruments
- Know how to conduct final performance evaluation meeting
- Know and explain performance improvement/action planning for sports and recreation programs
- Explain performance improvement action plan template

Key Terms

Performance Evaluation

Performance Management

Performance Plan

Job Analysis Data

Job Design

Job Descriptions

Key Success Factors

Performance Monitoring

One-Way Approach

Cooperative Self-Evaluation
    Approach

360 Degree/Multiple Appraiser
    Approach

Quantitative Data

Qualitative Opinions

Performance Standard Categories

Numerical Rating Scales

Graphic Rating Scales

Essay Approach

Critical Incident Method

Work Standards Approach

Performance Improvement
    Planning/Action Planning

Performance Management and Evaluations

Frequently, program administration and personnel cringe when they think of being involved with performance evaluations. For administrators, performance assessments can often (1) be problematic to construct, (2) be challenging to be objective, and (3) expend sizable allotments of time. Employees habitually assume that performance assessments are being used to judge their worth to the operation and calculate their current and future employment with the organization. Additionally, because of their negative preconceptions, performance assessments can be deemed as faultfinding which, in turn, can lead to confrontations and a disintegration of unity in the program. This mindset toward performance assessments is erroneous. To realize the true benefit of performance evaluation, these opinions by all program members, must be completely eliminated. This can be accomplished by communicating a commitment to the concept of performance management throughout the program, rather than the often disparaging and disenfranchised year-end performance assessments. Administrators should consider performance management and performance evaluations as a way to preserve and enhance the program's competitive advantage by building a more qualified human resource asset. Every facet of the performance management and evaluation process should be thought of as a constructive, optimistic method for the development of each employee's professional future, rather than a perilous valuation of their significance to the program.

> ### HR Tip
> Achieving program and human resource goals and objectives is directly tied into the performance and accomplishments of the program's people. To ensure that they are performing adequately to achieve these goals and objectives, performance management and performance evaluations are essential.

Defining Performance Management and Performance Evaluations

Certain scholars consider performance management and performance evaluations as two separate elements of human resource management. It is this author's assertion that these concepts are mutually inclusive, where performance management is the system and performance evaluations is an instrument within that system. Progressive organizations look beyond the conventional one-time, year-end performance evaluation, employing a performance management model where performance evaluations are the culmination of the larger system.

Armstrong (2015) defines performance management as the continuous process of improving performance by setting individual and team goals which are aligned to the strategic goals of the organization, planning performance to achieve goals, reviewing and assessing progress, and developing the knowledge, skills and abilities of people. (p. 9)

As indicated, performance evaluations are the end-product of the performance management system. They are a systematic and formal process through which job-relevant strengths and weaknesses of employees are identified, observed, measured, recorded, and developed. Appraisal is important in the sense that unless it is proper, job performance cannot be properly diagnosed. (Deb, 2008, p. 19)

Performance management and concluding evaluations provide an opportunity to (1) celebrate excellent accomplishments by superior program personnel, (2) optimistically challenge average performers to achieve beyond expectations, and (3) positively alter subpar performances by underachieving personnel.

> ### HR Tip
>
> Performance evaluations are not punishment and should under no circumstances be used as such. They are for developing the individual to achieve program objectives and goals. Even the most difficult evaluations with underperforming program employees should be viewed as an opportunity to "turn around" the situation and cultivate the individual's talents.

Table 7.1 discusses the benefits and drawbacks of the performance management process and final performance evaluations.

Steps in the Performance Management Process

The performance management process defined here is comprised of three principal phases with seven individual steps. While the progression is remarkably easy to comprehend for its maximum impact on the program and employee, it is imperative that the implementation of each phase and step be precisely followed.

> ### HR Tip
>
> For every program member, the performance management process should be a distinctively individualized developmental and assessment progression. While foundational components of the system can be collected, transferred, and utilized for multiple program members, typically within the same program position/status, each individual member should have their own personalized performance management plan and resulting performance evaluation.

Phase One: Performance Planning and Development

1. Administrators should dissect the previously collected job analysis data, job design construct, and formal description of the sports or recreation program position.

2. From this job information, (1) assemble and describe the position's goals and objectives, (2) inventory the primary responsibilities for the position, and (3) itemize the key success factors (traits, behaviors, and competencies) for effectual fulfillment of the positions responsibilities, designed to accomplish of the position's goals and objectives.

3. Catalog a definitive list of tangible performance standards expected for the position. These standards will be the foundation for the quantitative and qualitative evaluation measurements for the position.

4. Review the program member's previous performance appraisals to provide background and assist in developing the current period's performance plan and assessment criteria.

5. At the *beginning* of the evaluation period, the direct supervisor and employee review the job design and description, primary responsibilities, key success factors, and tangible performance standards for the program position. A mutual agreement is the ultimate goal of this session.

TABLE 7.1 Performance Management and Evaluations

Benefits	*Drawbacks*
(a) Introspective Analysis provides a chance for self-examining professional and personal developments as the foundation for career planning.	a) Cost and Time are required resources in performance management.
(b) Focuses Operations center the program's operations on tasks and accomplishments, rather than subjective opinions.	b) Human Element can sometimes be difficult to overcome to maintain objectivity without allowing personal bias/feelings to invade the process.
(c) Promotes Consistency and Uniform Execution which brings internal operational efficiency for the program.	c) Stressful or difficult is a common perception of evaluations when an employee is under performing. Administrators typically do not like discussing deficient performance. Often times confrontation voidance and internal defense mechanisms prevail. This can manifest in "turning a blind eye," open hostility, and/or passive aggressive reactions.
(d) Refocused Emphasis on Job Responsibilities provides a clear picture of job expectations and responsibilities which can minimize an employee's anxiety of unknown expectations. The employee can focus on critical aspects of their position because they have a clear understanding of key success factors.	d) Haphazard Commitment to performance management and evaluations can cause irreparable damage to the individual and program. Sporadic and with little emphasis, can make evaluations confusing, irrelevant, and thus squander significant program resources.
(e) Changing Attitudes and Behaviors can have a cascading impact on operations. If positively perceived, they can infuse a vested interest atmosphere throughout the entire program.	e) Developing Tangible Measurement Criteria through standards and measurements can be a problematic, daunting task with certain program positions.
(f) Administrative Clarity that encompasses all program stakeholders, can give administrators a true picture of what is actually happening in the operation. Each individual's performance can be examined in the overall scope of the program, and help determine training needs, validate the selection process, reevaluate job designs/descriptions, modify program and human resource plans, in succession planning, and amplify the utilization of the future human resource asset in the program.	
(g) Strengthen the Sports or Recreation Program's Culture furnishes administrators with an opportunity to develop a powerful, influential rapport with individual program members, which contributes to a high achievement culture.	
(h) Individuality reinforces the importance of the individual in the overall scheme of the operation. Program members understand their integration into the entire structure and its overall achievements.	
(i) Human Resource Administrative Core is the foundation of the employee's internal human resource file. This data is critical when assessing promotions, additional responsibilities, downsizing or layoffs, incentives and rewards, scheduling, and succession planning/depth charts.	
(j) Minimizing Litigation can reduce or eliminate lawsuits from wrongful termination, discriminating treatment, equity issues, etc., if consistent and thorough in application.	

Step #5 is not a "one-way street." The program employee, with their hands-on expertise in the position, should have an unmistakable voice in the job factors listed. They may identify various real-world job performance applications that could readjust the performance plan and measurement criteria significantly (for an increase or decrease in performance assessment standards). In other words, this step is a cooperative agreement on the critical factors of the position and how they are going to be measured. Without this give-and-take relationship, the employee will feel detached from their position and lack investment in achieving personal and program goals and objectives.

At this meeting, all criteria should be definitive, and a written performance plan should be (1) retained for review in the individual's program file as well as (2) given to the program employee for their reference and guidance.

Phase Two: Performance Monitoring

Throughout the evaluation period, the program member should "check-in" periodically with the supervisor to review progress toward their performance standards, as established in the performance plan. For example, if an evaluation period is one year in duration, an employee and supervisor could "sit down" every three months and review the quantitative and qualitative progress of the employee toward their pre-established plan and categorized standards. These discussions can focus on major factors of the position and whether any adjustments need to be made in the plan and individual standards. Independently, the program supervisor monitors and records their observations on the employee's quantitative and qualitative progress throughout the period. An open dialog and coaching during performance monitoring is a salient key to achieving performance measures.

Phase Three: Performance Reviews

At the end of the performance plan's time frame, a final performance review is conducted. It should be implicitly understood that if the administrator or supervisor and program employee are working the performance management system correctly, the final performance evaluation meeting should have no shocking revelations, disclosures, or performance bombshells. Steps for conducting this review will be discussed later in the chapter.

HR Tip

After the final evaluation review meeting the performance management process starts again immediately. It is important to understand that it is a continuous process in which performance is a non-static element that requires ongoing attention.

Approaches to Final Performance Reviews

Traditional. The traditional one-way performance evaluation approach is just that: a one-way conversation where the direct supervisor conducts the performance assessment session with little or no feedback from the program employee. As one can surmise, this method is counterproductive, and negates the entire performance management concept. Its authoritarian nature is prohibitive to an approachable, open dialog and is easy to see that compared with newer, more positive and inclusive approaches, this method does nothing to enhance program performance. Instead, the more progressive cooperative self-evaluation, 360 degree, and multiple appriaser approaches have yielded positive results in performance, satisfaction and operational enhancement.

Cooperative Self-Evaluation. Prior to the final performance review session, the program employee completes a written assessment of their own performance following with the established performance plan and its distinctive performance standards and measurements. It is then copied and submitted to the program supervisor before the final performance review session, where both the individual's self-assessment and the program's performance evaluation are reviewed. The comparison of the individual categories can have three possible outcomes. First, the program employee and administrator see "eye-to-eye" on performance standards and measurements, and both documents validate this conclusion. Second, performance comparisons between both documents illuminates slight/negligible variances. Or, third, considerable disconnects are discovered between performance standards and measurements. No matter what scenario transpires, this cooperative self-evaluation approach presents an outstanding opportunity to have a beneficial, focused dialog on the overall position, the principal job functions, key success factors, performance standards and measurements, and the individual's execution and accomplishments. Slight variances between the two documents (positive or negative) can be reconciled easily. Obviously, large disconnects should trigger significant dialogue for resolution. No matter what the comparison of evaluations show, at the end of the meeting, the supervisor and program employee should be in agreement with performance standards and measurements for each category. Any performance issues that remain unsettled should be well recorded. Both documents, along with any relevant meeting notes, should be retained in the program employee's file.

HR Tip

For a productive and cooperative self-assessment system, the format of the employee's self-assessment form should be pre-established and constructed with as much direct correlation to the program's performance evaluation form. If possible, it is recommended that the official program evaluation form and the self-assessment form be as close as possible in categories, evaluation criteria, and narrative opportunities.

As with every type of interaction within a program, there will be some limitations. Fallon and McConnell (2007) describe several cautions about cooperative self-evaluations:

Self-appraisal can be a productive component of a performance appraisal system. However, self-appraisal is not appropriate for everyone. Some employees are intimidated by it. Others are apprehensive, fearing the possible consequences of rating themselves too high or too low. Self-appraisal is most appropriate for higher-level technical employees, professionals, supervisors, and managers. While self-appraisal has the potential for success, many hourly employees are suspicious of the process and management's intent when using it.... While some people rate themselves higher or lower than may be appropriate, research has repeatedly shown that the majority of employees rate themselves no higher, and frequently lower, than their supervisors rate them. (p. 238)

To curtail these shortcomings, administration must continuously communicate throughout the performance management process, their observations of the individual's performance, and listen to the program employee's opinions and perceptions of their performance. If the supervisor is executing the performance management process appropriately, large disconnects (or revelations) should be curtailed or eliminated.

360 Degree/Multiple Appraiser Approach. This approach works on the same premise as the cooperative self-evaluation approach, but adds additional data to the performance management review.

Jobs are multifaceted, and different people see different things. As the name implies, 360-degree feedback is intended to provide employees with as accurate a view of their performance as possible by getting input from all angles: supervisors, peers, subordinates, customers, and the like. (Snell & Bohlander, 2012, p. 358)

The 360 Degree approach could be used to incorporate the program employee's own self-evaluation (as described previously).

There are a few distinct problems with this approach. The first and most serious relates to truthfulness from all the appraisers. An individual may have their own agenda and construct their evaluation to benefit themselves, rather than providing honest, dispassionate responses to a particular program employee's evaluation. For example, if promotions are competitive within the program, a peer evaluation may reflect negatively or deleteriously toward a rival program member to bolster their own chances of receiving the promotion. Second, the higher number of appraisers, the more synchronized the data collection coordination must be (some would say "running around after" to collect data). Further, the more data collected, the more difficult it is to tabulate and assimilate it into a coherent and accurate summation and layout.

Standardized Performance Evaluation Instruments

While an unlimited number of evaluation instruments and variations and modifications exist, this textbook will examine four primary evaluation instruments applicable to sports and recreation programs.

No matter the type of evaluation instrument a sports or recreation program is utilizing, backup documentation should be used to (1) authenticate as many quantifiable performance standards and measures and (2) bolster and reinforce subjective, qualitative judgements. For example, a performance standard could be used by an assistant college baseball coach to monitor and strengthen the team's semester and annual academic results. The standard and measure could be based on the team's aggregate grade point average (GPA). The quantitative objective for the team's GPA could be a mutually agreed upon and publicized 3.0 GPA (out of 4.0). At the final performance review meeting, all "hard" statistical academic data should be presented to evaluate this performance standard. Additionally, because of the power and retention capacity

TABLE 7.2   Potential Performance Standard Categories

Teamwork and cooperation

Professional experience

Professional development – seminars and continuing education

Public speaking, external committee work, and program representation

Interpersonal one-on-one communication

Creativity and decision making

Personal judgement

Situational assessment and decision making

Academic performance – graduation rates and GPA

Athletic performance – wins and losses, post-season honors, etc.

Efficiency and outcomes

Organizational proficiencies

Innovation

Ancillary contributions to sports or recreation program

Emotional appropriateness

Attendance

Consistency in work output

Stakeholder, donator, and booster interactions

Technical and administrative expertise

Recruiting athletes

of HRIS systems and computers, all statistical data and backup documentation should be retained, along with the program member's final performance review instrument.

Table 7.2 presents some of the possible program performance categories which could be incorporated into most performance evaluation instruments. Undoubtedly, each program position will accentuate different performance categories. Some of these categories can be quantified, while others are judgement based.

Numerical Rating Scale. While there are an abundant number of assessment instruments available, an uncomplicated numerical rating scale (as illustrated in Figure 7.1) could be the most straightforward and suitable mechanism for use in a sports or recreation program.

From the sample in Figure 7.1, the subsequent assertions can be extrapolated about numerical rating scales. They are simple to create, structure, and employ; are capable of being tailored to any/all exclusive sports or recreation program positions; have quantitative performance standards and measurements; can provide opportunities for written clarifications and professional opinions (as short qualitative comments); and can supply category-by-category ratings as well as, through totaling all categories, the entire quantitative job rating for the individual.

Performance Category: Team Academic Achievements
Performance Standard and Measurement: Aggregate Team Grade Point Average of 3.0 (out of 4.0, with no athlete below a 2.25)
Numerical Assessment:

Excellent	Exceeds Expectations	Meets Expectations	Improvement Needed	Not Acceptable
5	4	3	2	1

Evaluator's Comments:

_____
_____
_____
_____
_____
_____

FIGURE 7.1   Numerical Rating Scale

A modification to the numerical rating scale is a graphic rating scale where a continuum is drawn and the evaluator places an X or a checkmark where they think the program member resides in a particular standard. Figure 7.2 is a representation of this evaluation instrument.

The principle drawback to graphic rating scales is they are non-quantifiable. The benefit to this approach is they provide a compelling visual depiction of where a performance falls on an unambiguous scale.

Performance Category: Team Academic Achievements
Performance Standard and Measurement: Performance Standard and Measurement: Aggregate Team Grade Point Average of 3.0 (out of 4.0, with no athlete below a 2.25)
Graphic Assessment:

X
_____
Excellent   Meets Expectations   Not Acceptable

Evaluator's Comments:

_____
_____
_____
_____
_____
_____

FIGURE 7.2   Graphic Rating Scale

Performance Category: Team Academic Achievements
Performance Standard and Measurement: Performance Standard and Measurement: Aggregate Team Grade Point Average of 3.0 (out of 4.0, with no athlete below a 2.25)

Evaluator's Comments:

_____
_____
_____
_____
_____
_____

FIGURE 7.3   Essay Performance

Essay Approach. Under this evaluation instrument,

> no quantitative approach is undertaken. It is an open-ended appraisal of the employees. [The] evaluator describes in his own words what he perceives about the employee's performance. While preparing the essay on the employee, the rater considers the following factors: (a) Job knowledge and potential of the employee; (b) employee's undertaking of the company's programmes, policies, objectives, etc., (c) The employee's relations with co-worker and supervisors; (d) the employee's general planning, organising, and controlling ability; and, (e) the attitudes and perceptions of the employee in general. (Aquinas, 2009, p. 95)

The limitations and complications with the essay approach are apparent. Writing essays can be enormously time consuming. To finalize just one performance evaluation essay (with possibly 10-15 performance standard categories) could reasonably take hours. Administrators and supervisors could rush, restate, or word-for-word duplicate the same comments to accelerate completion of numerous essay evaluations, thus defeating the purpose of individualized performance enrichment. Furthermore, the administrator completing the essay assessment may have poor writing skills, which, not only portrays the evaluator in a negatively, but it depreciates the importance and professionalism needed to validate a program employee's performance. Finally, essays can be perceived, and can actually be totally opinion based. Without quantitative factors to guide the evaluator, they can have an appearance of containing bias, showing favoritism, and, in some cases, overt dislike. To support written comments, backup documentation and statistical data should be presented during the performance review and retained permanently in the program employee's personnel file. Figure 7.3 is an illustration of an essay assessment.

Critical Incident Method. Arthur (2004) describes the critical incident method of evaluating employees and its biggest shortcoming, as simply keeping a log of all the positive and negative behavior of each employee. At the employee's scheduled performance review, this log is used to develop a detailed picture of the employee's performance. This technique helps managers avoid the "recency bias," in which greater weight is assigned to more recent incidents. (p. 135)

The central issue associated with keeping a log of critical incidents, besides recalling only the most current performance actions and behaviors, rather than the entire evaluation period's performance actions and behaviors is in (1) observation opportunities and (2) the mindset and attitude of the evaluating supervisor. A disengaged supervisor may not interact with a program employee and therefore will have insufficient observation opportunities and critical incidences to record. Conversely, a hands-on supervisor may have too many occurrences or actions to observe, differentiate, and record. A cynical or distrusting administrator may only record negative incidences by the program employee. On the other hand, an upbeat, optimistic administrator may selectively remember and record only affirmative, constructive actions by the employee. Thus, for this approach to be legitimate, the direct supervisor or evaluator must have consistent interactions and observation opportunities, be a comprehensive recorder of actions and activities, and have neither a positive or negative attitude toward the job and program employee. Figure 7.4 is a sample design of a critical incident category.

Performance Category: Team Academic Achievements
Performance Standard and Measurement: Aggregate Team Grade Point Average of 3.0 (out of 4.0, with no athlete below a 2.25)

Critical Incident #1
Date of Incident:
Description of Incident:

_____

_____

_____

_____

Evaluator's Comments:

_____

_____

_____

_____

_____

_____

FIGURE 7.4   Critical Incident Performance

Work Standards Approach. While the above evaluation instruments have a blended and a sizeable portion of their assessments as either objective measures or subjective, opinion-based judgements, the work standards approach is almost completely quantitative in nature. Rue, Ibrahim, and Byars (2016) define the work standards approach as "a method of performance appraisal that involves setting a standard or an expected level of output and then comparing each employee's level to the standard. Generally, work standards should reflect the average output of a typical employee" (p. 231). Each performance category, standard, and measure is defined quantitatively as to what is commonly produced by the position and what is agreed upon at the beginning of the performance management process. Those numbers are the baseline

---

Performance Category: Team Academic Achievements
Standard and Measurements:
1. Aggregate Team Grade Point Average of 3.0 (out of 4.0)
2. No athlete below a 2.25
3. All Freshman Completing Required Learning Lab Hours (4 hours per semester week)
4. All Academic Probationary Student-Athletes Completing Learning Lab Hours (6 hours per semester week)
5. 25% of Team on Academic Honor Roll

Standard and Measurement #1: Aggregate Team Grade Point Average of 3.0 out of 4.0
Actual:
+ or – Variance:
Comments:

Standard and Measurement #2: No athlete below a 2.25
Actual:
+ or – Variance:
Comments:

Standard and Measurement #3: All Freshman Completing Required Learning Lab Hours
(4 hours per semester week)
Actual:
+ or – Variance:
Comments:

Standard and Measurement #4: All Academic Probationary Student-Athletes Completing Learning Lab Hours (6 hours per semester week)
Actual:
+ or – Variance:
Comments:

Standard and Measurement #5: 25% of Team on Academic Honor Roll
Actual:
+ or – Variance:
Comments:

FIGURE 7.5   Work Standards

for the category and the individual program employee's targeted goals. At the end of the evaluation period, the "numbers are added up" and recorded on the evaluation instrument.

> **HR Tip**
>
> Obviously, some job functions cannot be quantified with performance quotas. In these cases, an amalgamated approach could be used, which mixes different performance evaluation instruments. For example, a blended construct could utilize the numerical rating scale approach for qualitative and opinion-based performance standard categories, while the work standards approach could be utilized for strictly quantitative categories.

Evaluation instruments must be managed and conducted properly. If inconsistent and improperly administered, performance evaluation documentation can be used against the program in litigation proceedings. Paul Falcone (2005) succinctly describes this potential situation:

> When employees are terminated for cause and bring wrongful termination actions against prior companies, judges and arbitrators look to the consistency in a company's written communication in order to justify the termination and determine which party prevails. This written record is typically found in the form of written warnings and annual performance reviews, laid out side by side on a table as exhibits. But which one is more important in an arbitrator's eyes: the annual review or the written warning? Generally speaking, the annual appraisal is given more weight in legal deliberations because it covers an entire year's work...the annual appraisal is generally viewed as the "anchor" document that evidences the company's formal communication record with its worker. (p. 8)

> **HR Tip**
>
> No matter how unpleasant and uncomfortable a performance evaluation, it is critical that the conversation and documentation be as accurate and as dispassionate as possible. To "soft sell" or avoid addressing unacceptable performance issues can lead to serious difficulties in the sports or recreation program's future.

How to Conduct Performance Evaluations: Guidelines and Suggestions

Conventional recommendations, procedures, and tips for conducting final face-to-face performance evaluation review meetings are provided to assist program administrators properly plan for and conduct performance evaluations.

1. Prepare in Advance. With all business meetings, one should always be as organized and prepared as possible. This assertion is exceptionally significant when conducting performance evaluation reviews.

2. Clarity. Prior to the conference, make sure the program employee understands and is comfortable with the (1) overall performance management process and (2) the final evaluation instrument.

3. Present All Relevant Documentation. No matter what, all performance evaluation documents (instrument and accompanying support data, originals and copies) should be ready for distribution and examination at the performance review meeting. Both the program employee's evaluation packet and final program performance forms should be sequentially ordered and based on the review elements to be discussed.

4. Know the Employee's Job. Some program administrators supervise dozens of program positions. It can be burdensome to recall all of the complexities and intricacies of each position. Prior to the actual performance review meeting, briefly reexamine the specific position's responsibilities, environmental elements, key success factors, and overall hierarchical strata in the program. It would also be prudent to prepare a copy of the latest job description for reference at the meeting.

5. Listen. During the evaluation review, make a concerted effort to listen to the program employee. They can explain (1) why they achieved certain results, (2) what mitigating factors hampered the completion of certain tasks, (3) how they can improve in the future, and (4) how they feel about the work, position, and program.

6. Be Straightforward. Sports or recreation program personnel will appreciate an administrator who is upfront, honest, and sincere. The indispensable side effects of this tactic are transparency and minimized misinterpretations ormisunderstandings.

7. Emotional Neutrality. At all times, keep emotions out of the performance evaluation discussion. Emotions can spawn corresponding emotions, and even amplified emotions. An extreme emotional environment can cloud judgement and obstruct (or even totally block) information being transmitted.

8. Empathy. Be supportive and, in some cases, sympathetic throughout the entire review session. A simple but useful strategy is to imagine experiencing the review meeting from the employee's point of view.

9. Enlist Program Employees. To be of consequence, program employees must contribute input in the appraisal meeting. Without their participation, the evaluation loses value for the individual and program. With extroverted personnel, encouragement is not necessary, however, introverted individuals may need to be "drawn out" and actively enlisted into the session. Ask questions, wait for responses, and follow-up on responses to keep the dialog relevant and ongoing. Once more, the information derived will be meaningful to the sports or recreation program.

10. Positive Atmosphere. Keep the performance review meeting as positive and motivational as possible. This type of ambiance is conducive to free-flowing ideas and improvements.

11. Performance Problem-Solving. When discussing performance concerns, delineate what the issues are, and provide viable solutions. Solicit solutions from the program employee as well.

12. Interconnectivity. Employees must appreciate the interconnection of performance management and evaluations to (1) extrinsic organization rewards, (2) promotions, (3) job security, and (4) job satisfaction.

13. Overachievers. While the primary function of final performance reviews is for acknowledgement and, in some cases, improvement, overachievers being evaluated should also know their limitations and stretch objectives. A program employee who consistently exceeds expectations is a highly valued asset. Unfortunately, these individuals often push themselves to "the breaking point." The supervising administrator should recognize this and not contribute to their self-inflicted professional burnout. A performance evaluation review is an excellent opportunity to address this possible conundrum and discuss ways to continue high productivity while having a balanced life outside work.

14. Signatures. For internal human resource records, all evaluation instruments should be signed by all relevant parties. These signatures indicate acknowledgement of the review session and documentation.

HR Tip

All performance evaluations should retain the highest level of confidentiality and should be discussed with only the most directly involved administrators. As with all human resource personnel interactions, privacy is a mandated obligation.

Performance Improvement Action Planning

When there are considerable disparities between a program employee's performance standards and measures and actual performance results, corrective improvements can be accomplished in an action plan.

> Action planning requires HR program participants to develop detailed plans for accomplishing specific objectives related to the program. Usually prepared on the organization's customized form, an action plan shows what is to be done, by whom, and when. The action plan approach is a straightforward, easy-to-use method for determining ways in which participants can implement improvements. (Phillips, Phillips, & Smith, 2016, p. 131)

From this definition, an individualized performance improvement plan, based on a performance issues (missing targets and underperforming in performance measures and standards) is as follows:

> A performance improvement plan is a tool to monitor and measure an employee's deficient work products, processes, and/or behaviors to improve performance or modify behavior. It should be constructively and clearly communicated how the inadequate performance determination was made, what corrective and/or disciplinary action will be taken, by whom and when, and when and how the individual's performance will be reviewed again. A performance improvement plan

should be created in partnership with the employee to help address the performance obstacles being faced and to increase the employee's commitment to the plan and to behavior change. (Phillips & Gully, 2014, p. 270)

The construction of a performance improvement action plan is uncomplicated and clear-cut. Figure 7.6 provides a basic template for constructing a sports or recreation program's performance improvement action plan.

Program Employee:
Program/Division:
Date of Performance Review:
Performance Category:
Established Performance Standards and Measurements:
Actual Program Member's Performance:
Action Plan Steps (if applicable):
Step #1 –
Step #2 –
Step #3 -
Behavioral Modifications/Expectations (if applicable):
Administrative Review Points (Chronological progression toward performance improvements):

Review Point Date #1:
Expectations:

Review Point Date #2:
Expectations:

Review Point Date #3:
Expectations:

Consequences of inactivity or poor progression toward performance improvement:

Employee Signature:
Date:
Program Supervisor Signature:
Date:

**If the sports or recreation program employee has multiple deficiencies in performance, this form could be (1) used for each performance standard area or (2) modified into one all-inclusive form.

FIGURE 7.6   Performance Improvement Action Plan Template

> **HR Tip**
>
> The turn-around and success of a sports or recreation program employee's performance can often be contingent upon the administrator's commitment to the action plan. While the onus for completing the action plan's progression is on the individual, it is essential that review dates be strictly followed by supervisors as well as conducting periodic (informal) conversations based on corrective improvements.

> **HR Tip**
>
> Action plans are living documents. They should not be used for discouragement or termination, but for re-motivation and correction. Action plan expectations should be realistic and achievable.

Summary

A sports or recreation program's success directly relates to its personnel's performance. To ensure this success through proficient, focused performance, a systematized and functioning performance management process and performance evaluation instruments are essential. Sports and recreation program employees, through a participative step-by-step process, will have a palpable "voice" in how their positions establish and achieve goals and objectives. Their final performance assessments will provide them with critical information on whether they achieved, exceeded, or missed program and personal standards. If drastic inadequacies in a program employee's job performance are recognized and documented at the end of the performance cycle, a performance improvement action plan can be developed to correct the individual's work deficiencies.

References

Aquinas, P. G. (2009). *Human resource management: Principles and practice*. New Delhi, India: Vikas Publishing House.

Armstrong, M. (2015). *Armstrong's handbook of performance management: An evidence-based guide to delivering high performance* (5th ed.). London, England: Kogan Page.

Arthur, D. (2004). *Fundamentals of human resource management* (4th ed.). New York, NY: AMACOM.

Deb, T. (2008). *Performance appraisals and management: Concepts, antecedents and implications*. New Delhi, India: Excel Books.

Falcone, P. (2005). *2600 Phases for effective performance reviews: Ready-to-use words and phrases that really get results*. New York, NY: AMACOM.

Fallon, L. F., & McConnell, C. R. (2007). *Human resource management in health care: Principles and practice*. Sudbury, MA: Jones and Bartlett Publishers.

Phillips, J. M., & Gully, S. M. (2014). *Human resource management*. Mason, OH: South-Western/Cengage.

Phillips, J. J., Phillips, P. P., & Smith, K. (2016). *Accountability in human resource management: Connecting HR to business results* (2nd ed.). New York, NY: Routledge.

Rue, L. W., Ibrahim, N. A., & Byars, L. L. (2016). *Human resource management* (11th ed.). New York, NY: McGraw-Hill.

Snell, S., & Bohlander, G. (2012). *Managing human resources* (16th ed.). Mason, OH: South-Western/Cengage.

Review and Discussion Questions

1. Define performance management.

2. What are performance evaluations?

3. What is the win-win benefit of performance management and evaluations?

4. What administrative clarity can performance management and evaluations provide the sports or recreation program?

5. Discuss the time and cost drawbacks of performance management and evaluations.

6. What are the three phases in the performance management process?

7. Describe the seven steps in the performance management process.

8. Why should a sports or recreation program employee have a voice in their performance management process?

9. What is the one-way approach to final performance reviews?

10. What is the cooperative self-evaluation approach to final performance reviews?

11. What is the 360 degree/multiple appraiser approach to final performance reviews?

12. Name and describe five possible performance standard categories.

13. Why is it important to have back-up documentation for final performance evaluation review meetings?

14. What are numerical rating scales?

15. What are graphic rating scales?

16. What are some limitations to the essay evaluation instrument?

17. Describe the work standards evaluation instrument.

18. If inconsistent and improperly administered, what are the litigation concerns for performance evaluation instruments?

19. Why is listening important in final performance evaluation review meetings?

20. What is emotional neutrality in final performance evaluation review meetings?

21. What is a major concern in dealing with overachievers?

22. What are performance improvement action plans?

23. What are the major categories in a performance improvement action plan?

Application Exercises

1. From online research, construct a numerical rating scale evaluation instrument for one of the following positions:
   - Head strength and conditioning coach (professional – any sport)
   - Facility and equipment coordinator (city recreation department)

- Professional minor league baseball manager

The evaluation instrument should have 10–15 relevant performance standards categories and performance standards and measurements (see Figure 7.1).

2. From online research, find a high-profile college coach (any sport, any level) who has experienced performance issues. These issues can range from underperforming teams (win/loses) to off-court or field concerns and behaviors. From their situation, construct a performance improvement action plan to correct their various issues. Use Figure 7.6 as a template for your performance improvement action plan.

Human Resource Management Term Project
Individual/Group Written and Oral Presentation

You and your group are the new administrators for a small private community center (YMCA, YWCA, JCC, etc.) program. The department is growing rapidly and has no formalized performance management and evaluation system in place. Design (from the ground up) a performance management program for this organization.

Elements:

- Research human resource performance management programs that can be used by the operation. Use HR sources (online and journals) to do your research.

- Justify each component of the performance management program and why it would be appropriate for the operation.

- Discuss new software and hardware requirements, costs, and benefits of the performance management program.

- Develop a comprehensive performance evaluation instrument(s).

Term Project Criteria:

- Oral presentation
    - Develop a 30-minute presentation that details the program's performance management and evaluation system.

    - Prepare for a 15-minute Q & A session after main presentation.

    - Create PowerPoint slides and visual aids to supplement the presentation (hard copy to be submitted prior to presentation).

    - Conduct extensive external research to justify your selections.

- Written presentation
    - For all members of the audience, prepare a performance management and evaluation presentation packet. The packet should include:
        ○ Introduction
        ○ Performance management program
        ○ Selected performance evaluation instrument
        ○ Criteria for performance management system implementation (timelines, documentation, procedures, etc.)
        ○ Conducting performance evaluations; procedures and tips
        ○ Conclusion

chapter eight

Reward Systems

Chapter Objectives

- Understand the role of rewards management in sports and recreation programs
- Define intrinsic and extrinsic rewards
- Understand the fundamental elements involved in financial compensation
- Understand the difference between exempt and nonexempt employees
- Understand methods for internal job compensation evaluation
- Understand market value pricing and salary surveys
- Explain four primary ways for salaries and wages to be adjusted/increased
- Understand a variety of incentive-based reward systems
- Understand the elements of an organizational benefits package
- Understand the concept of pay equity and its impact on an organization

Key Terms

Program Rewards
Rewards Management
Intrinsic Rewards
Extrinsic Rewards
Financial Compensation
Base Pay, Hourly
Overtime Pay
Minimum Wage Restrictions
Base Pay, Salary
Exempt Employees
Nonexempt Employees
Fair Labor Standards Act
Piece-Rate
Differential Piece-Rate
Internal Job Compensation
   Evaluation Method
Positional Ranking

Job Grades
Point and Dollar Valuing
Computerized Valuation
Salary Surveys
Seniority
Merit Performance Pay Increases
Cost of Living/Across the Board
   Raises
Year-End Performance Pay
Incentives
Reward Differential
Short-Term Incentives
Long-Term Incentives
Health Related Benefits
Medical Insurance
Health Savings Account
HMO Programs

PPO Programs
Hospital/Clinical/Surgical
   Insurance
Emergency Room Coverage
Dental Insurance
Vision/Eye Care Insurance
Prescription Reimbursement/
   Insurance
Insurance Related Benefits
Life Insurance
Short-Term Disability
Long-Term Disability
Accident Insurance
Critical Illness Insurance
Downsizing/Early Retirement
   Insurance
Business Travel Insurance

Continued

169

Time Off/Leave Benefits
Paid Personal Time Off
Medical/Sick Leave
Bereavement/Compassion Leave
Jury Duty
Community Volunteer Service
Compensated Holiday Time Off
Religious Time Off
Sabbatical/LOA
Military Obligation Paid Leave

Maternity Leave
Retirement/Pension Benefits
Defined Contribution
    Retirement Programs
401k
Individual Retirement Accounts
    (IRAs)
Defined Benefit Plans
Employee Stock Ownership
    Options

Employee Assistance and
    Wellness Programs
In-Kind Scholarship Programs
    for Dependents
Daycare for Family Members
Cafeteria Benefit Plans
Pay Equity
Organizational Equity

Program Rewards

There is no subject in business that can generate such penetrating and impassioned discussion as rewards management. When administered appropriately, rewards management can provide a sports and recreation program with a balanced, well-ordered working environment. Regrettably, if mismanaged, rewards management can have disastrous wide-ranging consequences on the psyche of the sports or recreation program. By not extending competitive and equitable rewards, a program can experience short-term profits, but ultimately suffer long-term difficulties, especially retaining its outstanding employees.

> Rewards management is based on well-articulated philosophy—a set of beliefs and guiding principles that are consistent with the values of the organization and help to enact them. These include the beliefs in the need to achieve, fairness, equity, consistency, and transparency in operating the rewards system. The philosophy recognizes that if HRM [Human Resource Management] is about investing in human capital from which a reasonable return is required, then it is proper to reward people differently according to their contribution (i.e., the return of investment they generate). (Armstrong, 2006, p. 624)

The three primary areas of rewards management are financial compensation, incentives and bonuses, and benefits.

Intrinsic and Extrinsic Rewards

Before a discussion can be made on the subject of human resource essentials in sports or recreation program financial compensation, incentives and bonuses, and benefits, administrators must appreciate the principles of intrinsic rewards and extrinsic rewards.

> Intrinsic rewards are largely a function of job content... the individuals themselves derive and administer intrinsic rewards. To the extent that the intrinsic rewards reside in the job itself and that workers administer them, the organization does not have much control over them as it has over extrinsic rewards, such as pay and bonuses. (Chelladuria, 2006, p. 232)

Intrinsically driven rewards differ from employee to employee. Each individual will have divergent internal levels of satisfaction based on the completion and success of program undertakings. A key purpose of the step-by-step interview process (detailed in Chapter 5) is to hire and retain program employees who have a passionate intensity of intrinsic enthusiasm to accomplish the responsibilities of the position for which they were hired. Never underestimate this passionate zeal in an individual. It can induce them to undertake and achieve program assignments (through their heightened level of personal satisfaction in their job) beyond basic work duties. Additionally, this passion is contagious and can permeate itself throughout the program.

Extrinsic rewards, which are remunerations such as salary, incentives, bonuses, and program related benefits and "perks," are determined by the economic situation of the program, the importance of the position, and the credentials and experiences of the employee. Sports and recreation administrators, coaches, and general personnel can be eligible for compensation that compare with any corporate employee. Their rewards and benefits can include salaries or wages, commissions, performance bonuses, vacation and sick leave, pension and retirement, profit sharing, worker's compensation, and more. Simply stated, the concentration and variety of extrinsic rewards is dictated by the organization's fiscal condition and identifiable circumstance.

Different Types of Financial Compensation

While sports or recreation program rewards should be viewed holistically, the core item of any position's rewards package is financial: direct monetary compensation. It is the primary component of a position that attracts potential employees to a sports or recreation program and is frequently a strong factor in their retention. Organizations often examine financial compensation management primarily on its upfront financial risk (money committed) and ending with return on its investment (productivity generated). Employees often look at financial compensation as a profound statement from the organization and its administrators of their perceived worth to the program.

The subsequent definitions of compensation are straightforward, but essential and provide foundational choices for administrators in making compensation decisions for sports or recreation program employees.

Base Pay, Hourly. A hourly base pay system is a fixed, predetermined hourly rate of pay in which the employee is paid for the hours worked. Provisions are established to compensate the employee for overtime hours that can include, but are not limited to (1) working over an eight-hour day and (2) working over a 40-hour workweek. The standard overtime rate is 1½ times the hourly rate. For example, a clerical worker, whose standard hourly rate is $15.00 per hour, would make $22.50 per hour for any time worked over eight hours in a day, or 40 hours in a standard work week. Hourly pay increases can also be determined for shift differential pay (working outside normal operating hours) and holiday pay. The federal national minimum wage in 2019 is $7.25 per hour. This rate does not account for any state-by-state modifications/increases.

Base Pay, Salary. A salaried base pay is essentially a fixed annual amount, customarily distributed weekly, semi-monthly, or monthly, that does not change and is remunerated without regard to the volume of occupational output or time worked. In essence, while the individual is employed, they are guaranteed to receive a fixed amount on fixed dates based on their annual salary agreement.

Exempt and Non-Exempt Employees. Employment exemption status has recently generated new regulatory scrutiny and enforcement from the Fair Labor Standards Act (FLSA) and the Department of Labor in regard to overtime pay. According to Mathis, Jackson, Valentine, and Meglich (2017), "exempt employees hold positions for which they are not paid overtime. Nonexempt employees must be paid overtime" (p. 407). To determine if a position is exempt from overtime pay, Table 8.1, derived directly from the US Department of Labor's website are used by US businesses to aid administrators in properly compensating employees based on their status.

As with a majority of human resource decisions, it is strongly advised to meet with legal counsel to correctly determine the exemption status of new and current sports or recreation program positions. The Department of Labor website is an excellent source for exemption and other labor regulations.

From Table 8.1, it can be deduced that some sports or recreation program positions are totally exempt from overtime, while others could be classified as salary with overtime, based on the salary rate, and some positions would be classified as nonexempt and eligible for overtime.

Piece-Rate Compensation. Piece-rate compensation structure is based on the precise productivity of an employee. Basically, the employee is compensated on the number of completed units produced at an agreed upon price per unit. Differential piece-rate establishes a standard level of output for a designated period of time and pays a higher rate for every unit above the standard, and lower rates if the standard is not met. For example, in an eight-hour day, a standard level of output for an employee is 50 units per day. This number should be established by cumulative averages and valid measurements. At 50 units per day, the employee will receive $3.00 per unit. If the employee produces 60 units, the first 50 are compensated at $3.00 per unit and the remaining 10 could be assigned a differential compensation at 3.50 per unit. Conversely, if an employee does not meet the standard level of output for an eight-hour work day, they may be compensated $2.75 per unit instead of $3.00. While this compensation system in sports or recreation programs could be problematic, it is nevertheless possible and is a widely-used structure.

Designing Reward Systems

Two primary areas are used to determine and construct compensation systems in a sports or recreation program. These are job evaluation, and external market value pricing.

Job Evaluation Methods. Job evaluation determine sports or recreation program rewards by an internal examination of each position for (1) its operational components, based on job analysis data, (2) assessing those components and functions for their worth to the operation, and (3) comparing each job within the operation for its importance and value to the entire program.

> The outcome of a traditional job evaluation process is a set of job classifications, perhaps expressed as a formal hierarchy of jobs…. Traditional job evaluation involves the comparison of jobs in a formal, systematic way to identify their relative value to an organization. It has an underlying premise: that some jobs are worth more than others. (Price, 2011, p. 436)

TABLE 8.1 U.S. Department of Labor Exemption Regulations

Exemptions	• Some employees are exempt from the overtime pay provisions or both the minimum wage and overtime pay provisions.
	• Because exemptions are generally narrowly defined under the FLSA, an employer should carefully check the exact terms and conditions for each. Detailed information is available from local Department of Labor offices.
	• Following are examples of exemptions which are illustrative, but not all-inclusive. These examples do not define the conditions for each exemption.
Exemptions from Both Minimum Wage and Overtime Pay	• Executive, administrative, and professional employees (including teachers and academic administrative personnel in elementary and secondary schools), outside sales employees, and employees in certain computer-related occupations (as defined in DOL regulations);
	• Employees of certain seasonal amusement or recreational establishments, employees of certain small newspapers, seamen employed on foreign vessels, employees engaged in fishing operations, and employees engaged in newspaper delivery;
	• Farmworkers employed by anyone who used no more than 500 "man-days" of farm labor in any calendar quarter of the preceding calendar year;
	• Casual babysitters and persons employed as companions to the elderly or infirm.
Exemptions from Overtime Pay Only	• Certain commissioned employees of retail or service establishments; auto, truck, trailer, farm implement, boat, or aircraft sales-workers; or parts-clerks and mechanics servicing autos, trucks, or farm implements, who are employed by non-manufacturing establishments primarily engaged in selling these items to ultimate purchasers;
	• Employees of railroads and air carriers, taxi drivers, certain employees of motor carriers, seamen on American vessels, and local delivery employees paid on approved trip rate plans;
	• Announcers, news editors, and chief engineers of certain non-metropolitan broadcasting stations;
	• Domestic service workers living in the employer's residence;
	• Employees of motion picture theaters; and
	• Farmworkers.

Continued

TABLE 8.1 (*Continued*)   U.S. Department of Labor Exemption Regulations

Partial Exemptions from Overtime Pay	• Partial overtime pay exemptions apply to employees engaged in certain operations on agricultural commodities, and to employees of certain bulk petroleum distributors.
	• Hospitals and residential care establishments may adopt, by agreement with their employees, a 14-day work period instead of the usual 7-day workweek if the employees are paid at least time and one-half their regular rates for hours worked over 8 in a day or 80 in a 14-day work period, whichever is the greater number of overtime hours.
	• Employees who lack a high school diploma, or who have not attained the educational level of the 8th grade, can be required to spend up to 10 hours in a workweek engaged in remedial reading or training in other basic skills without receiving time and one-half overtime pay for these hours. However, the employees must receive their normal wages for hours spent in such training and the training must not be job specific.
	• Public agency fire departments and police departments may establish a work period ranging from 7 to 28 days in which overtime need only be paid after a specified number of hours in each work period.

Source: U.S. Department of Labor. (https://www.dol.gov/whd/regs/compliance/hrg.htm#8)

HR Tip

When using any of the internal job compensation evaluation methods for developing compensation structures, keep in mind that the assessments are for the position being valued, not the current or past individual in that position. The tangible, unbiased information gathered from the position's job analysis (Chapter 4) should be the prime source for the evaluation.

Table 8.2 shows various fundamental approaches for internal job evaluations that could be used by sports and recreation programs to determine compensation.

Market Value Pricing using Salary Survey Research. A salary survey is used to determine the actual real-world market value and compensation structure for professional employment positions. Dessler (2013) describes salary surveys as "aimed at determining prevailing wage rates. A good salary survey provides specific wage rates for specific jobs. Formal written questionnaire surveys are the most comprehensive, but telephone surveys and newspaper ads are also sources of information. (p. 369)

Additionally, Dressler (2013) discusses both governmental sources and pay data websites to utilize when constructing market value data on various professional positions.

TABLE 8.2   Internal Job Compensation Evaluation Tactics

Positional Ranking	In a depth chart of perceived importance, rank the positions in the operation from the most important to least and develop a pay structure on those determinations.
Job Grades	Create a job grade structure based on different levels of job responsibilities, skills needed, experience required, and other relevant criteria, and place jobs in those grades. Each job grade has a pay range on which to compensate employees.
Point and Dollar Valuing	Examine specific functions of each position and assign either points with relative values, or actual dollar amounts for each task. The total of all tasks, either in points or dollars, will determine the position wage/salary.
Computerized Job Valuation	Input job functions and responsibilities into a software program with a preset algorithm designed to values the position.

Website	*URL Link*
U.S. Department of Labor, Bureau of Labor Statistics National Compensation Survey	www.bls.gov/bls/wages.htm
Salary	https://www.salary.com/
JobStar	jobstar.org/tools/salary/sal-prof.php
CNN Money	cnnmoney.com

(p. 369)

The main advantage for applying market pricing is its ability to stay actively competitive in creating and maintaining compensation levels. In other words, "you know where you stand" in comparison to other similar sports or recreation programs when it comes to rewards and compensation. The difficulty in using this method is monitoring external markets (in this case sports or recreation operations) to determine if there are any major environmental changes which could impact the program's compensation structure.

Adjustments and Compensation Augmentation

There are four primary ways for employee salaries and wages to be adjusted: senority, merit performance, cost of living, and year-end increases.

Seniority increases are based on time served with the operation. They are not based on productivity, but rather on loyalty to the operation. A distinct advantage is this method is easy to design and implement. For every level in which "years of service" are defined, a designated percent a wage or salary is given. Another primary advantage is in its equity. Its primary disadvantage is its disregard for exceptional performance.

Merit Performance Pay increases are based on performance. Under this system, if an employee has exceptional performance and output for the program, they will see a merit-based raise over and above any other pay increase, thus rewarding and strongly encouraging increases in employee performance. The difficulty is often related to it subjectivity, as many merit-based pay increases are based on performance assessments, in which bias (either positive or negative), could have serious financial consequences for program employees.

Cost of Living/Across the Board Raises are similar to seniority raises but are determined by external economic factors. Once again, the percentage applied equitably, but the incentive to sports or recreation program employees to focus on the operation and its goals is depreciated.

Year-End Performance Pay increases, based on pay for performance categories and definitive results, are best described by Banfield and Kay (2012):

> Rather than simply awarding a bonus payment, performance-related pay usually refers to the system used to calculate the pay raise awarded to the individual, which is linked to a measure of his or her performance over a given period of time. Pay raises tend to be awarded annually for salaried and professional staff, but might be awarded at other intervals depending on the scheme in place. The performance element might be the whole of the award or an additional amount. (p. 326)

Performance raises are not bonuses but actual year-end salary increases, based on the overall output of the individual.

Incentives and Bonuses Practice

The first question that arises with incentives and bonuses is, Why use them? The answer is unmistakably clear. Whether they are individual, group, or program-wide in nature, incentives and bonuses are incredibly motivational to program employees. If a definitive link exists between one's performance and the potential incentives being offered, it can be used for amplifying productivity, enhancing quality, expediting completion times, reaffirming safety management targets, improving teamwork and program cooperation, and, ultimately, fulfilling the sports or recreation program strategies and goals.

HR Tip

Incentive programs should at all times be utilized as positive motivators for program employees. They are not for internal competition, but rather for celebration of accomplishments.

Phillips and Gully (2014), in their textbook *Human Resource Management*, have defined three key concepts in incentive-based reward systems: reward differentiation, short-term incentives, and long-term incentives. Reward differentiation is based on performance rather than giving all employees the same reward. Differentiating rewards allows the organization to communicate to the majority of employees that "Your performance was good, and you are getting the targeted rewards." The smaller

TABLE 8.3   Types of Program Incentives and Bonuses

- One-time cash or equivalent bonus for organizational performance: wins, successful activities, GPA, community involvement
- Courtesy vehicles for personal/program travel
- Auto insurance and gas allotment for travel
- Travel per diem or direct travel reimbursements for travel
- Program-related merchandise
- Unlimited periodic free of charge use of program facility and equipment
- Sanctioning independent merchandise agreements
- Gift cards for entertainment, dinning, merchandise, or gasoline
- Vacations and trips (private travel costs)
- Attendance at conferences and specialized instruction
- Free attendance at award ceremonies and banquets
- Facility or reserved optimal parking location
- Unrestricted therapeutic medical examinations and free program training services
- Restricted/unrestricted meal programs
- Participation in organization gain/profit-sharing programs
- Full or partial summer sports camp profits
- Health club memberships
- Professional memberships associated program position
- Accommodation/housing stipends
- Tuition reimbursement or free of cost professional development courses
- Free credit union banking
- Free tax services (planning and filing)
- Financial planning and legal counsel services
- Extended program employment contracts
- Use of program credit cards
- Providing program cell phones
- Retail discounts with sponsoring venders

group of high performers receive the message, "Your performance was outstanding and your rewards are above target." (p. 326)

Phillips and Gully (2014) go onto describe short-term incentives as one-time, variable rewards used to motivate employee behavior and performance for typically in a period one year or less. (Long-term incentives are intended to motivate employee behavior and performance that support company value and long-term organizational health. (p. 328)

Several fundamental guidelines assist with creating and deploying incentives in sports and recreation programs. It should be noted that some incentives are directly related to exceeding performance standards, while others are "upfront incentives" already built into or could be permanently added to a sports and recreation program position. These "perks" of the job, proactively incorporated to increase productivity, heighten performance expectations, retain personnel, and increase the overall attractiveness of the position.

The initial and most important guideline in utilizing incentives and bonuses is economic. A sports or recreation program's incentive system must be economically feasible, or within the operation's financial means. This can necessitate administrative creativity while still maintaining fiscal responsibility.

Incentives must be universally known throughout the operation for accomplishments that are "over and above" expected and required job functions. Clearly communicated incentive criteria, whether the measures from standard assessments of job responsibilities, tangible innovations, extra assignments and duties, should be plainly understood, suitable for the program's operation, and directly tied into the program vision, mission, values, and strategic goals. The incentive benchmarks cannot be giveaways or, conversely, out of reach of being accomplished. Incentives should be challenging but achievable.

The renumeration (payment/distribution) of incentives should be as soon as they have been earned. The quicker incentives and bonuses are distributed, the more the actual exceptional performance will be reinforced. Additionally, the payment/distribution of special incentives and bonuses should be visible to other sports or recreation program members as program-wide motivators.

Finally, for sports or recreation program emoloyees to be receptive to an incentive program, they must (1) have confidence in the administration to oversee and manage the program, (2) have trust and assurances the incentive system is equitable and fair, and (3) perceive the incentive to be attractive and desirable to entice involvement. Without these three aspects, full or even partial participation could be problematic.

> **HR Tip**
>
> Often times the tangible incentive earned is secondary to the actual recognition received by the incentive system that increases program employee motivation and job satisfaction. Distributing incentives at public events, such as banquets and awards ceremonies can impact the program employee's long-term motivation far beyond and long after the real incentive has been forgotten.

Benefits Options

Program employee benefit packages are developed from a philosophical perspective, as well as financial outlook. If a sports and recreation program is employee centered and 100% committed to its workforce, it will— within all resource restriction—attempt to provide the most advantageous benefit program for all of its internal stakeholders. Table 8.4 lists the potential components of a sports or recreation program's benefit package. This listing is outside of federal and state required benefits (e.g. unemployment, Social Security/ Medicare, worker's compensation, etc.).

The quantity and complexity of conceivable employee benefits is beyond the scope of this textbook. When creating a complete benefit program or adjusting current benefits, it is strongly recommended to employ a benefits specialist or consultant. These expert professionals can adeptly develop or remodel

TABLE 8.4 Components of an Organizational Benefits Package (Partially or Fully Funded)

Health Related	Medical insurance
	Health savings account
	HMO programs (health management organizations)
	PPO programs (preferred provider organizations)
	Hospital/clinical/surgical insurance
	Emergency room coverage
	Dental insurance
	Vision/eye care insurance
	Prescription reimbursement
Insurance Related	Prescription reimbursement/insurance
	Long-term disability
	Accident insurance
	Critical illness insurance
	Downsizing or early retirement insurance
	Business travel insurance
Time Off/Leave	Paid personal time off (PTO program)
	Medical or sick leave (personal reserve or illness banking)
	Bereavement/compassion leave
	Jury duty
	Community volunteer service
	Compensated holidays and special days: birthdays, family events
	Religious time off
	Sabbaticals/leave of absence
	Military obligation paid leave
	Maternity leave
Retirement/Pension	Defined contribution retirement programs (portable)
	401k
	Individual retirement accounts (IRA)
	Defined benefit plans (employer administered investments, nonportable)
	Employee stock ownership options
Miscellaneous	Employee assistance and wellness programs
	In-kind scholarship programs for dependents (within a network of colleges and universities)
	Daycare for family members; child or senior care (facility or subcontracted)
	Cafeteria benefit programs

a program's comprehensive benefits package based on the operation's philosophy, needs, and financial situation.

If the program has resources and would be considered large or substantial in terms of the number of employees, departments, and divisions), a benefit option could be to offer a cafeteria benefits program (also known as flexible benefits). A cafeteria benefits program allows employees

> to put together their own package by choosing those benefits that best meet their personal needs. Under this arrangement, the organization will establish a budgeted amount that it is willing to spend per employee, and the individual is then allowed to decide how to spend the money. For example, some employees may want more life insurance because they have a young family, whereas others may prefer to spend more on health insurance coverage because they have a spouse with a debilitating illness. (Luthans, Luthans, & Luthans, 2015, p. 94)

The significant key for a cafeteria program delivering constructive benefits is having sound consultations from expert benefits specialists throughout the entire process. While these programs can be complex in the variety and number of benefit choices, they need to be in the best interest of every individual involved. Providing program literature in advance of benefit selection, as well as private consultation (the day of an individual's open enrollment) can help facilitate the best benefit package for all program employees.

Pay Equity, The Right Managerial Practice

The idea of pay equity stems from the inclusive concept of organizational equity (or equity theory). Equity theory states that "employees compare their inputs (efforts) and outputs (rewards) with those of other employees. If an employee believes that he or she is being unfairly rewarded for efforts, compared to a fellow employee, then dissatisfaction will result" (Mills, Mills, Bratton, & Forshaw, 2007, p. 225). Pay inequity, when exposed—and it will be exposed—can radically impact

- the quality and condition of outputs;
- quantity of outputs;
- workforce attendance and punctuality;
- individual job enthusiasm and fulfillment;
- employee attitudes on working with other stakeholders;
- respecting and underscoring safety protocols; and
- physical and emotional investments into the sports or recreation programs mission and strategic goals.

When inequitable discrepancies are apparent in a sports and recreation program, it often goes far beyond an inadvertent miscalculation in someone's rewards and workload. Inequity, in any form, can be a core philosophical issue in a program in which people are being treated differently for comparable contributions. With more and more transparency in business operations, inequitable situations will be accentuated and in public view. This can generate major internal issues, such as high turnover, personnel frustration, collapse of group cohesion, and legal issues or liabilities, as well public relations difficulties. The solutions to program inequity are easy to remedy, and are based on sound, commonsense business practices. Pay according to preestablished and universally known formulas. Be overtly transparent in all rewards and pay situations. Base rewards and pay on definitive positions, seniority formulas, and tangible contributions to the operation, rather than the person in those positions. Know the market value of each sports or recreation program position. When an inequitable situation is unearthed, proceed immediately to resolve the issue. Finally, schedule periodic equitable pay audits which examine, not only at internal reward practices, but other similar program reward systems. A pronounced motto of the sports or recreation program should be "Treat everyone equally."

Summary

To keep your "team" of sports or recreation program employees together and functioning efficiently, rewards management is an operational area that needs ongoing attention. Through financial compensation, incentives, bonuses, and benefits, administrators can construct attractive reward packages that will assist in recruiting and retaining exceptional talent. If the concept of internal pay equity is emphasized, an atmosphere of fairness and teamwork will be fostered.

References

Armstrong, M. (2006). *The handbook of human resource management practice* (10th ed.). London, UK: Kogan Page.

Banfield, P., & Kay, R. (2012). *Introduction to human resource management* (2nd ed.). Oxford, EN: Oxford University Press.

Chelladuria, P. (2006). *Human resource management in sport and recreation* (2nd ed.). Champaign, IL: Human Kinetics.

Dressler, G. (2013). *Human resource management* (13th ed.). Upper Saddle River, NJ: Pearson.

Luthans, F., Luthans, B. C., & Luthans, K. W. (2015). *Organizational behavior: An evidence-based approach* (13th ed.). Charlotte, NC: Information Age Publishing.

Mathis, R. L., Jackson, J. H., Valentine, S. R., Meglich, P. A. (2017). *Human resource management* (15th ed.). Boston, MA: Cengage Learning.

Mills, A. J., Mills, J. C., Bratton, J., & Forshaw, C. (2007). *Organizational behavior in a global context*. Peterborough, Ontario, Canada: Broadview Press.

Phillips, J. M., & Gully, S. M. (2014). *Human resource management*. Mason, OH: South-Western/Cengage Learning.

Price, A. (2011). *Human resource management* (4th ed.). Hampshire, UK: South-Western/Cengage Learning.

United Sates Department of Labor, Classifying Exempt Status. Retrieved from https://www.dol.gov/whd/regs/compliance/hrg.htm#8

Review and Discussion Questions

1. What is rewards management?

2. Define intrinsic rewards. Define extrinsic rewards.

3. What is hourly base pay?

4. What is salary base pay?

5. What are the basic stipulations for overtime pay?

6. What is the difference between an exempt and a nonexempt employee?

7. What is differential piece-rate compensation?

8. What are some internal job compensation evaluation methods? Describe each.

9. What are salary surveys? Name some external source for salary surveys.

10. What are seniority wage/salary increases?

11. What are merit performance pay increases?

12. Why use incentives and bonuses?

13. What is the incentive concept of reward differentiation?

14. What are cafeteria benefit programs?

15. What are some issue that can arise with pay inequity?

Application Exercises

1. Research three job postings for community center program positions online. From Table 8.1, determine if the positions are exempt or nonexempt. Detail your conclusions.

2. Choose any branch of the United States military or United States government (local, state, federal) that utilizes pay grades. For each pay grade level describe: (1) range of compensation and benefits and (2) specific positions.

3. You are the Athletic Director for a major university athletic department. You are actively recruiting a prestigious basketball coach to complement your department's already strong core of coaches. From Table 8.3, construct an attractive incentive and bonus package. Base your incentives and bonuses on external market research for these types of positions and individuals. Justify your final conclusions.

Discipline, Grievance, Corrective Action, and Employee Separation Administration

Chapter Objectives

- Understand the concepts of employee relations and employee discipline and the significance of due process

- Apply real-world application guidelines for a program disciplinary system

- Understand a stage-by-stage, level-by-level disciplinary system for a sports and recreation program

- Understand and apply parameters for administering discipline in a program

- Understand the step-by-step grievance process for a sports and recreation program

- Understand, prepare for and conduct grievance procedures

- Understand and apply corrective action planning and personnel coaching in a sports and recreation program

- Develop and implement a corrective action plan

- Understand the terms and concepts associated with employee separation by downsizing, voluntary resignation, involuntary separation or employee termination from a sports and recreation program.

Key Terms

Employee Relations
Employee Discipline
Grievance Process
Corrective Action Planning
Employee Separation
   Administration
Punishment
Employment Separation
Disciplinary System

Performance Expectations
Behavioral Expectations
Oral/Verbal Counseling
Written Notices
Suspension
Termination
Administering Discipline
Grievance Procedures
Grievance Committee

Policy and Procedure Manual
Corrective Action Coaching
Downsizing
Voluntary Resignations
Letter of Resignation
Separation Checklist
Exit Interview
Involuntary Separation/Employee
   Termination

Systematizing Formal Employee Interactions

Sports and recreation programs do not operate in an idealistic, utopian world. Regrettably, there are some professional instances where program administrators and supervisors must have performance expectation and behavior "conversations" with their internal stakeholders. Being proactive and hands-on in one's management approach can, in most circumstances, curtail performance problems and discourage detrimental behaviors. Will employee engagement with program members eradicate personnel issues completely? The most simple and straightforward answer is no, it will not remove these circumstances. Nevertheless, it will furnish an operational environment that will allow program employees a choice in how they perform and behave.

From an administrative viewpoint, there are two schools of thought when it comes to employee discipline, grievance procedures, corrective action planning, and separations. The first, and what is now becoming obsolete by enlightened, employee centered organizations, is employee relations, interactions, and discipline are strictly for punishments, termination, and legal protection. Contemporary and innovative sports and recreation programs see employee discipline, grievance procedures, corrective action planning, and separations as opportunities for program improvement and competitive advantage.

From the individual program employee's perspective, employee relations are about having personal rights and assurances for impartial, reasonable treatment. They require a clear understanding of performance expectations while being guided toward personal and professional development. This psychological contract is affirmed by the program's official policies and procedures relating to disciplinary actions, grievance procedures, corrective action planning, and fair employment separation.

Finally, the most significant key to having compelling, clear-cut employee relations and interaction relates to communication within the operation. A sports and recreation programs with well written policies and procedures and sound communication systems for employee interactions will experience more internal harmony and an enhanced sense of teamwork.

HR Tip

Employee interactions such as discipline, corrective actions, grievances, and separation, are operational elements that few administrators "look forward" to being involved with. Nevertheless, having pre-established systems in-place can lessen this managerial apprehension and angst.

Having established systems may jeopardize the at-will status of certain employees. See Chapter 2 for additional information pertaining to at-will employment.

Program Disciplinary System

Wilkinson, Bacon, Redman, and Snell (2010), characterize four main employee discipline goals:

(a) ensuring consistent treatment of employees by clearly specifying standards for employee conduct; (b) ensuring that employees are aware of organizational expectations and the consequences of problem behavior; (c) ensuring employees have the opportunity to modify their behavior (except under conditions where doing so would create undue risk for the organization); and (d) ensuring that mangers can take progressively more severe action to obtain compliance with organizational expectations. (p. 323)

From these disciplinary goals, there are some significant real-world applications that must be acknowledged and utilized.

Consistent Treatment. Persistently affirm and enforce throughout the operation that "no one is above the law." All sports or recreation program stakeholders, from intern level to executive administration, should be held equally accountable for all of their actions. To do otherwise would be disheartening to program members and, in-turn, would disintegrate the entire disciplinary system. Additionally, inequitable or disproportionate treatment could set in motion litigation and adverse public sentiments towards the sports or recreation program.

Comprehension of Expectations. It has to be made unmistakably clear throughout the selection process, onboarding, orientation, training, and day-to-day operations the performance and behavioral expectations of the sports or recreation program. Without this clarity, it is unreasonable to discipline or reprimand employees for unspecified expectations.

Modification of Behavior. It is only reasonable that sports or recreation program employees be given an opportunity and sufficient time to rectify and amend their performance and behavior, provided the offenses are (1) not breaches of core values, (2) serious infringements on personal freedoms of other program employees, and/or (3) unlawful acts. This is at the foundational core of corrective actions as a positive change agent.

The Corrective Discipline Matches the Undesirable Performance and Behavior. The adage, "The punishment must fit the crime," is emblematic of equitable distribution of reasonable, judicious discipline. Punishments for undesirable behaviors that are too austere or harsh or too-lenient can diminish and even destabilize a program's disciplinary system.

Employee Rebuttals. Described elsewhere in this chapter, program employees should have a legitimate voice to repudiate or refute any impending disciplinary actions they deem to be false, impartial, and unequitable. The belief in due process is paramount in a fair-minded disciplinary system.

Step-by-Step Disciplinary Process. What determines the specifics of a progressive disciplinary policy? One obvious factor is the nature of the behavior an organization is attempting to discourage. When counterproductive behaviors are relatively mild, an organization can tolerate a number of infractions before severe consequences are warranted. However, for some behaviors, even one instance cannot be tolerated (Jex & Britt, 2014, p. 367).

With impartiality and equitable justice in mind, it will be up to the collective members of the program, along with legal counsel, to determine which detrimental performances and behaviors will have which category of disciplinary action. It is significant to note that the sports or recreation program should identify and determine the appropriate disciplinary actions for as many conceivable negative performances and behaviors as possible. In other words, it is important for all program employees to know the ramifications for unacceptable behavior and actions in advance. Having a straightforward, comprehensive list of violations and their subsequent disciplinary actions will eliminate any confusion when administering the appropriate corrective action. Table 9.1 provides a detailed progressive disciplinary system.

A few additional recommendations to remember about disciplinary systems:

- Repeat or subsequent low level transgressions by an employee will move through the stages and levels of discipline system until the behavior stops.

- Serious program violations pass over lower levels of disciplinary actions directly to an appropriate level action.

- Always provide a complete disciplinary system outline to new employees at orientation.

- The program's disciplinary process should be periodically reviewed and updated at organizational meetings or seminars.

- If the employee declines to sign or endorse the disciplinary action being taken, note and witnessed this action directly on the disciplinary action form.

- Employees should know their right dispute or challenge disciplinary actions (typically in disciplinary Stages 2 and 3). If they choose to dispute a disciplinary action during the meeting, they should be informed of the procedural steps of the program's grievance process (hard copy or online access).

Administering Discipline

Rue, Ibrahim, and Byars (2016) developed five essential guidelines for administering discipline that can be adopted by a sport and recreation program.

1. Avoid hasty decisions.
2. Document all actions and enter the evidence in the personnel file.
3. Thoroughly and fully investigate the circumstances and facts of the alleged offense.
   a. Notify the employee of the nature of the offense.
   b. Obtain the employee's version of the circumstances, reason for the actions, and the names of any witnesses.
   c. If suspension is required until the investigation is complete, inform the employee:
      i. To return 24 to 72 hours later to receive the decision.
      ii. That there will be reinstatement with pay if the decision is in the employee's favor.
      iii. Of the discipline to be imposed if it is not in the employee's favor.
   d. Interview all witnesses to the alleged misconduct. Obtain signed statements if necessary.
   e. Check all alternative possible causes.
   f. Decide whether the employee committed the alleged offense.

TABLE 9.1 Progressive Disciplinary System

Stage 1: Oral/Verbal Counseling	Between the program member and the direct supervisor. A reasonable action is for the supervisor to apprise their direct administrator of counseling discussions with employees.
Level 1 **Oral/Verbal Counseling (Not Documented)**	Disciplinary counseling for marginal/negligible transgressions. The supervisor—employee counseling session will have minimal (if any) supplementary or ongoing advisements and no recorded documentation.
Level 2 **Oral/Verbal Counseling (Documentation)**	For persistent marginal offenses or more serious transgressions. This level's supervisor—employee dialog necessitates accompanying documentation for reference. The counseling notes will become a permanent record in the employee's internal HR file.
Stage 2: Written Notices	Because of the severity of these violations, the witnesses (who have no input into disciplinary discussions and are absolutely neutral) should be required to (1) take detailed notes during the discussion and (2) provide their notes as addenda to the written disciplinary form.
Level 1: Written Notices (Program Documentation)	For undesirable/harmful behavior by the employee that would be classified as severe. This level and significance of the violation and disciplinary action is recorded on an established form, which is signed and retained in program employee's permanent file. The violation and procedure of the written notice is discussed at an official conference with an independent, impartial witness in attendance. All who partake in the disciplinary discussion sign the written notice documentation.
Level 2: Written Notice (Program Documentation and External Organizational Documentation)	This form of discipline is for continued undesirable or harmful behavior and more serious transgressions against program ideals, personal and program safety, core policies and procedures, etc. Written documentation is the same as in Level 1 except the written disciplinary documentation is retained in both the employee's program HR file, as well as in the organization's permanent records. Because of the severity of these kinds of violations, it is reasonable to have an organization administrator in attendance to witness the conference.
Stage 3: Suspension and Termination	It is prudent to videotape all suspension and termination conferences.
Level 1: Suspensions	For behaviors and actions of the most acute and serious nature. Discipline includes the employee being suspended from their program job responsibilities and duties. The duration could be fixed (through preestablished policies) or set through an advisory session with the organization's executive administration. All suspensions must be completely authenticated and documented with the absolute knowledge and backing of all program and organizational administrators. If desired, the employee can bring legal representation to suspension meeting.

Continued

TABLE 9.1 (*Continued*) Progressive Disciplinary System

Level 2: Termination	For the most detrimental and grave behaviors and actions. This dismissal level involves termination of the employee from all program responsibilities and duties. Because of the definitive nature of this type of discipline, all participants should be well represented in the meeting. Retaining all-inclusive written records is compulsory.

4. Determine the appropriate discipline for the employee. Consider:
   a. Personnel record: length of service, past performance, past disciplinary record. Has corrective discipline ever been applied?
   b. Nature of the offense.
   c. Past disciplinary action for other employees in similar situations.
   d. Existing rules and disciplinary policies.
   e. Provisions in the labor contract if one exists.

5. Advise employee of the nature of the offense, the results of the investigation, the discipline to be imposed, and the rationale behind the discipline. (p. 364)

HR Tip

It is vital that all parties involved with administering discipline to an employee regulate or control all emotional responses and reactions throughout the process.

Grievance Policy

For any disciplinary system to function properly, sports or recreation program empoloyees must know they have due process, or formal recourse to challenge and defend themselves against unwarranted, imbalanced, or even fraudulent disciplinary actions.

Mathis, Jackson and Valentine (2014) assert that due process, like just cause, is about fairness and protects employees from unjust or arbitrary discipline or termination. Due process occurs when an employer is determining if there has been employee wrongdoing and uses a fair process to give an employee the opportunity to explain and defend their actions. This typically involves thoroughly investigating all employment actions and giving individuals an opportunity to express their concerns to objective reviewers of the facts in the situation. Due process represents ethical and respectful treatment of employees; companies that fail to utilize such a process risk being seen as unethical. Organizational justice is a key part of due process. (p. 578)

To guarantee organizational justice, safeguard due process, and ensure the fair-minded integrity of the entire sports or recreation program, the operation should have a clearly defined procedural grievance system available for its personnel.

TABLE 9.2   Stages of the Grievance Process

Stage 1   The employee under reprimand must (1) inform all pertinent individuals (organization executives, administrators, and direct supervisor) in writing (hard copy electronic) of their intention to dispute a disciplinary charge or other employment action and (2) communicate their precise account of the incident or actions in question.

Stage 2   The organizational executives and administrators will organize a timely grievance conference (with impartial in-house program employees, as well as unbiased individuals independent of the program) to assess the legitimacy of the disciplined employee's petition. Furthermore, program administrators will deliver a formal written verification to the disciplined employee affirming (1) that a grievance committee meeting will convene, (2) the purpose of the initial committee meeting, (3) verification of the individuals serving on the committee, and (4) the date and time of the committee meeting.

Stage 3   At the initial meeting, if the committee believes the employee's disciplinary circumstance necessitates additional consideration, an official hearing will be convened. If the committee concludes the disciplinary action to be in agreement with established disciplinary policies and procedures, an official statement will be delivered to the disciplined employee describing the committee's conclusions and judgement.

Stage 4   If warranted (from Stage 3), an official hearing will be called to examine detailed documentation, protocols, previous precedence evaluations, and eyewitness interviews. The official disciplinary grievance conference should be recorded (via written transcriptions or video recording) by a neutral observer.

Stage 5   Following the official hearing, the grievance committee will make its final decision regarding the incident and the disciplinary action being appealed. The program member will be notified in a formal letter (typically within 24 hours) of the grievance committee's final decision.

Grievance Procedures. As discussed, all disciplinary systems should have an established grievance procedure to allow sports or recreation program employees a chance to challenge or appeal the discipline being administered. Thus, a straightforward comprehensive grievance process should be clearly defined in the program's policies and procedures manual. If a grievance process has not been established within the program, one should be developed as soon as possible. As with all human resource management practices, the grievance procedure, preceding its permanent incorporation into the program's policy and procedure manual, must be evaluated by independent legal counsel. This examination will certify that every stage in the grievance progression is within acceptable legal constraints. Table 9.2 is a sample of a stage-by-stage grievance process that can be adapted by a sport and recreation program.

Additional recommendations about grievance procedures:

- Contingent upon the seriousness of the transgression and disciplinary action being recommended, legal guidance (for both the employee and organization) may be a reasonable part of the proceedings.

- The grievance committee should be comprised of nonpartisan people for neutrality and objectivity.

- The program supervisor (who recommended the disciplinary action) must furnish the grievance committee with all operational records and incident information reinforcing their judgement to reprimand the employee. During the grievance process, the program supervisor should have no communication with grievance committee members (unless called upon to provide evidence during the official hearing).

HR Tip

Unfortunately, grievance procedures may not always resolve a situation. If the circumstance necessitates, and all parties agree, an independent arbitrator could be utilized to solve a particularly thorny disciplinary grievance issue.

Corrective Action Planning

There is a distinct opportunity during the disciplinary meeting to lay out a corrective action plan to improve orchange the program employee's unacceptable performance, behaviors, or actions. In other words, as an alternative to just coming down on the employee for what they did wrong during the disciplinary meeting, there is a distinct opportunity to turn a negative into a positive by presenting a way to rectify their undesirable performance, behavior, and actions. By doing so, the corrective action plan strategy circumvents personal criticisms and concentrates strictly on the performance, behaviors, or actions to be modified or eliminated.

Corrective action plans, which can be employed for all levels of discipline (except, understandably, termination), can be based on a coaching style approach. Lussier (2015) has devised a four-step coaching method that can be employed for correcting disciplinary and performance issues, extrapolated here.

Step 1. Describe the current performance. Using specific examples, describe the current behavior that must be changed, focusing on improvement, not the wrong behavior.

Step 2. Describe desired performance. Describe to the employee in detail exactly what desired performance isexpected. Show how they will benefit from following your advice.

Step 3. Get a commitment to change. When dealing with an *ability* issue, it is not necessary to get employees to verbally commit to the change if they seem willing to make it. However, if employees defend their way and you're sure it's not as effective, explain why your proposed way will work better. If you cannot get employees to understand and agree, get a verbal commitment. This step is also important for *motivational* issues, because if the employees are not willing to commit to the change, they will most likely not make the change.

Step 4. Follow up. Remember that some employees do what managers *inspect* (imposed control), not what they *expect*. You should follow up to ensure that employees are behaving as desired. (p. 433)

There are a number of pertinent details in developing, conveying, and implementing a corrective action plan.

1. The corrective action plan should have the full-endorsement of all individuals involved in the disciplinary action, especially the employee being reprimanded.

2. During the review session, it should be made perfectly clear that there are identifiable consequences for the employee if they do not adhere to the corrective action plan.

3. The corrective action plan should be in writing. For minor offenses, a basic outline of action needed will suffice. For pronounced and serious offenses, a detailed blueprint of corrective steps should be provided. This plan should (1) be maintained in the employee's human resource file, (2) be given to the employee at the conclusion of the meeting, and (3) copied to all relevant administrators and supervisors.

4. While the supervisor will be supporting and assisting the employee with the corrective action plan (through periodic feedback controls and intermittent coaching advice), the tangible completion and fulfillment of the plan's goals and targeted actions is solely in the individual's "hands."

5. The supervisor should be accessible to the employee to answer questions related to the corrective action plan. However, the employee should acknowledge that the supervisor's availability has some commonsense conditions and limitations. In certain situations, contingency supervision could be provided.

6. The supervisor producing the corrective action plan should appreciate the fact that the specified negative performances, behaviors, and actions could take time to modify or extinquish. Establish and agree upon performance and behavioral goals, as well as a timeline for the corrective action plan. Dangerous and exceptionally detrimental performance actions and behaviors should be eliminated immediately.

7. Sports or recreation administrators should be benevolent toward the situation the employee is experiencing; they could be under tremendous pressure and must be treated professionally and with consideration, empathy, and compassion. Listening to the employee's concerns and trepidations is an essential component of being supportive.

8. At the end of the agreed upon timeframe, the supervisor and employee should meet to examine and discuss their assessments of the corrective action plan and its execution. With as much quantitative data as possible, the supervisor should examine established action plan goals and compare them to concrete outcomes. If the goals were exceeded, the employee should be commended. If goals were met, this would also be a time for praise and compliments. If goals were not met, first investigate if there are mitigating circumstances that impacted the corrective action plan. Second, listen to the employee's rationale for why certain negative performances, behaviors, or actions were not modified or eliminated. Finally, plot a course of action that can include (1) formulating a new corrective action plan with adjusted goals and identifiable targets or, unfortunately, (2) commence with additional disciplinary actions, as determined in the progressive system.

Employee Separation Administration

While the concluding component of this chapter section is devoted to the process of involuntary separations and employee terminations, two employee separation scenarios may occur outside of the employee's purview and control, but will certainly affect them: downsizing and voluntary resignations.

Downsizing

When a sports or recreation program's long-term strategies and goals do not coincide with its personnel composition, the regrettable consequence can be downsizing individual employees or whole departments. For example, if administrators determine that an individual athletic program or team no longer fits within its long-term mission, goals, and objectives, the entire athletic program or team could be downsized. Unfortunately, another motivation for downsizing could be financial, either to reduce expenditures and monetary shortfalls, or to enlarge profitability or bottom-line results. Whatever the reason, an organization should not consider downsizing lightly. The impact of downsizing on the operation could have considerable repercussions on the retained employee morale, long-term personnel retention, and redistribution of workloads.

Luthans et. al (2015) provide several resourceful methods to prevent downsizing decisions from negatively affecting program personnel. Some of these include: (1) finding personnel who are interested in reduced hours, part-time work, job sharing, leaves of absence, or sabbaticals to work in the community; (2) networking with local employers regarding temporary or permanent redeployment; (3) using attrition effectively by examining whether a job needs to be filled or can be eliminated; (4) developing multistep voluntary early retirement packages; and (5) cross training so trained people are ready to step into new job openings within the firm (p. 240).

> **HR Tip**
>
> Sports or recreation program employees who are being laid off due to downsizing should know that the action has nothing to do with their personal job performance. They are not being terminated for cause, but rather a strategic decision that is necessary for the long-term benefit of the sports or recreation program. While, on the surface, this may not seem important, in the long run, it could have a profound effect on how downsized employees remember the sports or recreation program and their self-worth.

If there is no other alternative but to downsize individuals or departments, administrators should consider employee placement and assistance programs. These programs can help downsized personnel with financial support (severance packages), job search and placement services, education and retraining programs, increased extension of benefit packages, and general professional and personal counseling.

Voluntary Resignations

Well-known established protocols should be in place for employees to follow, should they decide to voluntarily resign their position with the sports or recreation program. However, employees are not obligated to comply with the process the program has established (other than returning any workplace property). A basic resignation procedure could be as follows:

1. The employee, in writing, submits a letter of resignation to their direct supervisor. This letter should contain the employee's complete name, position title, and final date of work. Typically, line or staff employees provide a standard two week notice, while supervisory and administrative personnel provide one-to-three-month separation notice.

2. The direct supervisor immediately copies and distributes the resignation letter to all relevant administrators and the human resource department.

3. The human resource department provides the resigning employee with a separation checklist. This checklist itemizes details the for separation and final pay, such as returning keys/key cards, parking passes, office equipment, program apparel, and program files. When completing the checklist, the employee should collect authorized initials to verify completed items. When the list is complete, the employee submits it to human resources for approval and retention.

4. An exit interview should be scheduled and conducted within the timeframe of the employee's separation notice. Sharma (2016) describes exit interviews as an interview held with an employee who is leaving the organization voluntarily, stating that the purpose of an exit interview is to find out the reasons why the employee is leaving or to provide counseling and assistance in finding a new job. The feedback received from exit interviews can provide the employer a better insight into what is right and wrong about the company. The assumption behind exit interviews is that employees who depart from the organization have no stake and are likely to give free and frank opinions. (p. 258)

5. Human resource management should provide the Information Technology (IT) department with the last date of employment for the program employee. IT should schedule a complete shutdown of all of the employee's internet, intranet, email, and program systems access on that date. Additionally, IT should physically remove the separating employee computer memory and collect all external hard drives, flash drives, and CDs.

6. While it is not a mandated component of the resignation process, a "farewell" gathering for the resigning employee is a good way to show and preserve goodwill.

Involuntary Separation and Employment Termination

Even after adhering to all human resource laws and regulations, disciplinary protocols, corrective action planning, and individual coaching support, there will be times where employment must be terminated. It goes without saying that these dismissal judgements could be problematic for a supervisor or administrator. Having a definitive process for involuntary separation or employment termination in-place can lessen, to some degree, the apprehension and emotional response associated with these adverse and unpleasant occurrences. It is imperative that once established, separation procedures for downsizing, voluntary resignation, and especially involuntary separation and employment termination be approved by the sports or recreation program's legal counsel prior to implementation.

While the involuntary separation and employee termination processes can vary from program to program, Sommerville (2007) provides some valid criteria when conducting termination procedures and conferences.

1. The prudent manager will have proper documentation to support the decision to terminate.

2. A signed statement that the employee has received a copy of the employee handbook and is familiar with the organization's rules and regulations is essential.

3. Management should have documentation that supports any written warnings, verbal warnings, and previous disciplinary issues, and that the documentation should be current and relevant.

4. It is often prudent to have another manager present who may act as a witness during the termination proceedings.

5. Management should determine through state and local laws the requirements for issuing an employee's final paycheck and for collecting company property such as uniforms, keys, and other such items.

6. Management should keep the details of the termination confidential on a need to know basis only.

7. Perhaps one of the most important actions that management can take when forced to terminate an employee is to leave the employee with dignity. (p. 303)

Summary

The magnitude of having strong, well-defined employee relation systems in a sports or recreation program is unmistakably clear. Systemizing processes in employee discipline, grievance procedures, corrective action planning, and separations will present administrators with tangible guidelines for program operations, while providing sports or recreation program employees with measurable performance and behavioral expectations. While each operation will have its own unique employee discipline progression, grievance process, corrective action planning, and separation systems, there are vital protocols that should be followed that protect both the sports or recreation program and employees from future irreparable harm.

References

Falcone, P. (2017). *101 Sample write-ups for documenting employee performance problems: A guide to progressive discipline and termination* (3rd ed.). New York, NY: AMACOM.

Jex, S. M., & Britt, T. W. (2014). *Organizational behavior: A scientist-practitioners approach* (3rd ed.). Hoboken, NJ: John Wiley and Sons.

Lussier, R. N. (2015). *Management fundamentals: Concepts, applications, and skill development* (6th ed.). Thousand Oaks, CA: Sage.

Luthans, F., Luthans, B. C., & Luthans, K. W. (2015). *Organizational behavior: An evidence-based approach* (13th ed.). Charlotte, NC: Information Age Publishing.

Mathis, R. L., Jackson, J. H., & Valentine, S. R. (2014). *Human resource management* (14th ed.). Stamford, CT: Cengage Learning.

Rue, L. W., Ibrahim, N. A., & Byars, L. L. (2016). *Human resource management* (11th ed.). New York, NY: McGraw-Hill.

Sharma, F. C. (2016). *Human resource management: Latest edition*. Agra, India: SBPD Publications.

Sommerville, K. L. (2007). *Hospitality employee management and supervision: Concepts and practical applications*. Hoboken, NJ: John Wiley and Sons.

Wilkinson, A., Bacon, N., Redman, T., & Snell, S. (2010). *The Sage handbook of human resource management*. Thousand Oaks, CA: Sage Publishing.

Review and Discussion Questions

1. When it comes to employee relations, what are administration's two possible "schools of thought"?
2. From an employee's perspective, why are employee relation systems important?
3. Define employee discipline.
4. In employee discipline, what is consistent treatment?
5. In employee discipline, what is modification of behavior?
6. What are the three stages of a progressive disciplinary system?
7. What are the six levels of a progressive disciplinary system?
8. In the progressive disciplinary system, describe Suspensions.
9. What should happen if an employee declines signing their disciplinary action documentation?
10. What are the five essential guidelines to administering discipline?
11. Define due process.
12. List and describe the stages in the grievance process.
13. What is corrective action planning?
14. What are the four coaching steps in corrective action planning?
15. Why should a corrective action plan be in writing?
16. What should happen at the end of a corrective action plan's agreed upon timeframe?
17. What is downsizing?
18. What are some resourceful methods to avoid downsizing?
19. What are employee placement and assistance programs?
20. List and describe voluntary resignation procedures.
21. Describe involuntary separation/employee termination.

Application Exercises

1. Research three real-world athletic program or recreation program disciplinary systems. Critique each for depth, coherent structure, and applicability.
2. You are the Executive Director for a local city parks and recreation department. You have an employee, while having exceptional abilities and knowledge, is:
   - consistently tardy;
   - often found surfing the web on their cell phone;
   - apathetic toward departmental meetings and does not participate; and
   - absent from external club events and matches.
3. Develop a corrective action plan, with specific behaviors, performance expectations, and timelines, to improve this person's performance.
4. Develop, from the ground-up, a written warning/notice document.

Human Resource Management
Term Project
Group Written and Oral Presentation

You and your group are the new Assistant Athletic Directors (various positions) for a large NCAA Division I Athletic Program. While the organization is considered a sizeable NCAA signatory institution, it has no formalized disciplinary, corrective action, grievance, or separation procedures in its operation. Your self-managed project group has been tasked with designing (from the ground up):

1. Disciplinary System
2. Corrective Action Program
3. Grievance Procedures
4. Employee Separation Processes

Elements:

- Research human research disciplinary, corrective action, grievance, and separation procedures that can be used by the operation. Use HR sources (online and hard copy) to do your research.
- Justify components of each step-by-step process and why each step would be appropriate for the athletic program.
- Delineate possible violations and how they would be processed through the disciplinary system.
- Develop appropriate disciplinary documentation instruments.
- Design a corrective action program, with appropriate documentation, that could be used by the athletic program for disciplinary issues.
- Create a grievance system for use by athletic program members. Delineate the grievance progression and provide all appropriate documentation and forms.
- Outline the steps involved with employee separation (voluntary and involuntary). Create exit interview documentation for the new system.
- Elaborate on the estimated costs for the implementation of the four new personnel systems and processes.
- Discuss new software and hardware requirements of the four new personnel systems and processes.

Criteria:

Oral Presentation

- Develop a 30-45-minute presentation that describes the four new systems for this NCAA program.
- Prepare for a 15-minute Q & A session after main presentation.

- Create Power Point slides and visual aids to supplement the presentation (hard copy to be submitted prior to presentation).
- Conduct extensive external research to justify your selections.

Written Documentation

Create all appropriate written documentation (in a presentation packet) for all attendees of the oral presentation. The written presentation packet should be well organized and easy to reference during the presentation.

chapter ten

Safety Management and Wellness Programs

Chapter Objectives

- Understand the concept of safety management
- Identify the financial and personal costs and importance of workplace safety and cultivating a safety culture in sports and recreation programs
- Understand the tactics and methods for developing a safety culture
- Identify and establish safety policies, procedures, and protocols in a sports and recreation program
- Develop a workplace safety program steps
- Identify and understand safety training areas for sports and recreation programs
- Collect and measure safety statistical data
- Understand incident/accident reporting systems for sports and recreation programs and to construct and utilize incident/accident reports
- Define and understand safety audits
- Identify and create a sports or recreation wellness program
- Understand and explain the concept of an Employee Assistance Programs (EAP's) and provide such resources in a sports and recreation program

Key Terms

Workplace Injuries and Illnesses
Safety Culture
Cultural Integration
Safety Policies and Procedures
Program-Wide Safety
Team-by-Team Safety
Individual Position-by-Position
   Safety
Safety Protocols
Safety First Attitude
Safety Training Programs
National Safety Council
Program Equipment

Crisis Training
Active Shooter Training
Online/E-Learning
Just-in-Time Training
Frequency Rate
Disabling Rate
Severity Rate
Management by Walking
   Around
Safety Audits
Benefit Providers
Medical Health Plan Provider(s)
Health Insurance Supplier

Local Community Centers
Program Coordinators
Child Care Specialists
Chiropractic and Massage
   Services
Safety Course Instruction
Mental Health Counselors
Stress Reduction Specialists
Family Counseling
Personal Counseling
Employee Assistance Programs
   (EAP's)

Continued

Emotional/Psychological Assistance Programs

Drug/Alcohol/Substance Abuse Testing, Intervention, Rehabilitation

Gambling Addiction Treatment

Occupational Stress and Burnout Therapy

Elder Care

Financial and Legal Counseling

Physical Assistance Programs/ Lifestyle Choices Support

Weight Management and Onsite Dietitians

Lunchtime Conditioning

Ergonomic Equipment

Safety Management

By now, the underlying theme of this text should be clear: sports or recreation program personnel are the most valuable asset to the operation; the assurance of their safety is indispensable in that foundational assertion. Protecting this asset is accomplished through safety management. In the book *Safety Management in a Competitive Business Environment*, Sinay (2014) defines the concept of occupational safety management by the following paragraph:

> Occupational Safety Management includes all activities related to carrying out and stating the threat extent. When assessing the extent of a threat as a negative event, it is necessary to state the possibility of its occurrence and assess the extent of possible consequences due to the effect of a negative event, that is, assess the risk. Then it is necessary to assess if the extent of the risk is acceptable. If the risk is higher than acceptable, then it is necessary to execute measures to decrease it or to completely eliminate it. (p. 1)

From this perspective, all internal stakeholders must become sensitive to workplace safety hazards and their effect on the program. In other words, each program employee must consider, evaluate, and discuss any potential safety issues, which could range from being remotely possible to imminent.

Costs Associated with Workplace Safety Issues

As one can imagine, the actual tangible costs to all U.S. industries relating to workplace safety (in financial dollars, pain and suffering of its personnel, and negative internal and external public relations impact) is unbelievably high. The following passage is from OSHA's (Occupational Safety and Health Administration) website. It illuminates the financial burden workplace safety places on U.S. businesses.

In addition to their social costs, workplace injuries and illnesses have a major impact on an employer's bottom line. It has been estimated that employers pay almost $1 billion per week for direct workers' compensation costs alone. The costs of workplace injuries and illnesses include direct and indirect costs. According to OSHA, the Occupational Safety and Health Organization, (n.d.), direct costs include worker compensation payments, medical expenses, and costs for legal services. Examples of indirect costs include training replacement employees, accident investigation and implementation of corrective measures, lost productivity, repairs of damaged equipment and property, and costs associated with lower employee morale and absenteeism.

TABLE 10.1 Fatality and Workplace Injury Statistics

Workplace Injuries and Illnesses

Year	2017	2016	2015
Cases involving days away from work	882,730	892,300	752,600
Median days away from work	8	8	8
Sprains, strains, tears	311,330	317,530	421,610
Back injuries	148,780	154,180	191,450
Falls, slips, trips	183,440	229,240	309,060
Total	2.8 M	2.9 M	2.8 M
Rate per 100 FTE	2.8	2.9	2.8

Fatal Occupational Injuries

Year	2017	2016	2015
Total (all sectors)	5,147	5,190	4,386
Roadway Incidents (all sectors)	1,299	1,252	1,138
Falls, slips, trips (all sectors)	887	849	800
Homicides (all sectors)	458	500	703
Rate per 100K FTE	3.5	3.6	3.4

Source: From the U.S. Department of Labor, Bureau of Labor Statistics, (http://www.bls.gov/iif/oshwc/cfoi-chart-data-2017.htm)

From the actual statistic of workplace injuries and illnesses, the US Department of Labor's Bureau of Labor Statistic has even more alarming data (see Table 10.1). There were approximately 2.9 million non-fatal workplace injuries and illnesses reported by private industry employers in 2016, at a rate of 2.9 cases per 100 full-time equivalent (FTE) workers. Further, 2016 marks the third consecutive increase in annual workplace fatalities and the first time more than 5,000 fatalities have been recorded by the Census of Fatal Occupational Injuries (CFOI) since 2008. The fatal injury rate increased to 3.6 per 100,000 full-time equivalent (FTE) workers from 3.4 in 2015, the highest rate since 2010. From these two governmental sources alone, it is easy to appreciate the importance of workplace safety and why it has become a serious, sobering issue that warrants a sports and recreation organization's absolute focus.

The Groundwork – Developing a Safety Culture

Once the sports or recreation program and its internal stakeholders acknowledge and grasp the magnitude of a safety conscious work environment, the question then becomes, How does the program develop a safe and secure work environment? The answer originates with creating and promoting a safety atmosphere and culture.

McKinnon (2014) defines a safety culture as how the organization behaves with respect to safety when no one is watching.

> It is the organization's safety personality…. This means that the safety aspects of the business are no longer an add-on or a nice-to-have, or something that is required by law, or forced upon them by a serious loss event, but simply part of the business all day, all night, 24/7. This embedded commitment to safety, which has become the way the organization does business, becomes the safety personality of the organization, and that is the safety culture of the organization and the workplace that it operates. (pp. 1-2).

To cultivate a safety atmosphere and culture, there are some vital ideas and strategies to consider.

Core Value of the Program. As discussed in Chapter 3, a vital component in the operational plan and its ensuing human resource plan is delineating the core values of the operation. It is essential that a focal core value of the sports or recreation program be its steadfast obligation to maintain a safe and healthy work environment for all of its personnel.

Publicized and Promoted. Not only should program produce resilient and compelling core safety ideals, it must publicize and call attention to these principles time and again. To take the "words from the page" to actuality, everyone must be frequently reminded of their significance. There must be a universally known and communicated 100% unconditional commitment to safety. If not put in use, it is window dressing that is waiting for a catastrophic accident to transpire.

Program Employee Engagement. The adage, "All hands-on deck," is apropos to the discussion of program safety.

In a strong safety culture, every employee feel a responsibility for safety and pursues it every day. Employees are willing to identify unsafe behaviors and conditions and take steps to correct them. An organization's safety culture is influenced by:

- Management and employee attitudes
- Supervisor priorities, accountability, and responsibilities
- Management and employee norms, beliefs, and assumptions
- Employee safety training and motivation
- Manager and employee involvement and commitment
- Production and financial pressures
- Actions employees take (or do not take) to correct unsafe behaviors and situations

(Phillips & Gully, 2014, p. 384)

Cultural Integration. Safety cultures and high-performance cultures are not mutually exclusive. One might assume that each is unconnected and counterproductive to the other. That conclusion would be erroneous, and in fact, the opposite is true. A safe work environment is one which has fewer worker associated absences, less financial liability, fewer mistakes and less rework, and, through its renewed job focus, is highly productive.

Conversion to a Safety Culture. To design and transform a program culture often takes demolishing the previous culture and the authentication and support for that culture. There is a clear-cut technique that can be used to transform a program's culture: unfreezing, changing, refreezing. The change mechanism works as follows:

- **Step 1 Unfreeze.** Break down the previous culture of unsafe (and possibly hazardous) practices by definitively pointing out these unsafe and frequently embedded habits/routines/methods.
- **Step 2 Change.** Through tangible strategies, change the safety culture of the program.
- **Step 3 Refreeze.** Once the culture has been altered to one of "safety first," refreeze the culture.

While the concept of cultural change is easy to absorb, in practicality, the exertion to modify (or completely transform) a program's culture can be substantial. For example, if an athletic program has had a long history of disregarding essential safety practices, "melting" this atmosphere in Step 1 unfreezing could be arduous and lengthy.

Why Develop Safety Policy and Procedures?

A policy is a predetermined course of action, established as a guide to accepted business strategies and objectives. A procedure is a method by which a policy can be accomplished; the procedures provide the instructions necessary to carry out a policy statement. (Page, 2002, p. 17)

In essence, policies are pre-determined guidelines and rules, while procedures are the "how-to-do" processes to complete program tasks. As one can surmise, safety policies and procedures are the tangible, written statements that guide internal stakeholders through safety practices and actions associated with their positions and overall sports or recreation program operation.

> ### HR Tip
> Safety policies and procedures form the basis for all safety related communications within the program, such as (1) interdepartmental safety memos, (2) safety posters, (3) email safety reminders, and (4) documents for safety committee meetings. Therefore, the safety policies and procedures should be articulated appropriately in straightforward language and be shared or distributed for easy access and reference.

When constructing safety policies and procedures for the first time, begin with an open format meeting or brainstorming session with all sports or recreation program personnel. The fundamental levels of safety policies and procedures should encompass:

Program-wide safety concerns (facilities, equipment, travel protocols, emergency procedures, etc.),

Group-by-group safety concerns (identifying inherent group-specific concerns/hazards),

Individual position-by-position safety concerns (based on job analysis data and job descriptions).

Because safety policies and procedures will directly contribute to the sports or recreation program's safety culture and safety management, it is important that they be professional and thorough.

Establishing Safety Protocols

With all of the diverse sports and recreation programs, it would be virtually impossible to examine all of the possible safety protocol areas for each operation. Each sports or recreation program and its collective stakeholders must independently categorize and establish safety protocol targets for their distinct situation. However, several general safety protocol areas that fundamentally encompass all programs are identified in Table 10.2, and provide a solid foundation on which to build.

Training: A Safety First Attitude

Never make the assumption that safety techniques and measures, no matter how rudimentary and commonsensical they may seem, are presently known and correctly employed. One assumption by program administrators could set in motion disastrous program-wide consequences. Verify that safety practices are known and accepted through open communication and persistent training.

> **HR Tip**
>
> Before a training program is created, every internal program member should be vested into the overall safety culture instilled in the sport and recreation program. Without a commitment to the safety culture, program personnel will not take seriously the individual safety processes and procedures required of their positions.

TABLE 10.2 Safety Protocol Areas

General facility maintenance	Floor-to-ceiling
Cleaning schedules	From administrative offices to locker rooms
Equipment usage and repair	From office equipment to athletic equipment
Personnel restrictions	Access and responsibility based on training and certifications
Work environment	Lighting, air ventilation, heat/cold, weather, etc.
Job rotation	For positions with repetitive tasks
Clothing	Appropriate gear as well as hygienic apparel
Transportation	Travel to-and-from competitions, work sites, and special events
Building and campus security	In conjunction with local/campus police
Fan interaction	Practices for exchanges and security

TABLE 10.3 Effective Workplace Safety Training Program

Step 1	Determine what safety training is needed	First ask if training can solve the problem at hand.
Step 2	Identify workspace safety training needs	Correctly identify the specific training required to address the knowledge gap.
Step 3	Identify satefy training goals and objectives	Set clear and measurable learning goals and objectives
Step 4	Develop workplace safety learning activities	Consider methods, materials, and resources to most effectively convey the message.
Step 5	Conduct safety training	Schedule and conduct the training in a clear and organized way.
Step 6	Evaluate workplace safety training program effectiveness	Evaluate training by asking trainees for feedback, supervisors their observations and analyze workplace data.
Step 7	Improve safety training program	Critical reexamination of methods, presentations, key concepts, and skills.

Source: National Safety Council.

Developing a Safety Training Program. The National Safety Council has created a straightforward seven-step process to create an effective workplace safety training program. Table 10.3 is an outline of their process.

As with establishing safety protocol areas, it would be impossible to define all of the possible safety training needs for all programs. However, there are a few training areas that are universal and cross all program boundaries.

Program Equipment. All internal stakeholder must have a functioning familiarity and understanding of the safe and proper operation of all program equipment. Demonstration and hands-on training should be utilized for this objective.

Facilities. Program stakeholders must be cognizant of every conceivable hazardous condition in the entire program facility. A facility condition walk-through with program personnel could be a valuable training strategy.

New Facilities and Equipment. Anytime new or unfamiliar facilities and equipment are being used, program members should be mindful of conceivable safety contingencies and concerns. As for new equipment, safety inspections of the equipment should be conducted prior to its incorporation into operations. If the equipment is new to the operation or an ultramodern mechanism that has never been employed by any program, it would be a sensible to have a manufacture representative available to demonstrate the proper usage of the equipment (or to have detailed instructional videos available).

First Aid/CPR. Due to the physical nature of sports and recreation program operations, it is a reasonable precaution to have all internal stakeholders safety trained by the American Red Cross in first aid and CPR.

Crisis Training. All foreseeable crisis eventualities should have an established protocol and, consequently, be assimilated into the safety training program. Crisis contingencies in areas such as individual and team travel, fan abuse and threats, athletic/activity related injuries, and non-related injuries should be included in possible scenarios to highlight in training sessions.

Fire Drills and Evacuation Training. In conjunction with community or municipal fire professionals, a sports and recreation program should have extensive and periodic facility evacuation drills. Evacuation drills should be regularly scheduled, conducted, and instantly evaluated. All drill times should be recorded for reference and used to improve response time as well as evacuation training.

Active Shooter Safety Training. Because of the ever-increasing risk of an active shooter event, a sports or recreation program should devise and conduct an active shooter training program and stage repetitive drills in conjunction with local police. If possible, the video recording of these sessions should be downloaded for future program use.

Online Safety Training/Personalized Refresher Courses. The various personnel training methodologies discussed in Chapter 6 can all be adapted and applied to safety training. However, e-learning programs and refresher courses are perfect ways to augment face-to-face, "on the floor" safety training courses. Snell, Morris, and Bohlander provide a persuasive reasoning for incorporating e-learning into sport and recreation safety training:

> E-learning transforms the learning process in several ways. First, it allows the firm to bring the training to the employees rather than vice versa, which is generally more efficient and cost effective…. E-learning also allows companies to offer individual training components when and where they need them. Offering employees training when and where they need it is referred to as **just-in-time training**. It helps alleviate the boredom trainees experience during full-blown training courses, and employees are more likely to retain the information when they can immediately put it to use. (Snell, Morris, & Bohlander, 2016, p. 277)

Therefore, in concert with other methods of safety instruction, e-learning is a valuable teaching method that can be accessed whenever and wherever needed.

Analyzing and Measuring Program Safety

To benchmark and calculate the impact of safety management and safety training programs, it is necessary to track every safety incidence. Rue, Ibrahim, and Byars (2016) have defined three key measurements for tracking the safety record of a program.

Frequency Rate. Ratio that indicates the frequency with which disabling injuries occur.

Disabling Rate Work-related injuries that cause an employee to miss one or more days of work.

Severity Rate. Ratio that indicates the length of time injured employees are out of work.

(p. 340)

While these three measures quantify safety from a work loss perspective, it is also reasonable to maintain and tabulate accident and injury data, no matter how insignificant or minor the incidences and injuries may seem. A general rule should be, that no injury is too small to acknowledge, respond to, and record.

HR Tip

Collecting safety data is only the first step in safety management analysis. It is important that the collected data be more than just recorded information for legal and regulatory compliance. The data should be analyzed and used to (1) target areas of concern, (2) compare to other sports or recreation programs (or departments within the overall organization), (3) alert and focus internal stakeholders, and (4) develop new and better ways of ensuring program employee safety. Simply stated, safety data is used to make and improve safety decisions in the future.

Accident Procedures

Sports and recreation programs should anticipate and train for as many foreseeable safety incidents as possible. While the number and range of injuries is immeasurable, the operation should have a proactive step-by-step process that can be deployed in a wide assortment of circumstances. As with all elements of a safety management culture, critical accident management should be a principal component of the safety training program Each program employee should be instructed in and required to perform emergency accident procedures when on sports or recreation program business. The procedures could easily be in the form of a laminated safety procedure card which (1) enumerates the program's step-by-step emergency procedures, (2) has all relevant emergency phone numbers (e.g. hospital, ambulance/EMT services, program medical staff), and (3) internal administrative emergency contacts.

Some fundamental actions should be prioritized when developing accident safety procedures, as outlined in Table 10.4.

Accident Investigation. After the incident has been managed through the above procedures, if the accident is judged serious, an independent investigation may be necessary. This investigation should be conducted through either an internal third party, such as a designated safety manager in human resources, or by an external contracted or commissioned investigator.

In his book *Health and Safety Handbook*, Stranks (2006) gives a thorough and well defined step-by-step procedure for investigating accidents. The following list extrapolates the main points of his process:

1. Establish the facts surrounding the accident as quickly and completely as possible with respect to:
   a. the work environment in which the accident took place, (location, lighting);
   b. the facility, equipment, machinery involved;
   c. the system of work or working procedures involved; and
   d. the sequence of events leading to the accident.

TABLE 10.4   Emergency Accident Procedures

Priority Actions	*Secondary Actions*	*Administrative Actions*
React immediately to protect the individual(s) from any additional injury. Try to remain calm.	After priority actions, ensure the environment is safe and secure for incoming personnel or emergency services .	For incidences that would be considered minor or within certain established guidelines, complete an incident report.
Administer first aid or CPR as needed without delay, dispense necessary medical treatment. Command the situation.	Inform program administrators of the situation. Remove any program assets from potential danger.	For incidences that would be considered serious and atypical, launch an independent investigation and document the process.
Make (or delegate) emergency calls. Provide emergency services with a complete description of the conditions and location of accident.		
If the situation is still dangerous, remove all other personnel from the area. Use the safest exits (practiced in evacuation drills). Enlist adult supervision and assistance when removing underage participants to safety.		

Note: All emergency accident procedures should be examined by the sports or recreation program medical personnel, as well as legal counsel prior to implementation.

2. Take photos of the accident scene before anything is moved.

3. Identify all witnesses and make a list of witnesses.

4. Interview all witnesses in the presence of a third party and take full statements. (Witnesses should be cautioned prior to making a statement). Do not prompt or lead the witnesses. Witnesses should agree with any written statements produced, then sign and date these statements.

5. Evaluate the facts and each witness statement of events leading to the accident with respect to accuracy, reliability, and relevance.

6. Endeavor to arrive at conclusions as to both the indirect and direct causes of the accident on the basis of relevant facts.

7. Examine closely any contradictory evidence. Never dismiss a fact that does not fit in with the rest of the facts. If necessary, find out more.

8. Examine fully the system of work in the operation, in terms of the persons involved with respect to age, training, experience, level of supervision, and the nature of work (e.g. routine, sporadic, or incidental).

9. In certain cases, it may be necessary for facility and equipment to be examined by an expert.

10. Produce a written report indicating the stages prior to the accident and emphasize the cause of same. Measures to prevent a recurrence should also be incorporated in such a report.

11. In complex and serious cases, it may be appropriate to establish a small investigating committee.

The thorough investigation of accidents is essential, particularly where there may be the possibility of criminal proceedings by the enforcement authority and/or civil proceedings by the injured party and his/her representative. (pp. 157-158)

Note: All accident investigation procedures should be examined by the sports or recreation program's legal counsel prior to implementation.

HR Tip

With technology so readily available, video recording of witnesses' statements as well as pictures of the accident scene could be easily taken with cell phones. This is not to say that written statements should be abandoned; it is another resource to record and reference for analysis.

Incident and Accident Reports. Table 10.5 identifies the basic categories included in a typical incident or accident report.

Note: All incident/accident reports should be examined by the sports or recreation program's legal counsel prior to implementation.

TABLE 10.5   Incident Report Categories

Section 1 Reference Data	*Section 2* Incident/Accident Information	*Section 3* Incident/Accident Actions	*Section 4* Verification and Recording
Program/Department:	Detailed Description of Incident/Accident:	Actions Taken and by Whom (e.g. accident specific treatments):	Program Supervisor's Signature:
Supervisor in Charge:			
Report Written By:	Parties Involved in Incident/Accident:		Date:
Date of Incident/Accident:		Actions Taken and by Whom (administrative):	Receiving Program Administrator's Signature:
	Specific Injuries of Incident/Accident:		
Time of Incident/Accident:		Additional/Special Actions:	Date:
	Witnesses to the Incident/Accident:		
Location of Incident/Accident:			

Administration and Individual Obligations on Safety

Administration and Supervisor's Responsibility Toward Safety

There are several distinct components of safety management that are the obligation of sports or recreation administration (and direct supervisors). It goes without saying that for safety management to be successful, there should be an unconditional, top-down commitment to safety by program administrators. While the collective group or safety committees work to define the program's safety goals and ambitions, protocols, policies and procedures, administrators should authenticate and endorse each safety strategy and objective by making certain these are articulated (in written form) for the entire operation. Through Management by Walking Around (MBWA) and intermittent unofficial inspections, administrators should look for opportunities to reiterate the importance of safety protocols and actions. This hands-on approach to safety stresses continuous improvement and safety coaching.

Formally, athletic administration should administer safety audits. A safety audit is

> an in-depth analysis of facilities, management and employee, attitudes toward safety, managerial effectiveness in maintaining safety, and quality of the safety planning, as well as operation's conformity with safety regulations…. Overall performance in controlling the operation's safety is the audit quest, rather than simply determining existing safety oversights. Audit is comparable to inspection, but differs ordinarily in intensity with which the examination is conducted. (Aswathappa, 2005, p. 481)

Administrators can promote other areas and impact sports or recreation program safety by (1) developing safety initiatives and incentive contests for individuals and groups, (2) underscoring, during the interview process and orientation, safety protocols and training for all new hires, (3) incorporating tangible safety responsibilities into each job design and descriptions, and (4) supplying program members an anonymous 24 hour, 7 day a week safety hotline to report any apprehensions, concerning behaviors, practices, and conditions without the fear of reprisal.

Individual Responsibilities Toward Safety

The individual sports or recreation program employees also have clear-cut responsibilities toward program safety. Program stakeholders first must recognize and respect the magnitude of safe workplace practices for themselves and others. Their personal responsibility starts with knowing and following safety protocols and respecting all established safety policies, procedures, and actions. Unquestionably, they must hold themselves accountable for safety in the sports or recreation program. Employees must also comprehend that their safety viewpoints have practical value and they have a voice to express those insights. By whatever method—formal safety committee work or informal discussions—employees must appreciate that they are practicing contributors to a safe working environment. Finally, employees should recognize understand their safety rights, which are central to the program's safety management and culture.

Wellness Programs

The adage, You can lead a horse to water but can't make him drink, is remarkably applicable to a wellness program. Typically, wellness programs and their events, activities, presentations, counseling, are voluntary, non-compulsory activities offered to program employees, and are primarily implemented due to anas,"[e]mployer's desire to improve productivity, decrease absenteeism, and control healthcare costs [that] have come together in the wellness movement. Wellness programs are designed to maintain and improve employee health before problems arise" (Mathis, Jackson, & Valentine, 2014, p. 506). In other words, proactive wellness programs function under the assertion that content and healthy personnel collectively make a more efficient, energetic, and industrious workforce. Moreover, the quality of life for active wellness program participants is exponentially higher than the average, non-participating program employee. To have and participate in a wellness program is the quintessential win-win scenario for both the program and its employees.

As with virtually all business decisions, the first aspect to address is cost. How much will it cost to develop and implement a wellness program? Obviously, if a sports or recreation program has substantial resources, cost could be budgeted and absorbed within the organization's operating budget. Contracts can be sent out for bid pricing and services could be bartered (e.g. in-kind trade) to control expenses. If the sports or recreation program is functioning on a tight budget, viable strategies can be employed to provide services while maintaining fiscal responsibility. To create wellness opportunities while staying within one's budget, a feasible low-cost, but impactful strategy could be to offer annual or semi-annual wellness fairs. Inviting the program's benefit suppliers, as well as national associations and local community businesses can be a solid first step in coordinating a wellness program, as many of these operations can underwrite much of the cost of their attendance and participation. Table 10.6 provides a list of useful and appropriate wellness fair participants.

Participation by external organizations may charge fees associated with on-sight services. The cost of their should be negotiated before their participation, and publicized to attendees prior to the event. The Center for Disease Control and Prevention (CDC) provides numerous resources for partnering with external wellness programs and organizations.

> **HR Tip**
> Developing wellness programs can have a substantial bottom-line impact on the sports or recreation program, through increased productivity and work output, and through insurance cost reductions.

Ongoing Wellness and Health Programs

An organization can provide ongoing emotional and physical wellness activities and counseling to it stakeholders through an Employee Assistance Programs (EAP). The United States Office of Personnel Management defines an EAP as:

TABLE 10.6 Potential Wellness Fair Participants

Benefit Providers	Medical Health Plan Provider(s)
	Dental Plan Administrators
	Vision and Eye Care Insurance
	Health Insurance Supplier (Short-Term and Long-Term Disability)
Flu Shot and Vaccination Services	
Cardio Screening	Blood Pressure Testing
	Cardio Vascular Screening
Diabetes Screening	Blood Testing
Local Health Clubs	Personal Trainers
	Yoga Instructors
	Aerobics Instructors
	Martial Arts Instructors
	Cross Fit Trainers
Local Community Centers	Program Coordinators
	Child Care Specialists
	Summer Camp Administrators
Chiropractic and Massage Services	Fully Licensed Practitioners and Interns/Practicum Students
Hearing Tests	
Dieticians	
Local/National Fitness Clubs and Associations	Biking, Swimming, Hiking, etc.
Local Restaurants	Healthy Cooking Demonstrations
Nutrition/Vitamin/Heath Retailers	
Campus and Local Police	Safety Course Instruction
Local Hospital Representatives	
Mental Health Counselors	Stress Reduction Specialists
	Family Counseling
	Personal Counseling
Other Health Organizations	American Heart Association, American Red Cross, American Lung Association, American Cancer Association, local and national charitable operations, etc

TABLE 10.7 Potential EAPs in Sports and Recreation Programs

Emotional & Psychological Assistance Programs	*Physical Assistance Programs/Lifestyle Choices Support*
Substance abuse testing, intervention, rehabilitation	Weight management and onsite dietitians
Smoking intervention and treatment	Lunchtime conditioning
Gambling addiction treatment	Onsite daycare
Occupational stress and burnout therapy (home and work life balancing)	Ergonomic equipment (minimize repetitive motion injuries)
Anger management	Personal days
Child care	Social activities (achievement parties, team building, athletic teams, etc.)
Elder care	
Financial and legal counseling	
Family violence and abuse counseling	

a voluntary, work-based program that offers free and confidential assessments, short-term counseling, referrals, and follow-up services to employees who have personal and/or work-related problems. EAPs address a broad and complex body of issues affecting mental and emotional well-being, such as alcohol and other substance abuse, stress, grief, family problems, and psychological disorders. EAP counselors also work in a consultative role with managers and supervisors to address employee and organizational challenges and needs. Many EAPs are active in helping organizations prevent and cope with workplace violence, trauma, and other emergency response situations.

Table 10.7 provides a registry of potential EAPs that can be developed and implemented by a sports or recreation program. Depending on the organization and its resources, some of the EAPs can be located onsite, while other will be outsourced to local professionals. Only licensed professionals with impeccable service records should be considered for a sports or recreation program's EAP.

Summary

Safety management in a sports or recreation program is paramount. By developing an employee-centered safety culture, the program can create a work environment that increases productivity and long-term stakeholder retention. Through a cooperative system, administrators and program employees create safety policies and procedures, establish safety protocol and standards, appreciate and participate in safety training, and will be prepared to handle accidents and subsequent investigations.

Wellness programs are designed to provide assistance in maintaining and increasing personnel health and wellbeing. By utilizing wellness fairs and EAPs, sports and recreation program administrators provide a myriad of tools for program members to sustain mental and physical health and happiness in the workplace.

References

Aswathappa, K. (2005). *Human resource and personnel management: Text and cases* (4th ed.). New Delhi, India: Tata McGraw-Hill.

Mathis, R. L., Jackson, J. H., & Valentine, S. R. (2014). *Human resource management* (14th ed.). Stamford, CT: Cengage Learning.

McKinnon, R. C. (2014). *Changing the workplace safety culture*. Boca Raton, FL: CRC Press.

National Safety Council. (2013, November 25). 7 steps to create and effective workplace safety training program. [NSC Blog]. Retrieved from http://blog.nsc.org/7-steps-create-effective-workplace-safety-training-program

Page, S. (2002). *Best practices in policies and procedures*. Westerville, OH: Process Improvement Publishing.

Phillips, J. M., & Gully, S. M. (2014). *Human resource management*. Mason, OH: South-Western/Cengage.

Rue, L. W., Ibrahim, N. A., & Byars, L. L. (2016). *Human resource management* (11th ed.). New York, NY: McGraw-Hill Education.

Sinay, J. (2014). *Safety management in a competitive business environment*. Boca Raton, FL: CRC Press.

Stranks, J. (2006). *Health and safety handbook*. Burlington, MA: Elsevier Butterworth-Heinemann.

Snell, S., Morris, S., & Bohlander, G. W. (2016). *Managing human resources* (17th ed.). Boston, MA: Cengage Learning.

U.S. Department of Labor, Bureau of Labor Statistics. [website]. National Census of Fatal Occupational Injuries in 2016. Retrieved from https://www.bls.gov/news.release/cfoi.nr0.htm

U.S. Department of Labor, Bureau of Labor Statistics. [website]. Employer-Reported Workplace Injuries and Illnesses in 2016. Retrieved from https://www.bls.gov/news.release/osh.nr0.htm

U.S. Department of Labor. (n.d.). Occupational Safety and Health Administration [website]. Business Casof Workplace Injuries. Retrieved from https://www.osha.gov/dcsp/products/topics/businesscase/costs.html

U.S. Office of Personnel Management. [website] (n.d.). What is an employee assistance program (EAP)? Retrieved from https://www.opm.gov/faqs/QA.aspx?fid=4313c618-a96e-4c8e-b078-1f76912a10d9&pid=2c2b1e5b-6ff1-4940-b478-34039a1e1174

Review and Discussion Questions

1. Define the concept of safety management.

2. From OSHA 2016 statistics, what do U.S. employers pay per week for direct workman compensation costs?

3. In the U.S. in 2016, how many non-fatal workplace injuries and illnesses were reported?

4. What is a safety culture?

5. A sports or recreation organization's safety culture is influenced by what factors?

6. Describe the change mechanism unfreeze, change, refreeze.

7. What are the three fundamental levels of safety policies and procedures?

8. What are the seven steps to creating a workplace safety program for sports or recreation programs?

9. Why is first aid/CPR training so important in sports and recreation programs?

10. Explain e-learning.

11. Define these three terms: frequency rate, severity rate, and disabling rate.

12. What can safety data be used for?

13. What information should be on a laminate safety procedure card?

14. What are the priority actions in an emergency accident procedure?

15. What are the secondary actions in an emergency accident procedure?

16. What are the administrative actions in an emergency accident procedure?

17. Summarize the steps in an accident investigation.

18. What are the four sections of an incident report?

19. What is MBWA and why is it useful in sports and recreation program safety management?

20. What can an administrator do to promote and impact safety management?

21. What are employee wellness programs?

22. Name five potential participants and why they are appropriate for a sports or recreation program wellness fair?

23. What are employee assistance programs (EAPs)?

24. Name five emotional/psychological employee assistance programs.

25. Name five physical assistance/lifestyle choice employee assistance programs.

Application Exercises

1. Review a real-world athletic facility in the local area, with the permission of the facility's athletic administration/operators. Analyze the facility's (1) work environment safety, (2) emergency evacuation plan, (3) accident procedures/action steps, and (4) special safety circumstances. Be critical and specific in your analysis/critique.

2. From the information derived in exercise 1, develop a safety improvement plan for the facility. After academic review, submit the written safety improvement plan to the administrators or operators of the facility.

3. Construct, from the ground-up, a wellness fair event for a real or fictitous recreation program. Outline these events:

   - Goals and objectives

   - Dates and times

   - Location

   - Potential business partner participants

   - Anticipated attendance

   - Room and floor schematic

   - Incentive for attendance (promotional items, activities and entertainment, free testing, free services, etc.)

   - Evaluation system

chapter eleven

Ethical Strategies in Human Resource Management

Chapter Objectives

- Understand the concept, intricacies, and the importance of strong ethical standards in a sports and recreation program
- Explain the connection between a program's culture and its ethical core
- Understand the potential influences on ethical behavior
- Understand program leadership's role in establishing ethical standards
- Understand the function of ethical training in sports and recreation programs
- Identify a code of ethics and a code of conduct and their functions in a sport and recreation program

Key Terms

Ethical Behavior and Actions
Unethical Behavior and Actions
Ethical Standards
Program Culture
Upbringing/Background/
   Experiences
Greed/Financial Gain
Self-Serving Rationalization

Societal Influences
Coercive Leadership
Groupthink
Unethical Leadership
Prejudice/Discrimination
Blind Conformity/Loyalty
Interpersonal Dysfunctional
   Conflicts

Politicized Environment
Ethical Leadership
Ethical Training
Code of Ethics
Code of Conduct
Ethical Code of Conduct

Why Ethics Matter

The intricacies of interpretation applied to ethics is one of the most complex in our world today, evidenced by the myriad choices made by businesses, societies, and political systems the world over. Even among families, individuals within a family can show great disparity of meaning and influence. Before delving into the topic of ethical strategies in human resource management, it must be clear that the content of this chapter is not presented to sermonize and lecture the reader on what is ethically appropriate, or to identify specific behaviors or viewpoints that should be taken or adopted by administrators of a sport or recreation program. Throughout life, people will encounter literally thousands of personal and professional situations in which ethical choices must be made. No book can provide definitive answers to every potential situation. Ultimately, then, *ethics* can be considered a relative term rather than absolute.

But even in relative terms, general statements can be applied to ethics as a set of principles or a form of conduct and what that means in terms of influencing desired behavior in a sport and recreation program. In his book, *Human Values and Ethics in the Workplace*, Martin (2011) provides six themes that can be universally applied to the ethics.

1. *Customs and norms*, concerned with the agreements that societies reach about what is right and wrong.

2. *Social conformity*, concerned with the process of valuing actions as right or wrong or good or bad, which is distinct from other opinions and implies the ability to distinguish moral reasons from what other people think.

3. *Character*, through ethical actions that reflect back on what we think of persons (or organizations), which implies that people recognize themselves as moral agents responsible for their own actions.

4. *Principles*, which are universal and more than a fixed, blind set of rules of behavior, so it entails reasoning about behavior and choices.

5. *Altruism*, moral and ethical behavior distinguished apart from actions aimed at the person's own success, as unselfishness, or a concern for the welfare of others.

6. *Conduct*, how people act, aside from theoretical interest, or a motivation for choices of action in a manner consistent with the tenets above.

(Martin, 2011, p. 41)

HR Tip

Ethics are not laws. Human resource laws, as described in Chapter 2, are edicts, decrees, or formalized declarations established by a society through government legislated procedures. Ethics are introspective principles that vary greatly from individual to individual and typically are not enforced through a society's legal system. Could an ethical situation necessitate a law? If deemed important enough by a society, absolutely.

Creating, comprehending, and following ethical standards in a sports or recreation program is critical. Most importantly, it should be understood that ethical standards are not commodities or luxuries, but program necessity. Ethical standards legitimize the sports or recreation program internally for staff, coaches, counselors, and administrators, and externally for customers, supporters, boosters, and the general public. Human resource ethics and ethical standards for internal program stakeholders go beyond what is considered right and wrong, which are personal, subjective, often strongly held views. Ethical standards defined in the core ideals of the program's value statements can guide internal stakeholder behaviors, judgements, and, ultimately, actions. Establishing ethical standards for the operation's human resource personnel is a way to take individual, subjective ethical foundations from internal stakeholder upbringing, background, education, and experience and unify them into an organizational paradigm and culture. For external stakeholders, having strong and well publicized ethical standards provide a strong foundation for positive public relations, which increases patronage and sustainable competitive advantages. In essence, having admirable ethical standards, and living up to those standards, increases a sports or recreation program's brand value and public perception.

An undeniable connection exists between a sports or recreation program's ethical principles and its culture. There is some debate on whether a program's culture stems from its ethical principles or if the operation's ethical principles originate in its culture. Either way, the bond between the two and the impact they have on each other is irrefutable. A sports and recreation program with a strong culture that accentuates citizenship, professionalism, and social responsibility will also have sound corresponding ethical standards that shape the moral foundation of the operation. People in those programs will be more reflective and conscious of the cascading impact of their actions on individuals, groups, and society. Regrettably, the opposite is also true. Sports and recreation programs with weak cultures that emphasize a deliberate and sometimes malicious disregard for citizenship, professionalism, and social responsibility will likely have few or no ethical standards. The character of these operations will be disjointed, self-serving, and often self-destructive.

Unethical Behavior

What drives people to behave unethically? To counteract or prevent unethical behavior, it is first necessary to recognize some fundamental factors that can lead to its acceptance and adoption.

Upbringing, Background and Experiences. Harris and Hoffman (2002) state that each individual differs on the

> basis of background, involving educational, cultural, social, and ethnic dissimilarities. The differences in workers' backgrounds tend to influence the philosophical values of the workers. An individual's philosophy provides a set of guidelines or principles by which the individual's life is conducted. Because individuals' backgrounds are different, their philosophies tend to differ. Differences in philosophies will have a direct bearing on individual behaviors. (p. 377)

It should be recognized that just because individuals have divergent and conflicting upbringing, background, and experiences does not mean that they will have incompatible ethical standards. Conversely, individuals with very comparable if not indistinguishable upbringing, background, and experiences can have tremendously contradictory ethical philosophies.

Pressure. in the form of stress and anxiety can be both real and perceived. Real, tangible pressure in the workplace can be, for example, (1) bottom-line cultures where attaining one's quantitative goals is the only factor for performance assessments and job retention, (2) impracticable expectations where performance measures are set well beyond what an individual can realistically accomplish, (3) a hostile work environment which can make an individual anxious and defensive, (4) negligible authority to make decisions which, in turn, impacts the individual's job performance, (5) having an inhospitable physical work environment, (6) job insecurity, downsizing, and professional obsolescence, and (7) an unworkable balance of personal or family obligations with work responsibilities. Perceived pressure comes from internal fears and self-doubt. Each program stakeholder reacts differently to interpersonal confrontations, office politics, frustration, authority, and group dynamics.

Greed and Financial Gain. One of the most prevailing motivators for unethical behavior is greed. Knight and Willmott (2007) best define greed:

> When materialistic societies are conceived to be the most 'civilized,' the greed that they inspire is readily identified as an essential feature of human nature. On reflection, economic self-interest is found not to be an essential quality of human nature. It is, rather, an effect of how in contemporary, materialistic societies, the individual and wealth are elevated as key values. In short, greed has become a widespread, normal pattern of behavior—so widespread that economic self-interest is commonsensically regarded as inherent to human nature. (pp. 7-8)

Self-Serving Rationalization. Individuals, typically with an elevated and often misplaced opinion of themselves, can justify unethical behavior due to a prevailing belief in their own righteousness, prestige, and value to the sports or recreation program. They believe strongly in ethical standards for other individuals, but not for themselves. Moreover, their condemnation and vocal denunciation for others committing ethical violations can be severe, while their own unethical improprieties are often "rationalized away."

Societal Influences. Societal influences on unethical behavior can be immeasurable. Through traditional societal avenues such as television, movies, social groups, and publications to contemporary influences, such as social media, blogs, and websites, the power these societal outlets have on ethical behavior and, regrettably, unethical behavior is tremendous.

Coercive Leadership Approach. Kumar and Meenakshi (2009) define this situation, which is primed for unethical behavior, as

> the leader creates a reign of terror, bullying and demeaning his executives, shouting his displeasure at the slightest misstep… Employees feel disrespected and they lose their sense of responsibility. Unable to act on their own initiative, they lose their sense of ownership and do not feel accountable for their performance. Some employees are so disgusted with their leader that they vow not to do anything for him. (p. 115)

Sports or recreation program employees in this type of environment will care little or nothing about ethical or unethical behavior. Because of anger and frustration, they frequently try to hurt the organization, either through covert unethical sabotage or overt unethical activities. Feeling powerless, unethical behaviors by people in these strict authoritarian working conditions can often be a "call for help."

Groupthink. This phenomenon also known as Don't Rock the Boat thinking, can be a powerful contributor to intentional or unintentional ethical misjudgments. Due to forceful demands to conform, these groupthink errors of judgment can be in the form of actions taken or actions not taken.

> Groupthink results from pressures on individual members to conform and reach consensus. Groups and teams that are suffering from groupthink are so bent on reaching consensus that there is no realistic appraisal of alternative courses of action in a decision, and deviant, minority, or unpopular views are suppressed. (Luthans, Luthans, & Luthans, 2015, p. 318).

Unethical Leadership. Simply stated, zealous, passionate leaders have a powerful control over the sports or recreation program and its internal stakeholders. Whether for good or bad, they create the standard for the behaviors and actions of the operation. If for good, they can pilot the sports or recreation program through wide-ranging ethical conundrums. They "walk-the-talk" and have an unqualified commitment to ethical integrity. If for bad, they can motivate program personnel, through their strength of character and dynamic personalities, to perform behaviors and actions those personnel would otherwise never consider.

Weak leaders either through a laissez faire attitude or managerial incompetence set minimal operating guidelines and allow the group to fall into operational chaos. If the sports or recreation program is mature and self-sufficient, ethical standards can be self-regulated and maintained. If the program personnel are immature and inexperienced, environmental forces without leadership to guide them could overwhelm and drive them to desperate, unethical behaviors and actions.

Other Factors for Potential Unethical Behavior

Operational Strategies. Whether by deliberate design or unintentional happenstance, a sports or recreation program in their operational plan and subsequent human resource plan can strategize future policies, procedures, objectives, and tactics that are unethical.

Systemic Factors. Whether by deliberate design or unintentional happenstance, a sports or recreation program's operational systems could be established and utilized unethically. A simplistic but relevant example could be a payroll system that classifies full-time employees as independent contractors.

Prejudice/Discrimination. Discriminatory practices of any kind, especially individual or cultural are highly unethical and illegal and must be recognized as a possible contributor to unethical behavior and actions.

Blind Conformity/Loyalty. Having 100% loyalty to an organization, in this case, a sports or recreation program, is an admirable quality. Having blind conformity and devotion to an organization without questioning its motives, behaviors and actions, can be a contributor to a highly unethical environment.

Interpersonal Dysfunctional Conflicts. Interpersonal conflicts can be extremely emotional, and frequently lead to ill-advised encounters and unethical behaviors and action.

Politicized Environment. "Political activities are, by definition, not formally sanctioned by organizations. In other words, power and politics in organizations, by their nature, are a self-serving process" (Nahavandi, Denhardt, Denhardt, & Aristigueta, 2015, p. 417). If a sports or recreation program has a politicized internal environment, members, in their desire for power, may possibly use any means, including unethical behaviors, to gain influence and authority. For example, in a politicized environment where promotions are given by status and power rather than by performance measures, program employees may undertake any scheme or maneuver to gain an advantage (e.g., developing power alliances, setting group against group, or falsifying information on other personnel—these are just a small number of unethical actions that could be employed).

Below Market Rewards. Unfortunately, under-rewarding employees can often lead to unethical behavior and actions.

Ethical Behavior Is Everyone's Responsibility

The solution to the question, Who is responsible for ethical standards and conduct in a sports or recreation organization? can be answered fairly easy: everyone. From entry-level and base positions to the executive administration level, every internal stakeholder is accountable to each other. Individuals in leadership and supervisory positions have a special obligation to the organization and its ethical benchmarks. Phillips and Gully (2014) provide an excellent description of ethical leadership as:

> The demonstration of normatively appropriate conduct through personal actions and interpersonal relationships, and the promotion of such conduct to followers through two-way communication, reinforcement, and decision making.… Because ethical leaders are caring and fair, followers' relationships with them are built upon social exchange and reciprocity norms. An ethical leader's followers want to reciprocate the leader's supportive treatment with their own ethical behavior. Research has found that employees' perception of their supervisor's ethical leadership are positively related to their willingness to report problems to management, job commitment, and satisfaction with their supervisor. (p. 434)

Ethical leaders are uniquely focused on operational actions that are right and in everyone's best interest, they lead-by-example, and are 100% dedicated to training and instilling ethical ideals. In order to act ethically, the sports or recreation programpersonnel must be able to distinguish between ethical and unethical actions; It is here that sports and recreational program leaders commit to ethics training.

> The goal of ethics training is to help the organization avoid governmental and societal sanctions by preventing unethical and illegal behavior. During training, employees discuss a code of ethics, organizational procedures for reporting unethical behavior, ethical frameworks based on ethics theories, and case studies showing ethical and unethical decisions. (Champoux, 2017, p. 63)

Ethics training should be regarded as an ongoing endeavor of diagnosing and adjusting to new and challenging circumstances. An ethics team should be established to develop program processes to review and create, or revise ethical principles and requirements for all program personnel. These principles and requirements should be publicized throughout the entire organization.

HR Tip

A core concept in the development and launching of ethical standards in sports or recreation programs is in the assertion that ethics must be a two-way street. The organization's ethical obligations to its people must be an operational imperative, while the program employee's ethical obligation to the organization should be absolute. For an organization to achieve its ethical goals, reciprocity is key between the organization and its employees.

Constructing an Ethical Code of Conduct

Several scholars support isolating a code of ethics from a code of conduct. For example, in the textbook *Business Ethics: Ethical Decision Making and Cases*, Ferrell, Fraedrich, and Ferrell (2009) defend this approach in this way:

A code of **ethics** is the most comprehensive and consists of general statements, sometimes altruistic and inspirational, that serve as principles and the basis for rules of conduct. A code of ethics generally specifies methods for reporting violations, disciplinary action for violations, and a structure of due process. A code of conduct is a written document that may contain some inspirational statements, but usually acceptable and unacceptable types of behavior. A code of conduct is more akin to a regulatory set of rules and, as such, tends to elicit less debate about specific actions. (p. 214)

In broad terms, a code of ethics is a wide-ranging document that authenticates core ethical pronouncements, while a code of conduct is a more explicit and itemized management instrument with identifiable actions to be taken. For expediency, this text will not make a distinction between a code of ethics and a code of conduct, but will instead combine them as an ethical code of conduct, as a foundation and inspiration for ethical behavior of stakeholders while providing practical strategies and actions for specific ethical situations.

No matter what format one considers to write a code of ethics, when constructing individual and specific ethical codes of conduct, some salient directives should be followed.

1. Be clear about the objectives the code is intended to accomplish.

2. Get support and ideas for the code from all levels of the organization.

3. Be aware of the latest developments in the laws and regulations that affect your industry.

4. Write as simply and clearly as possible. Avoid legal jargon and empty generalities.

5. Respond to real-life questions and situations.

6. Provide resources for further information and guidance.

7. In all its forms, make it user-friendly.

(Hartman & DesJardins, 2008, p. 126)

Table 11.1 identifies some universal areas to consider when developing an ethical code of conduct. The sports or recreation program and its collective personnel together determine which areas should be (1) included and (2) defined in the ethical code of conduct.

> ## HR Tip
> A key element to establishing ethical cohesion among program members starts in the interview process. A fundamental criterion for new employee selection should be the individual's ethical make-up and their compatibility with the sports or recreation program's ethical standards. A negative disconnect between the individual's ethical foundation and the ethical standards of the sports or recreation program should be a red flag, and a strong consideration to preclude the candidate from joining the operation.

TABLE 11.1 Areas of Focus for an Ethical Code of Conduct

Cross-Cultural Sensitivity

Use of Inherent Power in Operation

Loyalty

Workplace Safety

Total Quality Commitment

Professionalism

Integrity, Respect, Positive Identity

Racial Equality

Gender Equality

Religious Acceptance

Emotional Intelligence

Citizenship and Civility

Honesty

Equity and Fairness

Embracing Demographic Diversity and Individuality

Coherent Organizational Justice System

Teamwork, Common Identity, and Collective Goals/Mission

Inclusive Family Atmosphere

Communication, Information Sharing, Transparency, and Feedback Systems

Professional Transparency and Positional Knowledge

Mutual Accountability versus Self-Interest

Trust and Cooperation

Empowerment, Creativity, and Innovation

Summary

The benefits of a sound, ethically focused sports or recreation program is immeasurable. Internal integrity and professionalism combined with positive external perceptions are a formidable combination that can furnish a distinct competitive advantage for the program. Prior to delving into ethical standards, an examination of what can cause individuals to act unethically is a prudent exercise. By comprehending these factors, administrators can guide the program through various situations to make ethical choices.

The basis for establishing and implementing ethical standards is the supposition that the entire operation should be vested in the developmental process and have meaningful input into what the sports or recreation program wants to emphasize as its moral foundation. Leadership facilitates inclusion and input by everyone in the program, and leads by example in every ethical circumstance.

A salient tool for the reiteration and emphasis of ethics in a sports or recreation program is the ethical code of conduct, which can be both inspirational directive in nature, and should be the core document for instilling and guiding the sports or recreation program's ethical ideals as well as a bonding element for the entire operation.

References

Champoux, J. E. (2017). *Organizational behavior: Integrating individuals, groups, and organizations* (5th ed.). New York, NY: Routledge.

Ferrell, O. C., Fraedrich, J., & Ferrell, L. (2010). *Business ethics: Ethical decision making and cases* (7th ed.). Mason, OH: South-Western/ Cengage.

Harris, O. J., & Hoffman, S. J. (2002). *Organizational behavior*. New York, NY: Best Business Books/ Haworth Press.

Hartman, L. P., & DesJardins, J. (2008). *Business ethics: Decision-making for personal integrity and social responsibility*. New York, NY: McGraw-Hill/Irwin.

Knight, D., & Willmott, H. (2007). *Introducing organizational behavior and management*. London, England, Thompson Learning.

Kumar, A., & Meenakshi, K. (2009). *Organizational behavior: A modern approach*. New Delhi, India: Vikas Publishing.

Luthans, F., Luthans, B. C., & Luthans, K. W. (2015). *Organizational behavior: An evidence-based approach* (13th ed.). Charlotte, NC: Information Age Publishing.

Martin, G. (2011). *Human values and ethics in the workplace*. Cherrybrook, NSW: Australia: G. P. Martin Publishing.

Nahavandi, A., Denhardt, R. B., Denhardt, J.V., & Aristigueta, M. P. (2015). *Organizational behavior*. Thousand Oaks, CA: Sage.

Phillips, J. M., & Gully, S. M. (2014). *Organizational behavior* (2nd ed.). Mason, OH: South-Western/Cengage.

Review and Discussion Questions

1. Describe the complexity involved with the term *ethics*.

2. What are some universal feature for the term *ethics*?

3. What are some of the benefits of ethical standards for sports or recreation program internal stakeholders?

4. What is the connection between a program's culture and its ethical standards?

5. What are some factors of real workplace pressure?

6. Define greed.

7. What is self-serving rationalization?

8. What is coercive leadership?

9. Define groupthink.

10. How can sports or recreation program leadership influence ethics (good and bad)?

11. What is blind conformity/loyalty? How can it contribute to unethical behavior?

12. What is the ethical impact of a politicized work environment?

13. Describe ethical leadership.

14. What is an ethical code of conduct?

15. What are the seven directives when constructing individual codes of ethics?

16. Name and describe three potential components in an ethical code of conduct.

17. How do ethics tie into the interview and selection process?

Application Exercises

1. Research and download a corporation's ethical code of conduct. From concepts presented in the chapter, critique the document.

2. Research and investigate a high-profile instance of unethical corporate (or sports or recreation organization) behavior. Describe the circumstances, unethical behaviors, and possible actions that could have been used to prevent the occurrence.

3. Research and complete a profile of an ethical leader (any profession – business, politics, sports, etc.). Highlight this individual's core ethical principles.

Human Resource Management
Term Project
Individual Written and Oral Presentation

The student will have a final individual project as a part of their course grade. The assignment will be divided into two graded components.

Component 1

The student will present a written paper on human resource management ethics topic. The paper will be 10–15 pages in length and will be written within accepted academic style (APA). All concepts should be well supported with current researched references.

Component 2

The student will present research findings on the written topic in a formal oral presentation. The presentation will be 15 minutes in length with a 5–10-minute Q&A session. Visual aids or PowerPoint slides will be utilized to assist with the presentation.

Term Project Topics

Age Discrimination

Americans with Disabilities Act

Women in the Workplace

Stereotypes

Workplace Stress

Sexual Harassment

Conflict Management

Cross-Cultural Sensitivity

Term Project Oral Presentation Structure and Template

Foundational components for designing and implementing an oral presentation for individual or group speeches for a sports or recreation management human resource course

Oral Presentation Purpose and Objectives

- Construct bonds with audience
- Convince and inspire audience
- Communicate materials to audience
- Foster professional interactions with audience

Foundations of the Communication Model

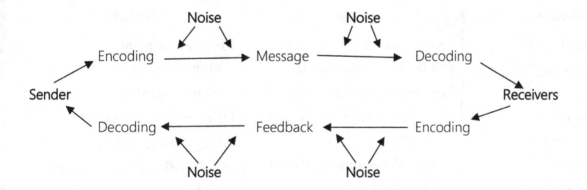

5 Steps in Planning a Formal Presentation

1. Establish goals and objectives of the presentation
2. Audience delineation and evaluation
3. Presentation timetable and limits
4. Succinct and relevant conveying of information
5. Determination of proper approach to dispense materials

Audience Analysis	Background assessment (experiences, education, socio-economic, etc.)
	Significant concerns and interest related to subject matter
	Assortment of cross-cultural backgrounds
	Viewpoints toward subject matter
	Sensitive toward subject matter
	Mental and physical condition of audience
Environmental Elements	Tangible Settings
	Social Settings
Feedback	Correct Interpretations
	Immediate Responses
	Explicit Verbalized
	Implicit Actions
Extemporaneous	Over Textual and Memorization
	Avoid Digressions
	Outline /Notes

Presentation Structure

Introduction	*Body*	*Conclusion*
Personal introduction(s)	Primary message and main points (3 or 4 maximum)	Revue major points (summarize)
Presenter(s) background and credibility	Logical progression	Action oriented (if appropriate)
Outline topic and major objectives	Flow from concept to concept – transitions	Drive home major points
Be concise and brief	Balance development of main points with details	Strong closing remarks
Attention grabber (audience specific)	Possible structure of body	Thank audience for attention/ attendance
• Quotation	• Time sequence – chronological or reverse	
• Anecdotes	• Categories and components	
• Humor	• Importance (most to least)	
• Rhetorical question	• Pre-established criteria	

Visual Aids

Main Types	Graphical Aids	General Tips
Power Point	Organizational Charts	Placement when appropriate in presentation
Posters	Flow Charts	Flow and geographic relationships
Flip Charts	Pie Charts	Audience specific
Smart Boards	Line Graphs	Technologically advanced
Slides	Bar Graphs	Information suitable
Video Clips	Maps	Easy to follow
Transparencies	Photos	Adequate for size of the room/ environment
Computer Online Web	Drawings/Schematics	Simple, brief, and uncomplicated (5-point rule)
Chalk Board		Titled
Animation		Timing – one every 1-2 minutes
		Dress rehearsal – prep in advance
		Triple checked
		Face audience when using visual aid

General Tips for Oral Presentations

1   Image, appearance and first impressions

2   Physical elements of the presenter

    Facial expressions

    Gestures

    Spacing with audience

    Eye contact; 180 degree technique

    Posture

    Natural movements

3   Articulation tips

    Pronounciations

    Word selection, audience specific

    Pitch, rate, volume, inflection and rhythm

    Positive words vs negative words

    Bias-free words: gender, age, sex, religion, disability

    Precise words vs. ambiguous words

    Redundancy in words and phrases

    Wordiness

4   Other general tips

Overcome internal barriers, introversion

Adaptability, contingency planning

Time and timing

Humor

Confidence; too much or too little

Friendliness

Enthusiasm

Put the brakes on concept

Introduce group members, have group facilitator

Resume Evaluation Checklist for Program Administrators

Evaluation criteria for incoming resume submissions can be utilized as a checklist when creating a pool of candidates for vacancies in a sport and recreation program. While there are no right or wrong formats and unlimited designs and layouts, some resumes, through their content and professionalism, work better than others. The typical resume format is either chronological or functional; the profession and position dictates which style or combination of styles will be most appropriate.

Key Questions

- Does the resume illustrate the bond between the applicant's competencies, depth, and accomplishments and the needs of the sports or recreation program?
- Is the resume tailored to the sports or recreation program or is it generic?
- Does the resume show the whole person, not just work experience and education?
- Does the resume sell the applicant without "hard selling?"
- Does the resume have significant time gaps?
- Does the first impression of the resume's presentation exude refinement and class?

Guidelines

- For entry level jobs, did the applicant limit the resume to one page?
- Did the resume utilize action words to illustrate the applicant's accomplishments?
- Does the resume employ an appropriate font (business)?
- Is the resume free of spelling/grammatical errors?
- Does the resume have good flow and spacing?
- If utilizing chronological style, are the categories in reverse chronological order?
- Was the resume paper 20-24 bond with matching envelops?
- Are there any inconsistencies that bring into question the resume's validity?

Resume Format

Heading	Name, title, address, phone numbers, email (business)
Job Objective	Attention grabbing and definitive
Administrative Qualifications **Managerial Qualifications**	Direct correlation between the applicant and the open position
Education and Certifications	Relevant coursework if work experience is insubstantial
	Academic awards
	Relevant certifications
Professional Experience	For each position, date (start/end years) and location (city/state),
	Description of the position, with at least 4 major responsibilities that relate to open position
	Narrative description or short bullet points
	Shows career progression (if possible) as well as stability
	Write in active voice (rather than passive)
Military Service	If applicable
Entrepreneurial ventures	If applicable
Honors, activities and awards	If applicable and relevant
Associations	Demonstrated leadership in this category
Campus activities	Responsibilities and accomplishments delineated
Community activities	Time duration for each
Professional memberships	

Appendix C

Undergraduate Internship Program Template

Program Composition

I. Mission Statement

XYZ University Sports Management Department is committed to provide the highest quality theoretical and practical sports and recreation management education for its undergraduate learners. The XYZ University Sports Management Internship Program is a targeted extension of this objective. The program is designed to:

- Give existing senior level students invaluable, real world occupational experience in leading sports and recreation management organizations.
- Cultivate enduring cooperative relationships with local, regional, and national sports and recreation organizations.
- Establish XYZ University as a viable supplier of superior entry level sports and recreation management employees and managers.
- To present conscientious, self-directed, and career-oriented student interns to sports and recreation organizations to assist in their operations and productivity.

II. Operational Overview

The operational abstract of the XYZ University Internship Program encompass the following six stages.

1. The Internship Program Director will, through interpersonal contacts, establish a foundation of ongoing sports and recreation management internships in the general location. The targeted number of continuous or perpetual internships should be 20-25, depending upon program interest and size of college or university sports and recreation management department. Additionally, special fixed term internships will also be solicited.

2. The undergraduate learner will formally apply and be interviewed for specific internships through the Internship Program Director. The student will be evaluated on the attached student prerequisite and provisos. All considerations will be made to match possible internship positions with the unique future aspiration of the learner.

3. Student who are qualified and selected will be set up with a traditional, formal interview at the specified internship location. The interview process will:
   - Match needs of the organization with qualifications of the management student.

- Determine cooperatively the working association between the management student and the organization. Issues such as job responsibilities, accountability, work hours, and job protocol will be discussed.
- Finalize the internship offer and acceptance.

4. On a weekly basis, the student will e-mail the Internship Program Director updates on the position, what relevant knowledge is being learned, and their distinct perspective of the internship.

5. The sports/recreation organization will be contacted every three weeks by the Internship Program Director to discuss the student's progress and ability to help the operation. While the conversations will be informal in nature, they will be utilized for the concluding evaluation.

6. At the end of the prearranged time frame for the internship, a formal evaluation will be completed by the sports/recreation organization's internship supervisor. Additionally, the student will present to the Internship Program Director a formal 1,000-word term paper discussing the comprehensive internship experience.

III. Student Criterion

The following is student prerequisite list for participation in the Internship Program. It is strongly recommended that **all** of the conditions must be met to be eligible for the program.

1. The student must be an XYZ University Sports/Recreation Management major.

2. The student must be at senior level status at time of internship (90 credits out of 120 semester hours). Applications for internships can be processed prior to senior status, but actual placement will not commence until senior standing has been achieved.

3. The student must have achieved a minimum overall of 3.0 GPA and a 3.25 GPA in sports/recreation management related courses.

4. The student must have a current resume and cover letter. These two documents will be submitted to the Internship Program Director at the initial interview as well as the sports/recreation organization internship interview.

5. The student must follow all interviewing procedures established by the prospective employer.

6. The student must commit 20 flexible hours per week for 14 total weeks for the internship. Hours are to be established by mutual cooperation between the intern and sports or recreation organization supervisor.

7. The student must have suitable transportation for internship.

8. On accepting the internship, the student must have a complete knowledge of the sponsoring sports/recreation organization's policies and operational procedures.

9. The student must recognize that the internship is:
   - an employment relationship with all of the associated duties and responsibilities;

- an external position in which conduct is a direct reflection on XYZ University and the Sports/Recreation Management Department; and

- a distinct privilege and recognition of their exemplary class work. As a privilege, it should not be taken lightly and the performance expectations are of the highest standard.

IV. Business Stipulations

The sports and recreation organization requisites for the internship program are straightforward and uncomplicated. The organization participating in the XYZ University Sports and Recreation Management Internship Program are required to:

1. Interview each prospective intern as they would a regular employee. Additionally, under the same premise, when hiring an intern, the individual should be treated no differently that any other worker.

2. Agree with the learner on job responsibilities, work schedules, and expectations.

3. Supervise the intern with the underling principle of teaching real world sports/recreation management practices, processes, and procedures.

4. Utilize the intern to the maximum of their abilities.

5. Complete a term ending final evaluation on the

   - work produced and contributions of the intern;

   - characteristics and aptitude of the intern; and

   - overall impressions of the intern.

Form 1 University Internship Course Agreement

Intern Name: _____

Daily Schedule:

    Monday _____   Tuesday _____

    Wednesday _____   Thursday _____

    Friday _____   Saturday _____

Job Duties – Primary:

_____

_____

_____

_____

_____

Job Duties – Supplementary

_____

_____

_____

Student's Signature: _____

Date: _____

Form 2 Internship Program E-Mail Template

Form 2 Weekly Updates

Intern Name: _____

Date of Update: _____

Job Duties Completed:

_____

_____

_____

Job Duties Pending:

_____

_____

_____

Comments:

_____

_____

_____

Form 3 Internship Program Student Checklist

Pre-Internship Items

1. Resume on file with internship program director
2. Initial meeting with internship program director
3. Internship contract completed by organization's direct supervisor
4. Copy of internship application
5. Copy of internship job description

Mid-Term Internship Meeting

1. Review internship log with documentation of job work and hours internship program director
2. Internship evaluation 1 from sports and recreation organization.

Post Internship Meeting

1. End of course paper (1,000 words on internship experience) to internship program director
2. Submission of internship log with documentation of job work and hours to internship program director
3. Internship evaluation 2 from sports and recreation organization

There should be one Internship Program Director visit to organization during term (mutually agreed upon time by all parties).

IRS Rules and Regulations for Employment Classifications

The Internal Revenue Service parameters and rulings specify the status of employees. Thus, it is imperative sports or recreation program administration to make the distinction for for all sport and recreation program postions, including administrators, supervisors, coaches, staff members, and unspecific personnel whether these positions are employees or independent contractors.

When evaluating personnel on their status, the engagement of both a lawyer and Certified Public Accountant is essential. These cautionary and preventive conferences could protect a sports or recreation program from expending considerable resources (time, money, personnel) in the future.

Two essential IRS webpages to review, with the operation's legal counsel and CPA are:

- IRS Independent Contractor (Self-Employed or Employee) found at http://www.irs.gov/ Businesses/Small-Businesses-&-Self-Employed/Independent-Contractor-Self-Employed-or -Employee
- IRS Independent Contractor Training Materials, Training 3320-102 (10-96) TPDS 84238I http://www.irs.gov/pub/irs-utl/emporind.pdf

Common Law Rules

The IRS clearly defines the the degree of control and independence of employees in three categories:

1. *Behavioral:* Does the company control or have the right to control what the worker does and how the worker does his or her job?
2. *Financial:* Are the business aspects of the worker's job controlled by the payer? (these include things like how worker is paid, whether expenses are reimbursed, who provides tools/supplies, etc.)
3. *Type of Relationship:* Are there written contracts or employee type benefits (i.e. pension plan, insurance, vacation pay, etc.)? Will the relationship continue and is the work performed a key aspect of the business?

Source: IRS.gov. (n.d.)

Businesses must weigh all these factors when determining whether a worker is an employee or independent contractor. Some factors may indicate that the worker is an employee, while other factors indicate that the worker is an independent contractor. There is no set number of factors that designates a worker as an employee or an independent contractor, and no one factor stands alone in making this determination. Also, factors relevant in one situation may not apply in another.

The keys are to look at the entire relationship, consider the degree or extent of the right to direct and control, and finally, to document each of the factors used in coming up with the determination.

Additionally, the IRS has a 20-area examination on whether a person is an independent contractor or an employee:

1. Must the individual take instructions from your management staff regarding when, where, and how work is to be done?

2. Does the individual receive training from your company?

3. Is the success or continuation of your business somewhat dependent on the type of service provided by the individual?

4. Must the individual personally perform the contracted services.

5. Have you hired, supervised, or paid individuals to assist the worker in completing the project stated in the contract?

6. Is there a continuing relationship between your company and the individual?

7. Must the individual work set hours?

8. Is the individual required to work full time at your company?

9. Is the work performed on company premises?

10. Is the individual required to follow a set sequence or routine in the performance of his work?

11. Must the individual give you reports regarding his/her work?

12. Is the individual paid by the hour, week, or month?

13. Do you reimburse the individual for business/travel expenses?

14. Do you supply the individual with needed tools or materials?

15. Have you made a significant investment in facilities used by the individual to perform services?

16. Is the individual free from suffering a loss or realizing a profit based on his work?

17. Does the individual only perform services for your company?

18. Does the individual limit the availability of his services to the general public.

19. Do you have the right to discharge the individual?

20. May the individual terminate his services at any time?

In general, "no" answers to questions 1-16 and "yes" answers to questions 17-20 indicate an independent contractor. However, a simple majority of "no" answers to questions 1 to 16 and "yes" answers to questions 17 to 20 does not guarantee independent contractor treatment. Some questions are either irrelevant or of less importance because the answers may apply equally to employees and independent contractors.

Consequences of treating an employee as an independent contractor: The IRS states, if you classify an employee as an independent contractor and you have no reasonable basis for doing so, you may be held liable for employment taxes for that worker.

Suggested Reading

IRS.gov (n.d.) Small Business and Self-Employed [website]. Behavioral Control https://www.irs.gov/businesses/small-businesses-self-employed/behavioral-control

IRS.gov (n.d.) Small Business and Self Employed [website]. Financial Control. https://www.irs.gov/businesses/small-businesses-self-employed/financial-control

IRS.gov (n.d.) Small Business and Self Employed [website]. Type of Relationship. https://www.irs.gov/businesses/small-businesses-self-employed/type-of-relationship

Appendix E

HR Practicum Project into Sport Management Curriculum

The essential premise behind any academic program's practicum project is to apply theoretical information attained through extensive coursework to real world situations. In the educational specialty of sports and recreation management, the most viable way for students to apply scholarly information into practical relevance is by practice. Student-developed human resource plans can enrich a student's education by allowing them to experience the entire process of designing and executing human resource strategies to an operational sports or recreation program. The stages involved for the integration of this practicum assignment into a college or university sports and recreation management or human resource management program of study. This appendix will include discussion of human resource planning guidelines, human resource plan templates, and grading rubric categories.

Practicum Rationale

An essential consideration in designing a practicum project for an undergraduate or graduate course should be the application of the student's sports and recreation management education. It is also an exceptional rubric for measuring a student's wide-ranging management knowledge, and the end product is the construction of a comprehensive human resource plan that can be implemented at a local or regional, small to mid-sized sports or recreation program.

The benefits of student-led development of human resource plans for sports and recreation organizations:

- Provide students with the opportunity to blueprint, construct, and implement practical applications from conceptual human resource management theories learned throughout their college experience

- Allow students to function in a real world, real time setting rather than using a stagnant case study or problem analysis methodology;

- Reiterate the substance of sport and recreation management and human resource management curriculum. In most cases, students will be challenged to re-examine coursework from prior years;

- Provide students with professional human resource management preparation in a controlled educational setting. The practicum allows students to transition and experience human resource management in sports and recreation environments while being soundly guided and mentored by experienced faculty practitioners;

- Develop community awareness for the quality of an institution's sports and recreation management students and their work product. This community consciousness can increase positive public perception or the college or university, which, in turn, can generate additional, higher quality applicants and local and regional corporate collaboration;

- Energize students in the learning process. The dynamic nature of the practicum lends itself perfectly to a a sense of accomplishment, much like they would experience in the real world.

- Refine a student's cognitive abilities by allowing them to think strategically and reason independently. This type of cognitive creativity is a major operational function of the human resource practicum and is ardently desired by sports and recreation organization employers.

- Work in a self-managed team environment that replicates future situations in the student's sports and recreation management or human resource management career.

The primary reasons sports and recreation organizations cooperatively engage in student-based projects, are practical. Such projects:

- furnish the organization with a free human resource plan, often of very high quality. This can provide a tremendous competitive advantage since most sports and recreation operations cannot afford the resources—mainly time and money—to construct their own human resource plan or to pay expensive outside consultants;

- allow sports and recreation program personnel to focus their human resource competencies and effort toward more effectual utilization;

- provid sports and recreation administrators with the ability to expand their attention from the day-to-day minutia of running a sports or recreation entity to re-examine long term goals and direction of human resource management;

- acquire an outside, objective view of the sports or recreation program's current human resource situation.

Practicum Overview

A human resource practicum is a far-reaching project intended exclusively for human resource and general sports and recreation management courses. Due to the demands and composition of the practicum, it should be integrated into the final semester of an undergraduate or graduate student's education. The practicum is the philosophical mindset of the student groups, from which two primary elements must be conveyed. First, the students are 'acting' as human resource management consultants for their sports or recreation administrators, staff, and organizations. As consultants, the team's main concentration will be to provide the operation with optimum achievable and ethical strategies and, ultimately, a quality human resource plan. While professional consultants receive monetary payments for services rendered, the student consultants get academic payment in the form of grades. Secondly, human resource plan groups must recognize that they are autonomous, self-managed teams with interdependent accountability to each other and the sports or recreation organization. Authority and empowerment should be a key ingredient of the team environment.

The selection of a sports or recreation organization in which to embed the practicum should meet four core criteria.

1. The organization is an authentic entity currently in business. Special exceptions can be made for new ventures that are an extension of a previously established sports or recreation program or department.

2. The organization does not have an operational human resource plan.

3. The operation is within a realistic and serviceable radius of the college or university.

4. The sports or recreation program administration or executive administrators can attend the group's final presentation of the human resource plan.

Outside these four standards, the choice of a sports or recreation entity is entirely up to the student group. It is advisable that the organization selected for the project be up to the student groups rather than the institution, department, or professor. Having students solicit and decide on their own organization vests them into the practicum process more enthusiastically. Their choices can come from networking family, friends, professional acquaintances, or from indiscriminate solicitations.

The three sections of the human resource plan practicum project include a prospectus overview, the written plan, and an oral presentation.

Practicum Design

Prospectus.   The initial 'practicum project entails having the student groups (ideally 3-5 members) create an authoritative prospectus of the proposed sports or recreation organization, its operations, and the rationale for the human resource plan. The prospectus, which is characteristically a 5-10-page document, presents a synopsis of the venture, as well as indispensable operational components. Questions and items in the prospectus can include but are not limited to:

- Location of the sports/recreation program, and how long has it been in operation
- Size of the venture (in personnel and number of programs
- Current structure of the sports/recreation management team and organization
- Basic environmental elements:
  - Competition
  - Target market demographics
  - Government and sports and recreation specific regulations
  - Social constraints
  - Economic
  - Natural
- Identify the organization's fundamental revenue stream
- Ways in which the sports or recreation program can distinguish their operation

- Launch details for the division or venture, if it is part of an established sports or recreation program

- Identify the organization's human resource stakeholders And strengths do they bring to the program

- Preliminary human resource SWOT analysis

- Geographic opportunities and concerns for the sports or recreation organization

- Why this particular sports or recreation organization was selected, and the benefits of a human resource plan for this organization

- Other details that are exclusive to the sports or recreation organization.

Important points the professor or instructor should consider in reviewing each prospectus: .

- Whether the terminology is pass/fail, go/no go, or approved/rejected, the prospectus should be a significant hurdle to overcome in the group's human resource plan development. A passing grade is an endorsement for the continuation of the practicum.

- The prospectus is the instructor's sole opportunity to scrutinize the necessity of the human resource plan and validity of the practicum. Once the prospectus is passed, approved or given the green light by the instructor's authority, the group can officially initiate the human resource plan project.

- The student consulting group should generate a written release that allows them to construct the venture's human resource plan. This release should be signed by the sports or recreation organization's principal administrator. Thatsignature constitutes a legitimate arrangement between the sports or recreation entity and the student group.

- An official thank you letter on college or university letterhead should be delivered to the program's administrator(s) from the Sports and Recreation Management Department Chair or Dean. The letter should detail the student group's objectives and the final product to be presented to the sports or recreation program.

The prospectus completion should be scheduled as early as possible in the academic term. Due to the work requirements of the other human resource plan elements, it is advisable to complete the prospectus within the first three or four sessions.

Practicum Operation

Once the prospectus has been endorsed by the course's faculty member, student groups should compose a thorough work distribution list and a detailed schedule for practicum completion. The course instructor should examine with the group the work distribution and timetables to ensure equitable task allocation, realistic feasibility of time schedules, and other peripheral curriculum commitments. Major checkpoints and deadlines should be integrated throughout the practicum timeline.

Student groups should establish five formal sessions with the sports or recreation organization administrators and staff throughout the course term, and include several informal meetings at the operation's convenience. The five formal meetings are described below.

Meeting One. The first human resource plan meeting encompasses group introductions and a tour of the facility and operations. It is strongly recommended that this meeting occur at the beginning of the course term; in most cases before prospectus is due. The objective of the meeting is to create a level of familiarity with all parties involved in the practicum and to assemble basic organizational information.

Meeting Two. The second human resource plan meeting is classified as the group module meeting. The primary purpose of this meeting is to collect and solidify information for the sections of the human resource plan. These sections in which all members contribute to the collective whole are comprised of

Section 1 - Operational Philosophy and Values for Human Resource,

Section 2 - Overview of Legal and Regulatory Components (as they relate to human resource)

Section 3 - Goals of Human Resource Management (long- and short-term), and

Section 4 - Human Resource Internal Assessment.

These human resource plan components are completed by the entire group as the core elements from which all other human resource plan segments emanate. In other words, all group members need to be "on the same page" with these sections for human resource plan consistency and cohesion. Due to the prerequisite nature of this group and sports or recreational program discussion, it should be scheduled into the practicum as early as possible.

Meeting Three. The third meeting with the sports or recreation organization should concentrate strictly on individual assignments in the human resource plan. Sections of the final plan that are normally prepared by individual group members are in Section 5 - Operational Components of Human Resources (current and future projections). Elements such as hierarchical structure, job descriptions, bod job descriptions, staff job descriptions, net human resource requirements and action plan, selection and hiring procedures, HRIS, orientation and training, performance management, reward systems, disciplinary system, and safety and health are all individually constructed. How the group defines and assigns these plan elements is determined by the completion dates, each student's level of expertise and strength, and the program's needs.

Meeting Four. The fourth meeting can be classified as the conclusive rundown or refinement session. During this meeting the group will fill-in any gaps of information needed to complete the human resource plan, confirm the completed written plan date, and verify the final presentation date, time, and format.

Meeting Five. The final group meeting with the sports or recreation organization is the official human resource plan presentation, which is discussed later in this appendix.

While there are five prearranged and structured meetings, there will be numerous informal visits and calls between the group or individual students and the sports or recreation program.

The key to a successful, productive session with sports or recreation administrators and staff is advanced preparation. The practicum instructor must communicate to the student groups that operation's administrators and staff members have tremendous time constraints and that their time is precious. Simply put, the more the group is organized and prepared for a meeting, the less time they will require from the administrators and staff, such preparation and professionalism, and ultimately the group and their project will be appreciated and received.

Research

Strong quantitative and qualitative research is central to the practicum. While the subjective human resource strategies designed by the group could be appropriate and applicable for the particular sports or recreation organization, solid research is needed to support these suppositions. The body of research employed by the student group is dependent on the level and capabilities of the students, the time allotted for the course and practicum, the sports or recreation environment in the geographic region, and the accessibility of current, relevant human resource secondary sources.

Written Human Resource Plan

As a central deliverable of the practicum, provided below is a conventional template which can be used in the construction of the actual hard-copy human resource plan. An extensive body of existing literature dedicated to human resource plan construction, can be adapted to sports and recreation human resource planning. It is advisable that the student groups construct their human resource plans from the 'ground up' rather than plugging strategies into a pre-established software program.

Resource Plan Breakdown

Section 1   Operational philosophy and values

Section 2   Overview of laws and regulations

Section 3   Short and long term goals of HR management

Section 4   Human resource internal assessment

Section 5   Current and future operational projections:

- HR information system
- Orientation and training
- Performance management
- Reward systems
- Disciplinary system
- Safety and health

There is no single standard format for a human resource plan. General sections are consistent but not order or format. Refer to Chapter 3 Appendix, p. 85 for an in depth discussion of each section of the Human Resource Plan.

The reputation of a college or university's Sports and Recreation Management Department in the community is keenly affected by all outside cooperative practica. Due to the direct external impact of the course's practicum, the written human resource plan must be thorough, complete and of superior quality

Student groups should consider the following suggestions intended to augment the quality and overall appearance of their written human resource plan.

- Provide a detailed table of contents.
- Createa a sectional format with headings and sub-headings. Major sections of the plan should be separated and clearly defined.
- Write in a clear cohesive way, so that the human resource plan reads as if one person wrote it. Flow and readability are important quality factors of the human resource plan.
- Review and provide accurate, error-free documents. The plan should be proofed and re-proofed before submission to eliminate spelling, grammatical and sentence structure errors.
- Quality materials and professional presentation. The paper, the ink, and the and business appropriate font are important.
- Control the plan by numbering and securing all copies for confidentiality.
- Provide the organization a flash drive of the human resource plan for future reference, review, and adjustments.

Oral Presentations

The oral presentation of the human resource plan to the administration of the sports or recreation organization should be described to the student groups as a business professional presentation with formal invitations and appropriate attire. The presentation should employ compelling visual aids to supplement the information being communicated. It is strongly suggested that the presentation be limited to a 30-minute time frame (+ or - 3 minutes) with a question and answer session of 15-20 minutes.

If the conventional course classroom is deemed unsuitable for a formal professional presentation, an alternative conference style room should be utilized. Due to the sensitive proprietary information being conveyed, most sports and recreational administrators will insist on a private, confidential presentation, and therefore may limit the audience.

Practicum Project Administration

An instructor must be mentally prepared for supervising an assignment of this intricacy and depth. Simply stated, this practicum needs a 100% commitment from all parties, including the faculty member. This extraordinary dedication from the faculty member entails not only embracing required course content but also the ongoing involvement and guidance with each student practicum group. Faculty members must have a well-rounded portfolio of subject knowledge and should have access to Sports and Recreation Management Department resources (other specialized faculty members) when the occasion and need arises. Instructors must be cognizant of their accessibility and the additional time commitment to the project. While accessibility is enhanced by modern communication methods, the most convenient being course webpages, e-mails, the extra time obligation can be considerable.

Grading the practicum is dependent on the instructor's introspective standards and expectations. However, there are some broad evaluation areas that can be applied collectively to all human resource plan projects.

Course rubrics should be utilized for both the final written human resource plan and oral presentations. The rubrics can help quantify subjective opinions. Generalized categories are identified here.

Oral Presentation Rubric

Preparedness	On Time Start-Finish-Total Time
	Technology/Power Point
	Room Set Up
	Human Resource Plan and Flash Drive Submitted
Introduction	Formal Introduction
	Items Covered
Body	Depth and Cognitive Work
	Assessment of Human Resource Strategies
Conclusions	Recap and Recommendations
Knowledge and Value of Content	Conveying the Critical Aspects of the Human Resource Plan
	Q&A Responses
	Q&A Overall Evaluation
Professionalism and Presentation Style	Transitions
	Dress
	Flow
	Overall
Power Point/Visual Aids	Number of Slides, Timing, and Reliance on Slides
	Appropriateness of Slides
	Overall

Written Human Resource Plan Rubric

Correct Human Resource Plan Format	Template, consistency in presentation, quality of presentation
Research Depth	Quantitative research, qualitative research, overall
Body and Sectional Completion	Depth, cognitive work, sectional depth
Grammar, Style, Sentence Structure, etc.	Errors, flow of presentation, overall
Content Relevance	Relevant and applicable human resource strategies, utilization of human resource theories

---

In grading the worth and quality of the student group's work, not only should the human resource strategies be considered, but also how well the group justified those strategic choices. In other words, the assessment of strategic validation should address not only the group's opinions but also the quantitative support through research to back those opinions.

Due to the sheer volume of work involved in the human resource practicum project, all group members must energetically contribute and participate in the entire process. The self-managed group model requires this, and must also include the ability of group to discipline or remove non-performers. The accountability process, which is dependent upon college or university policies may resemble the following:

> In the human resource plan practicum, a student may be removed from a group for non-participation in group work and activities. If group members feel that an individual is not contributing to the collective work required to complete the project, the group can submit a written statement to the instructor **detailing** the non-participation or transgressions of the student. This document must be collectively signed by **all** remaining group members. At this point, the documentation will be reviewed and the student will be given a zero for the project. The student can be reinstated if he/she can present tangible proof or documentation of project work and group contribution.

Further grading standards can be based on a 360-degree methodology. In other words, a student and their group's grade will be based on the faculty's assessment, a quantitative evaluation from the administration of the program, and peer evaluations within the group. It is up to each instructor to weigh each assessment tool.

Some additional guidelines for practicum success can consist of the following (in no special order):

- For the sports or recreation program's sense of security over proprietary information, confidentiality must be maintained. A security system for monitoring and protecting sensitive human resource data must be developed and maintained.

- Because traditional and non-traditional students have sizeable time restrictions, it may be necessary for student groups to use class time for group and individual off-campus visits. It is important to note that school policies pertaining to off-site and external work must always be followed.

- A fundamental success factor for the practicum is in allowing students the choice of which sports or recreation organization to work with. The ideal administrator is zealous about the process, accessible, communicative, and has a genuine need for a human resource plan. Conversely, a sports or recreation program administrator who is lethargic, distant, and uninterested are not likely to provide a positive experience, and should be avoided.

About the Authors

Richard Leonard, PhD is currently a Professor of Business Administration/Management at Flagler College in Tallahassee, Florida. His primary teaching focus is in Strategic Management with secondary instruction in Human Resource Management and Marketing. For eight years at Flagler, Dr. Leonard was the Department Chair for Business Administration and Accounting. His duties included curriculum improvement, complete human resource management of departmental faculty (full-time and adjunct), development of departmental initiatives, and participation in external departmental activities and promotions. In addition to his duties at Flagler College, Dr. Leonard was Distance Learning Faculty of Sports Management at the United States Sports Academy. His principal areas of instruction at USSA were in doctoral and graduate level courses in Strategic Management, Strategic Marketing, Human Resource Management, Event Planning, and Fundraising.

Dr. Leonard's main academic professional development concentration over the past 14 years has been publishing textbooks. Leonard's textbooks include *Fundraising for Sport and Athletics* (2nd Ed. 2016), *Summer Sports Camps 101: A Guidebook for Development and Operation* (2015), *Principles of Sport Administration* (2013), and *The Administrative Side of Coaching: Applying Business Concepts to Athletic Program Administration and Coaching* (3rd Ed. 2017). Additionally, he has written numerous articles in the field of sports administration. These articles, published by the American Volleyball Coaches Association—the governing body of the sport, encompass every aspect of sport management including planning, organization, human resource management, and strategic management.

Dr. Leonard earned a bachelor's degree in accounting from Robert Morris University, an MBA in management from Florida Metropolitan University – Tampa College, and a PhD in management from Walden University. He has certifications in Strategic Management and Leadership from the American Management Association, as well as certifications in Professional Learning, Collaborative Learning, and Classroom Management.

Dr. Leonard's professional knowledge and experience in sports administration is in the tangible, real-world development and operation of NCAA athletic programs. For six seasons, he was the Head Women's Volleyball Coach at Georgia State University in Atlanta, Georgia. Under his leadership as a head coach and program administrator, he led the team to a record of 144-69. His GSU team still holds the best winning percentage in school history at .676. He was named Trans American Coach of the Year in 2000, and the Atlantic Sun Conference Coach of the Year in 2001 and 2003. The GSU program won five different conference titles during that period, as well as a multitude of post-season individual awards.

Prior to Georgia State, Dr. Leonard spent four seasons as Associate Head Coach at Saint Louis University. During his tenure at Saint Louis University, the Billikens developed into one of the best volleyball programs in the Midwest. SLU compiled a 91-59 mark, including a 29-10 record and a trip to the Volleyball National Invitational Tournament.

Dr. Leonard's first coaching position was at the University of North Florida. The UNF Ospreys went to the NAIA National Championship in the first two years of intercollegiate competition. In the team's first season as an NCAA Division II member, UNF gained a top 15 national ranking and a number 1 ranking in the Southeastern United States Region.

Dr. Leonard was a member and player in the United States Volleyball Association from 1980 to 1997 and was AA rated. He was on four USVB regional championship teams and seven USVB semifinalist and finalists. During his playing career, his teams have won more than 125 tournaments and league championships.

Dr. Leonard served as a USVBA Regional Tournament Director and Regional Marketing Director. He is US Volleyball CAP Level II certified and US Volleyball Critical Thinking Seminar certified. He also has his ACEP certification.

Dr. Leonard's professional career has encompassed four managerial occupations, beginning with hotel and restaurant management, community center administration, athletic program administration and coaching, and academic administration. His supervisory positions in each occupation have had extensive human resource management duties. Aspects such as human resource planning, job designing and job description development, recruiting and selecting new employees, onboarding and new employee orientation, personnel training, and employee assessment are just a few of the human resource management functions he has been involved with throughout his professional career.

Jeffrey Kelly, Esquire. Jeffrey Kelly's experience in human resource management stems from both his legal experience as a licensed attorney in the State of Florida and practical experience as a supervisor. His legal career includes seven years serving as an assistant general counsel for the Florida Department of Revenue, one of the largest state agencies in Florida with over 4,500 employees. Mr. Kelly advised and represented the agency in all aspects of human resource issues including employee discipline, policy development, employment discrimination, FMLA, ADA, wrongful termination, collective bargaining, unemployment compensation, and veteran's preference claims. Mr. Kelly has also acquired practical experience in human resource management as a supervisor in three different positions. From 2007 to 2010, he supervised a team of seven attorneys and four assistants at the Department of Business Professional Regulation in a unit that prosecuted complaints against licensed contractors. From 2015 to 2017, Mr. Kelly supervised two attorneys in a unit that provided legal advice for the Florida Department of Revenue and represented the agency in various types of employment-related litigation. Mr. Kelly currently serves as a division deputy director at the Department of Business and Professional Regulation, where he assists in overseeing a division consisting of over seventy employees responsible for the licensing of various professions, including architects and interior designers, asbestos consultants, building code administrators, construction and electrical contractors, pilot commissioners, cosmetologists, barbers, and veterinarians.

Since 2006, Mr. Kelly has also served as an adjunct professor for Flagler College in Tallahassee, where he teaches courses in business law. Mr. Kelly obtained his bachelor's degree in criminal justice from University of Central Florida in 1999, and his juris doctorate from Florida State University College of Law in 2003.

Index